*Slum Imaginaries and Spatial Justice
in Philippine Cinema*

Slum Imaginaries and Spatial Justice in Philippine Cinema

Katrina Macapagal

EDINBURGH
University Press

Edinburgh University Press is one of the leading university presses in the UK. We publish academic books and journals in our selected subject areas across the humanities and social sciences, combining cutting-edge scholarship with high editorial and production values to produce academic works of lasting importance. For more information visit our website: edinburghuniversitypress.com

© Katrina Macapagal, 2021, 2023

Edinburgh University Press Ltd
The Tun – Holyrood Road
12 (2f) Jackson's Entry
Edinburgh EH8 8PJ

First published in hardback by Edinburgh University Press 2021

Typeset in Garamond MT Pro by
Servis Filmsetting Ltd, Stockport, Cheshire

A CIP record for this book is available from the British Library

ISBN 978 1 4744 5189 5 (hardback)
ISBN 978 1 4744 5190 1 (paperback)
ISBN 978 1 4744 5191 8 (webready PDF)
ISBN 978 1 4744 5192 5 (epub)

The right of Katrina Macapagal to be identified as author of this work has been asserted in accordance with the Copyright, Designs and Patents Act 1988 and the Copyright and Related Rights Regulations 2003 (SI No. 2498).

Contents

List of Illustrations   vi
Acknowledgements   viii

Introduction   1

Part I   Locating Philippine Urban Cinema
1   Spatial Justice and the Slum Chronotope   13
2   The Rise of Manila Slums and Philippine Urban Cinema   27
3   The Slum Chronotope in Philippine Cinema Genres and Modalities   36

Part II   Routes of Reading Philippine Urban Cinema
4   Kids in the Hood: Chronotopes of Passage in *Ang Pagdadalaga Ni Maximo Oliveros* and *Tribu*   59
5   Women Walking: Affective Chronotopes in the Melodramatic Imaginaries of *Kubrador, Foster Child* and *Lola*   82
6   Men on the Move: Chronotopes of Mobility in the Noir Imaginaries of *Kinatay, Metro Manila* and *On the Job*   107
7   Migrants in *Transit*: The Slum Chronotope and Chronotopes of In/Visibility in the Overseas Filipino Worker Genre   132
8   Sounds of Youth: The Production of Noise and Chronotopes of Performance in *Respeto*   156

Conclusion   175

Bibliography   180
Filmography   198
Index   200

Illustrations

FIGURES

4.1	Maximo walking into a *looban* in an early scene of *Ang Pagdadalaga ni Maximo Oliveros*	63
4.2	A scene that depicts symbolic lines of intersection among the figures of justice and injustice in *Ang Pagdadalaga ni Maximo Oliveros*	66
4.3	A clash between the Tondo gangs in *Tribu*	69
4.4	Ebet holding a toy gun while spying for a Tondo gang in *Tribu*	72
5.1	The ghost of Amy's son walks behind her in a scene where she gets lost in a *looban*. A scene from *Kubrador*	87
5.2	The ghost of Amy's son watches her just before she exits the film screen in *Kubrador*	89
5.3	John-John takes a piss just after bathing. A scene from *Foster Child*	93
5.4	Thelma and her son walk aimlessly in Manila's commercial district after John-John's discharge. A scene from *Foster Child*	96
5.5	Lola Puring battles wind and rain as she ascends concrete stairs, having just lit candles on the site where her grandson was murdered. A scene from *Lola*	101
5.6	Lola Sepa descends a prison staircase to visit her grandson, who has been charged with murder. A scene from *Lola*	103
6.1	Peping's masculinity is put to the test inside the van that traverses the city in *Kinatay*	112
6.2	Peping's moment of indecision in the bus that can take him back home. A scene from *Kinatay*	114
6.3	The armoured truck driving through one of the city's main thoroughfares in *Metro Manila*	117
6.4	Ong and Oscar overlooking the city in *Metro Manila*	119
6.5	Daniel's walk introduces the prison space that resembles a *looban*. Screen grab from *On the Job*	123
6.6	The final collision of masculinities in *On the Job*	128

7.1	Bridging the distance between migrant mother and daughter in *Transit*	149
7.2	An image from *Transit*'s montage of empty spaces set in Tel Aviv	152
8.1	The youth figures in *Respeto* on top of cemetery tombs, suggesting liminality	168
8.2	*Respeto*'s final tableau: a powerful melodramatic spectacle	172

Acknowledgements

Writing this book was not without challenges, especially in the middle of a global pandemic. I have my family and friends to thank for encouraging me to finish this book, despite and because of the injustices of the times and spaces we live in.

This book began as a PhD dissertation, which I would not have completed without the support of my supervisors from Queen Margaret University, Michael Stewart and Jeremy Valentine. Thank you as well to my PhD batchmates, Cornelia Heyde, Mariola Tarrega, Robert Munro, Christos Theodorakopoulos and Suzanne Zaremba for the company along the way.

Thanks to friends and former colleagues from the University of the Philippines (UP) where I began my academic pursuit. It goes without saying that my literary theory background has found its way into the pages of this book. My thanks to the kindness of senior academics from my home university that helped set off my UK postgraduate studies: Jose Wendell Capili, Ruth Pison, Pooching Testa, Aileen Salonga, Lily Rose Tope, Rolando Tolentino and Patrick Campos. I will always be grateful to the brilliant Edel Garcellano, whose sharp insights from my undergraduate years remain critical to my way of thinking, in and beyond the academe.

Thank you to former lecturers at the University of Westminster, David Cunningham, Harriet Evans and Marquard Smith, who supported my PhD pursuit and whose lectures initiated my interest in the subject of this book.

Thank you to Edinburgh University Press for the opportunity to publish this work. My thanks to EUP editors Gillian Leslie and Richard Strachan for the generous advice along the way.

Thank you to the UP Film Institute for providing copies of most of the films included in this study. I would also like to thank the filmmakers, Hannah Espia and Treb Monteras II for generously sharing copies of their films. Thank you to the filmmakers for creating the films included in this book, and granting kind permission to use screen grabs from their work. My thanks as well to filmmaker Baby Ruth Villarama, and fellow academic Rosa Cordillera for helping me connect with filmmakers for this book.

My sincere thanks to Bliss Cua Lim and Philippa Lovatt for all the encouragement. Your dedication to research in Asian cinema is inspiring.

Thank you to Carlos Piocos and Jayson Fajarda, for your patience in reading and commenting on early writing. I am grateful for the constancy of your personal advice and friendship.

Thank you to the members of my ever-reliable transnational support group who continue to spam my inbox: Lesther Libarios, Jojo Nem Singh, Anna Ramos, Rebekah Roque, Ted Tiñedo and Gabriel Valbuena. Your good-natured humour and competitive spirit absolutely helped me power through this project.

To friends who kept me sane: Dara Bascara and Rafael Maramag – your commitment to the struggle for social justice and our conversations about activism helped me think through the roadblocks I encountered in writing this book. Thank you for being constant sources of moral and emotional support.

To Jeno Villaverde and Anna Marie 'Meters' Mitra – our days and nights in London will always be a source of positive energy.

Thanks to friends who have given me advice and provided overall positivity along the way: Michael Balili, Louie Navarro, Roy Cuesta, Vladimeir Gonzales, Piya Constantino, Iggy Rodriguez, Kristine Alave, Rory O'Hara, Alyx Arumpac, Reagan Maiquez, Michael Andrada, Oscar Serquiña. Special thanks to Karl Castro for your advice on selecting illustrations. To my *Maginhawa* friends: Sharine and Mark Lim, Iris Pagsanjan, Dianne Roa – thank you for the parental wisdom.

Thank you to Anne and David, Louise and Howard for constantly expressing well-wishes.

I express my deep gratitude to my parents, Gil and Mayette, for the unlimited support and understanding. I also thank my siblings, and my 'family by heart' for always welcoming me home.

Finally, my thanks to Nick – I wouldn't have reached the finish line without you.

Introduction

> Today, now more than ever . . . class struggle is inscribed in space. (Lefebvre [1974] 1991: 55)

The COVID-19 pandemic struck at the time that I was revising this book for publication, a period beyond the range of this book's case studies of Philippine films set in Metropolitan Manila's slum imaginaries. President Rodrigo Duterte's regime, known for enforcing extrajudicial killings in the slums of Manila, implemented one of the longest 'hard' lockdowns in the world.[1] The lockdown exposed government neglect of the urban poor, who were forced to stay home in slum areas where social distancing is impossible, and with little government aid. Two weeks after the lockdown, a group of residents from the slums of Sitio San Roque who staged a protest demanding aid were arrested and detained. Following the arrest, Duterte issued a strong warning to lockdown violators, addressing the police and military: 'Shoot them dead.'[2]

History might have outpaced the films covered in this book, but the issues of spatial justice grounded on Manila's slum imaginaries that I examine here remain relevant as the government's neoliberal policies sustain the abandonment of the urban poor. Post-pandemic, just as slum inhabitants continue to assert their right to the city, I have no doubt that Philippine filmmakers will find new ways to imagine spatial justice grounded on the slum chronotope.

* * *

The slum imaginary looms large in the history of Philippine cinema, invoked heavily in a number of renowned films set in cities comprising Metropolitan Manila. Bursting with an estimated 4 million slum-dwellers, a figure that amounts to roughly 37 per cent of the total urban population of 12 million (Ballesteros 2011), it is not surprising that the slum spaces of the Philippine capital figure prominently in the country's cinematic imagery, whether they are used as primary setting or are strongly referenced throughout film narratives.

The images of poverty and squalor prompted by Manila's slum imaginary project themselves onto a larger scale, intersecting with what the United

Nations has called the 'urbanization of poverty' (UN-Habitat 2003: v). In this landmark report, the UN warns that close to a billion people inhabit the slums of the developing world. Urban historian Mike Davis (2006) dubbed the rapid urbanisation of poverty as the emergence of the 'planet of slums', painting an apocalyptic account of life in the shanty towns of the Third World – Manila included.

Philippine cinema's surge in independent digital filmmaking in roughly the last two decades can be set against this backdrop of the global urbanisation of poverty signified through the heightened visibility of slums, a period considered by some to be a new 'golden age' in the country's film history. This book examines selected examples of contemporary Philippine urban cinema – independently produced and internationally circulated films that prominently feature, reference or dialogue with Manila slums as setting.

This book has two broad aims: (1) to offer an interdisciplinary framework for reading films from the emerging genre of Philippine urban cinema that draws from urban studies, film studies and cultural theory; and in the process, (2) to make a case for Philippine urban cinema, and Philippine urban history in general, as a significant vantage point from which to understand imaginaries of narrative and subjective formation in the age of neoliberal global capitalism. As I hope to show, this study of Philippine urban cinema, while contextualised in local urban conditions, also dialogues with the larger context of global urban development.

This study of Philippine urban cinema can be located broadly at the intersections of film studies and urban studies, a terrain that takes into account existing forays into the discourse of the cinematic city, or the 'cinema-city nexus' (Shiel and Fitzmaurice 2001: 2). There is by now a vast source of literature that examines the relations between cinema and the city, with David Clarke's (1997) *Cinematic City* and Mark Shiel and Tony Fitzmaurice's (2001) edited collections arguably being the two most highly influential precursors. Both collections call for the productive linking of film studies with other disciplines, particularly sociology and geography. Shiel and Fitzmaurice (2001: 2) argue that sociological studies and film studies are mutually beneficial disciplines, as they are both concerned with the '*lived social realities* in a range of urban societies of the present and recent past'. As for human geography, Stuart Aitken and Leo Zonn's (1994) edited collection is generally considered the discipline's pioneering step towards actively linking geography with film.

It is only relatively recently, however, that the cinema-city nexus has been pursued in the study of films beyond Western contexts. There has been welcome interest in the study of films in the context of global cities (Andersson and Webb 2016; Krause and Petro 2003). An exemplary work that explores Indian urban experience through cinema is Ranjani Mazumdar's

(2007) *Bombay Cinema: an Archive of the City*. There is also growing interest in East Asian cities and cinema (Braester and Tweedie 2010; Zhang 2010). A more recent publication that converses with my own study is Igor Krstić's (2016) *Slums on Screen*, which explores the representations of slum spaces in world cinema, including some examples from this study's scope of films.

This book's foray into the cinema-city nexus activates what David Harvey (1973: 24) has called 'spatial consciousness' or the 'geographical imagination', a notion that underlies the very discipline of human geography (Massey et al. 1999). In his seminal work, *Social Justice and the City*, Harvey (1973: 24) describes the geographical imagination as the kind of thinking that 'enables the individual to recognize the role of space and place in his own biography, to relate to the spaces he sees around him, and to recognize how transactions between individuals and between organizations are affected by the space that separates them'.

This study does not use the term imaginary lightly as it relates to film analysis, taking after thinkers who have reinvigorated the concept as crucial to the understanding of the world. As Arjun Appadurai (1996: 31) has famously argued: 'the imagination is now central to all forms of agency, is itself a social fact, and is the key component of the new global order'. More specifically, this study examines slum films as forms of the urban imaginary, or what Andreas Huyssen (2008: 3) has described as 'the way city dwellers imagine their own city as the place of everyday life, the site of inspiring traditions and continuities as well as the scene of histories of destruction, crime, and conflicts of all kinds'.

The films I examine in this book reveal urban imaginaries that depict how the global underclass of slum inhabitants in the context of Manila's slum imaginaries stake their 'right to the city' through time-spaces of spatial justice. Henri Lefebvre's (1996) radical slogan for 'the right to the city' remains relevant in these times of urban crisis materialised in the rise of slums. Harvey (2008: 23) understands this slogan as the 'freedom to make and remake our cities and ourselves'. The urban poor – the subjects of the films examined in this book – are largely denied their right to this freedom, even as their lives and labour are indispensable to neoliberal capitalism. More significantly, the 'right to the city' is not just a territorial matter; it is, as Peter Marcuse (2009: 192) argues a 'moral claim founded on fundamental principles of justice, of ethics, of morality, of virtue, of the good'. The right to the city, or the urban poor's struggle for space, is what the films analysed in this book are able to imagine or render visible.

In keeping with the cinema-city nexus approach, this book's framework emerges from the combination of two key concepts drawn from human geography and critical theory – spatial justice and the chronotope. Broadly, this book examines how the narratives and characters of selected Philippine urban films might reveal imaginaries of 'spatial justice' through chronotopic analysis. These two concepts lay the groundwork for what I call the 'slum chronotope' – the discursive tool that underpins my analysis of Philippine urban cinema. The examination of the slum chronotope in the films included in this book, to my mind, is a valuable means to understand how space in this age of the urbanisation of poverty is produced and imagined by its inhabitants.

The concept of spatial justice, a term offered by urban theorist Edward Soja (2010), broadly argues that social justice can be approached productively from a spatial perspective. Spatial justice captures the critical value of analysing social issues in and through space, in a particular historical context. The concept is, of course, indebted to Lefebvre's [1974] (1991) highly influential thesis that space is a social product. Space is never merely just there, but is a product of social forces and relations, what Soja (2010: 4) calls the 'sociospatial dialectic'. I use justice in the broad sense of equality and fairness, as well as in the spatial sense of the urban inhabitants' struggle to participate in the production of space. In relation to film analysis, I explore how the narratives and characters configure and are configured by the urban spaces they inhabit.

The global urbanisation of poverty lends itself clearly to the perspective of spatial justice, with the rise of slums being spatial manifestations of how injustice is literally produced through space over time. Slumification is a clear and present example of social and material injustice produced and sustained in and through space, a direct result of the state's subscription to neoliberal capitalist policies that ultimately result in the dispossession of the urban poor. I frame Philippine urban cinema through the lens of spatial justice given its strong emplacement in the global landscape of spatial injustice, as signified by the use of the slum imaginary in the films' narrative and character configurations.

Combined with spatial justice, I use Mikhail Bakhtin's (1981) classic theory of the 'chronotope' (literally meaning time-space) in order to formulate the theory of the 'slum chronotope'. By now a well-known concept in literary and film studies, the chronotope refers to spatio-temporal elements in narratives that convey generic and representational value. The chronotope serves as the crucial artistic bridge that connects text and context, the imaginary and the real.

The slum chronotope is what I argue to be the crucial organising centre of Philippine urban cinema. I use the slum chronotope as an analytical tool in this study, from which I am able to explore other chronotopes configured through the film's generic configurations. As I will discuss further in the succeeding chapter, I deliberately use the word 'slum' to call to mind the discourse of poverty pornography invoked by the urban imaginary of slums in the Third World. The theory of the slum chronotope serves as a means to think through the social, political and ethical issues raised in the films, some of which have been charged with poverty pornography. By formulating the slum chronotope as a theoretical tool towards the purpose of locating and examining spatial in/justice, the study diverges from the sometimes limiting route of poverty pornography, shifting attention to the ways the narratives are productive in examining how the films' narrative and character configurations enable the production of space in spaces of injustice. In the study's film discussions, I locate other chronotopes particular to the genres enabled by the slum chronotope, which are able to shore up the ways by which the film subjects imagine or enact the struggle for spatial justice in and beyond the film worlds. The combination of spatial justice and the slum chronotope enables an interdisciplinary theoretical framework for examining the ways social justice is revealed in and through film narratives set in the particularities of Manila's slums and its larger urban landscape.

This book embarks on close textual analysis of how chronotopic dialogues in Philippine urban film narratives reveal and enable subjective formation through its character configurations, even if this formation is admittedly limited. The films I analyse arguably provide space and time for its characters to stake their claims in the struggle over the production of space in Manila's spaces of injustice. In all the films, the characters are located in times and spaces where they are compelled to make decisions that bring to fore the complexities of justice – and its related moral and ethical considerations – especially when framed within the politics of survival or the desire for a better future.

The past few years saw the resurgence of the Philippine slum chronotope in the global urban imaginary, not just in films, but in the international media coverage of the spate of extrajudicial killings in impoverished areas of Manila. Shortly after being sworn into office on 30 June 2016 with a landslide victory, President Rodrigo Duterte's anti-crime crusade took flesh, to borrow Bakhtin's words, in his rallying call to wage a war against drugs. During his campaign, Duterte promised a brutal war against drug pushers and users alike: 'When I become president, I will order the police to find those people [dealing or using drugs] and kill them. The funeral parlors will be packed' (Human Rights Watch 2017).

Nobody imagined Duterte's threat would come to pass. Subsequent reports in international media relayed the growing death toll in the slums of Manila following Duterte's anti-crime crusade. A CNN (2017) special report titled 'City of the Dead' includes a detailed map of a slum neighbourhood in Pasay City 'where some of the most shocking killings have taken place'. The report is accompanied by a series of harrowing images of dead bodies on the street. Time Magazine online posted a special series of photographs with the title: 'In Manila, Death Comes by Night' (Nachtwey 2017). In late 2016, a *New York Times* photo series on Duterte's war on drugs titled, 'They are Slaughtering Us Like Animals', shared widely on social media, won a Pulitzer Prize (Berehulak 2016). The online report featured a map of the forty-one sites of Manila where the photographer captured images of fifty-seven dead. Meanwhile, in a video report, *National Geographic* captured footage of blood-soaked *eskinitas* (small alleys) in the wake of five reported killings in one night alone (Hincks 2017). The international Human Rights Watch organisation reveals that the victims in Duterte's drug war are 'the country's poorest, most marginalised, most vulnerable citizens' (Mohan 2016). Duterte's war on drugs is a war on the urban poor (Wells 2017).[3]

In the era of Duterte's extrajudicial killings, the lifeless bodies of the urban poor literally and symbolically mark the streets of Manila's slums as spaces of injustice. At a time when the state's brazen disregard for the lives of the urban poor has become more visible, Philippine urban cinema's imaginaries of spatial justice also become all the more valuable. If we are to understand slumification as the materialised urban manifestation of global social injustice, it is possible to approach Philippine urban cinema with the intent of uncovering the spatio-temporal representations of social in/justice. The main question I strive to answer is this: How does Philippine urban cinema imagine spatial justice through its dialogue with the slum chronotope and the other chronotopic configurations it enables?

Chapters

Throughout the book's chapter discussions, I draw from interdisciplinary sources across critical theory, film theory, and urban and space theory in support of my general aim of locating spatial justice in representative Philippine urban films.

The book is divided into two parts. 'Part I: Locating Philippine Urban Cinema', sets up this book's theoretical tools, starting with the introduction of key concepts in Chapter 1. I also address some of the ethical issues surrounding slum films in this chapter, including poverty pornography and slum voyeurism. Chapter 2 introduces the theory of the slum chronotope in Philippine urban cinema, where I trace the rise of Manila slums as urban forms that reveal a history of spatial injustice in the global backdrop of neoliberalism. I then locate the slum chronotope alongside the development of Philippine cinema, with its earliest notable films being set in the ruins and squalor of Manila leading up to the contemporary independent wave of

Manila-based films. Chapter 3 examines the slum chronotope as it relates to particular genres and modalities situated in the Philippine context, providing the contours of the analysis of case studies in the second part of the book: these are the coming-of-age and teen film genre, the modalities of melodrama and noir, and the Overseas Filipino Worker genre (the migrant narrative unique in Philippine cinema).

In 'Part II: Routes of Reading Philippine Urban Cinema', I proceed to examine the film's case studies in more detail. In each chapter I examine the films more closely by locating other chronotopes within the particular genre or modality through which the films are framed. Each chapter builds upon the next and progressively expands the grounds covered by the slum chronotope, from the slums of Manila to the export of Manila's urban imaginary in the migrant narrative examined in the penultimate chapter, before returning to the slums of Manila in the final chapter. The arrangement of case studies in Part II can also be approached chronologically, illustrating the progressive development of Philippine urban cinema's themes and aesthetics over time, alongside the films' spatial expansion.

The first chapter examines two coming-of-age films, *Ang Pagdadalaga ni Maximo Oliveros (The Blossoming of Maximo Oliveros;* Solito 2006) and *Tribu (Tribe;* Libiran 2007). In these films, the time of childhood takes place in the slum spaces of *loobans* and the labyrinthine streets of Manila's Tondo district. In both films, I locate what I call 'chronotopes of passage' that serve as key moments in the narratives that facilitate the young protagonists' transition from childhood to another phase of maturity. The two films imagine opposing outcomes for the child protagonists. *Ang Pagdadalaga* depicts a narrative of escape for its queer character, while *Tribu* offers a narrative of entrapment for its child figure transitioning into a sense of manhood. However, both films portray the struggle for spatial justice through the ways the children appropriate spaces in carving out their future.

The second chapter is framed through the modality of melodrama in its examination of three female-centred films: *Kubrador (The Bet Collector,* Jeturian 2007), *Foster Child* (Mendoza 2007), and *Lola* (Mendoza 2010). In these films, I locate what I call 'affective chronotopes' configured by the spatial practice of walking, and framed through the mode of melodrama. I examine how the abject female characters appropriate space through their affective encounters and the spatial practice of walking, as the camera follows their movements within, through and away from the slums. I argue that the films are powerful depictions of resilience through the spatial practice of walking, which dialogues with the subjective power of affective labour embodied in the films' female protagonists.

In the third chapter, the male-driven narratives of *Kinatay* (Mendoza 2009),

Metro Manila (Ellis 2013) and *On the Job* (Matti 2013) are viewed through the lens of film noir. The films in this chapter cover even more ground in the urban space, as the male characters are shown to move to and from the slums. If the first two chapters are focussed on characters with limited mobility, the men in Manila noir are shown to struggle over the production of space through the politics of mobility. In all three films, I locate what I call 'chronotopes of mobility' in scenes of transit in which the male characters aspire to master the urban space. I argue that these examples of Manila noir offer imaginaries of spatial injustice, as the narratives reveal masculine anxieties in the ways the characters are able or unable to map urban space.

While the first three chapters are confined to the urban spaces of Manila, the fourth chapter expands the coordinates of the slum chronotope in the study's examination of the migrant narrative of *Transit* (Espia 2013). I argue that the slum chronotope can productively dialogue with what I locate as 'chronotopes of in/visibility' in the Overseas Filipino Worker genre. I read the film as exemplary in revealing the migrant worker's struggle for spatial justice in the foreign space, delinked from the rhetoric of national sacrifice.

In the concluding chapter, I return to Manila's urban space in my analysis of *Respeto* (Monteras II 2017), a hip-hop film specifically located in the district of Pandacan that resonates loudly with the country's sustained history of state violence. In this film the slum chronotope dialogues with 'chronotopes of performance' – instances in which the film's liminal youth characters produce space through the production of noise. The film's melodramatic closing shows the potential of urban cinema to address its spectators, to enjoin us to pause and listen to the sounds of violence in our times.

The films analysed in this study stand out from the growing body of work comprising the still-emerging independent wave of Philippine cinema in terms of subject matter, aesthetics, and local and international acclaim. I have chosen the films that are arguably more well known, as evidenced by local and international accolades and the frequency of references in existing literature. Three other factors influenced the scope of the study: first, the privileging of the slum space as setting or as point of reference – this means that the slum setting is fundamental and not just coincidental to the film narratives. My second consideration is international circulation, in order to support my assertion that these films can be emplaced in the larger frame of the global urban imaginary. Third, the films examined are all full-length narrative films, which lend themselves more fruitfully to the study's theoretical framework.[4]

This book is not at all an exhaustive study of Philippine urban cinema, and is undoubtedly also influenced by my own value judgement in terms of choice of films. I am well aware that there are many other films that could have been included in this study, had there been more time and space. But it is my hope that it spurs future research on the subject as the independent age continues to develop. I can point to three other issues in terms of the book's limitations. First, the book can no doubt be accused of privileging 'Imperial Manila' – a phrase used among Philippine academic circles that suggests the primacy of Manila-focused research at the expense of regional areas. While I cannot contest this charge, my hope is that it becomes a springboard for the study of films beyond Manila. I am also fully aware that there are three Mendoza films included in the study – which attests to the filmmaker's significance in what has been criticised as the new hierarchy in Philippine independent cinema. Finally, I recognise the limited period covered by the films (2005–17), owing to the limited time frame of the project, as well as the fact that the Philippine urban cinema continues to develop as I write.

While the slum chronotope persists in Philippine independent cinema, recent films have begun privileging rural spaces, suggesting the possibility of a new route for chronotopic analysis. The films of Lav Diaz are prime examples of the emergence of the rural chronotope, with many of his laborious epic works filmed in rural spaces, in contrast to the slice-of-life narratives more typical in slum films. Moreover, the rural chronotope might potentially converse with the emergence of regional festivals in the country, which are gradually picking up pace against the dominance of Manila-based festivals such as Cinemalaya.

Beyond Philippine cinema, this study's broad interdisciplinary framework can potentially be applied to the study of films from other urban contexts. As Andreas Huyssen (2008: 5) explains, urban imaginaries are mediated 'sites of encounters with other cities'. It is possible to locate the slum chronotope in the urban imaginaries of other megacities, in both Western and non-Western contexts. The theory of spatial justice can be located, for instance, in films set in Third World spaces within First World contexts where the built environment of the urbanisation of poverty takes flesh in different spatial forms.

At the heart of this book is my strong belief that films are cultural products that can configure the ways we think about the spaces and times we live in. This project of tracking spatial justice in Philippine urban cinema was borne out of my personal intent to come to terms with the nature of films that Philippine filmmakers are offering to the world. By taking a step back and rethinking my own limited understanding of slums as either spaces of despair or spaces of hope, I reached what I believe to be a more productive perspective, strongly underpinned by a socio-spatial dialectic: slums are spaces of injustice where people struggle everyday towards justice. With this view, this book makes a strong case for the significance of Philippine urban cinema as an emerging genre through which we can think through matters of social justice, not just within the Philippine context, but within the global imaginary of the urbanisation of poverty.

Notes

1. The whole of Metropolitan Manila was officially placed under 'general community quarantine' or total lockdown on 16 March 2020, which gradually expanded to the National Capital Region.
2. See '"Shoot Them Dead": Duterte Warns against Violating Lockdown' (Aljazeera News 2020).
3. While international media produced reports and documentaries in the early period of Duterte's war on drugs, the exemplary documentary *Aswang* (Arumpac 2019) stands out as the first Filipino-produced documentary on the subject, covering a period of three years.
4. Thus, I have opted to exclude the experimental works of prolific filmmaker Khavn Dela Cruz, even though a number of films from his vast body of work are set in the slums of Manila.

Part I

Locating Philippine Urban Cinema

CHAPTER 1

Spatial Justice and the Slum Chronotope

This chapter expounds on this book's key concepts of spatial justice and the slum chronotope, as well as contextualises the rise of slums in the age of neoliberal capitalism. I also address the related issues of poverty pornography and cinematic ethics that continue to beset works of Philippine urban cinema, which the slum chronotope productively dialogues with.

SPATIAL JUSTICE

Any conception of space is informed by Henri Lefebvre's highly influential thoughts in *The Production of Space*, where he principally argues that '(Social) space is a (social) product' (1974/1991: 26). Here Lefebvre introduces his spatial triad as what constitutes the production of space. These are: representations of space, spaces of representation and spatial practices. Representations of space refer to the 'dominant space of any society' (Merrifield 2013: 109), while spaces of representation are the spaces used and inhabited by human beings as part of everyday experience (Merrifield 2013: 109). Meanwhile, spatial practices refer to the ways we use space – they 'structure lived reality, include routes and networks, patterns and interactions that connect places and people, images with reality, work with leisure' (Merrifield 2013: 110). I reference this spatial triad throughout this book when I refer to the production of space in films.

This understanding that space is produced means that space is a site of conflict – it can be contested, appropriated and used in various ways that can benefit some, to the detriment of others. And it is in this way that space links with matters of social justice. I use social justice here in the broad sense of fairness and social equality, often relating to issues of ethics and moral judgement. However, it is important to recognise that justice is not an ahistorical philosophical idea. Social justice, especially as it relates to space, manifests itself through and in the historical production of space in various sociocultural contexts, which in this book is set within Philippine urban space, as well as against the larger backdrop of the global rise of slums. As Marxist geographer David Harvey (1997: 362) argues, social justice, while a 'universal' ideal, must 'be construed as a differentiated construction embedded in processes operating in quite different spatio-temporal scales'.[1]

This strong relationship between the production of space and social justice is what urban theorist Edward Soja foregrounds in his theory of spatial justice which is the general framework that guides this book. Briefly put, spatial justice pertains to a *perspective* that social justice has significant spatial dimensions. Soja (2010: 1) argues that the 'the spatiality of justice ... is an integral and formative component of justice itself, a vital part of how justice and injustice are socially constructed and evolve over time'. He goes on to say that there exists a '*socio-spatial dialectic*' in the struggle for justice, which means that social processes are influenced by the production of space and vice versa (Soja 2010: 4). Soja's endorsement of the term spatial justice, moreover, does not seek to replace spatial justice with social justice; rather, it pertains to a 'particular emphasis and interpretative perspective' of social justice *as* spatial (Soja 2010: 13).

Like Soja, urban theorist Mustafa Dikeç (2001: 1794) forwards 'the spatial dialectics of injustice' across his studies of space (2001, 2007, 2015). Dikeç defines this dialectic as such:

> the spatiality of injustice implies that justice has a spatial dimension to it, and therefore, that a spatial perspective might be used to discern injustice *in space* ... The injustice of spatiality, on the other hand, implies existing structures in their capacities to produce and reproduce injustice *through* space. (2001: 1792–3)

Dikeç goes on to relate spatial justice to the practice of emancipatory politics in and through space, as inhabitants claim their rights to participate in the ways space is shaped. This goes back to Lefebvre's rallying call for urban inhabitants to claim their 'right to the city', a slogan which Marxist geographer David Harvey interprets as: 'The freedom to make and remake our cities and ourselves' (2008: 23). The rise of the urbanisation of poverty shows that the global urban poor are essential to the survival of the planet, but are dispossessed of their right to participate formally in its production. This does not mean, however, that the urban poor do not produce space – in fact, slum inhabitants are crucial to the production of the city space, even as they are rendered invisible by those who own and control the formal means of producing space.

SLUMS AS MATERIALISED HISTORY OF SPATIAL IN/JUSTICE

The growth of slums globally is a significant aspect of urbanisation that lays bare the social production of space. The production of slum spaces links directly with the concerns of spatial justice, as it is an urban phenomenon that demonstrates the spatiality of justice and the injustice of spatiality.

The term 'slum' first emerged to mean 'racket' or 'criminal trade' (Davis 2006: 21) in nineteenth-century Europe. The term can be traced to Victorian London, used to refer at first to 'a room in which low goings-on occurred' (Dyos 1967: 8) or to parts of the city that are rarely frequented. In looking at the historical emergence of slums, what is clear is that there has never been a precise definition or description for these spaces. Even the values ascribed to slum spaces constantly evolve. As stated in the landmark publication collated by a group of over a hundred international researchers commissioned by the UN, there are two broad categories of slums: 'slums of hope' and 'slums of despair', the former described as 'progressing' settlements, the latter 'declining' (UN-Habitat 2003: 9). Among urban theorists, some view the rise of slums with optimism, such as the architect Rem Koolhaas (2000) who views the slums of Lagos as a model for future cities. Meanwhile, others take a more critical view of the rise of slums, with Mike Davis's (2006) *Planet of Slums* being a prime example.

While spaces that can be called slums do indeed exist in advanced capitalist countries, the slums that the UN is concerned with are those that have become more and more entrenched and visible in cities of the Third World. Consider this description that practically equates the Third World city with slum development: 'The extension of slums in developing countries is a product of 20th- and 21st- century urban growth and represents the very essence of the Third World city' (Bolay 2006: 285). There is a growing sense that the slums of the Third World are far worse than their Anglo-American counterparts. As *City* editor Howard Husock (2015) phrased it, with reference to Jacob Riis's photographs of New York slums in the 1880s: 'Riis's Manhattan, even at its roughest, was never that squalid. True, some 20,000 shacks once squatted on the site of what became Central Park. And certainly the Lower East Side was terribly crowded. But even the worst Orchard Street tenements were actual buildings, not tin-roofed shanties with dirt floors.'[2]

Slums in cities of the Third World, although different in every context, can be situated in the current age of neoliberal global capitalism, thanks to urban restructuring schemes endorsed by global financial institutions. In *Planet of Slums*, Davis (2006) grounds his analysis of slumification in the conditions imposed by debt-lending institutions to Third World borrowers following the worldwide financial crisis in the 1980s. According to Davis, the International Monetary Fund (IMF) and World Bank's (WB) structural adjustment policies can be blamed for the rise of slums in the Third World and the gradual retreat of the state in providing social services, as these policies strongly endorsed privatisation. Davis cites the UN-Habitat publication, *The Challenge of Slums* in reiterating that: 'The main single cause of increase in poverty and inequality during the 1980s and the 1990s was the retreat of the state' (Davis 2006: 43) – a direct consequence of IMF-WB structural adjustment policies.

The neoliberal project that has seen the unprecedented rise of slums in the Third World is part of the evolution of neoliberal global capitalism through the logic of what Harvey (2009) has called 'accumulation by dispossession'. One way that accumulation by dispossession reached a global scale was through the creation of international financial institutions. Harvey describes this process as internal to capitalism's logic of accumulating surplus capital and labour through urbanisation. Urbanisation creates cities where surplus capital and labour are continually absorbed and subsequently destroyed to allow the flow of capital. Slum formations and clearances illustrate this form of 'creative destruction', when generations of slum inhabitants are forcibly removed to make way for profitable infrastructure. As philosopher Slavoj Žižek (2009: 424) has put it, slums are 'the true "symptoms" of slogans such as "Development," "Modernization," and the "World market": not an unfortunate accident, but a necessary product of the innermost logic of global capitalism'.

Accumulation by dispossession has produced the world's 'surplus humanity' (Davis 2006: 174) – those who now constitute the informal economy of the urbanising world. As the global source of surplus labour, the informal economy of slum inhabitants has become integral to capitalist survival, even though slum dwellers are rendered invisible and are not recognised as full citizens of the state (Mahmud 2010). The city's paradoxical dependence on the dispossessed literally sustains accumulation, as the invisible spaces of the slums become the vast source of cheap labour that keeps cities alive (Mahmud 2010). As Tayabb Mahmud (2010: 144) explains: 'Rapid urban growth triggered by globalized economic circuits, along with diminished state capacities and resulting civil strife, is the recipe for mushrooming slums in the global South.' This neoliberal landscape of accumulation by dispossession is the broad context in which Philippine urban cinema and its slum imaginaries can be set against, while also grounded in the production of space particular to Philippine urbanisation.

THE CHRONOTOPE

If spatial justice allows me to contextualise Philippine urban cinema in the neoliberal age of global capitalism, the concept of the chronotope is useful for breaking down how films can be read as imaginaries of spatial justice. A term Mikhail Bakhtin borrowed from physics, the chronotope (time-space) refers to spatio-temporal configurations in literary texts through which narrative meanings are created and derived. Bakhtin describes the chronotope as the artistic form where time/space conjoin: 'Time, as it were, thickens, takes on flesh, becomes artistically visible; likewise, space becomes charged and responsive to the movements of time, plot and history' (Bakhtin 1981: 84). For Bakhtin, chronotopes are crucial to narrative formation, functioning as 'the organizing centers for the fundamental narrative events . . . the place where the knots of narrative are tied and untied' (1981: 250). As a spatio-temporal form of imagination, the chronotope is 'the primary means for materializing time in space, emerges as a centre for concretizing representation, as a force giving body to the entire novel' (Bakhtin 1981: 250). Bakhtin cites examples of places that can function as chronotopes, such as the road, the castle, the salon – forms which give rise to genre formation. For instance, he describes the chronotope of the castle to be 'saturated through and through with a time that is historical' (Bakhtin 1981: 246) so that it features prominently in the historical novel.

As well as being constitutive of narrative and genre, chronotopes have significant representational value. As Bakhtin (1981: 253) has powerfully argued: 'Out of the actual chronotopes of our world (which serve as the source of representation) emerge the reflected and created chronotopes of the world represented in the work.' At the same time, Bakhtin warns that there is no direct correspondence between reality and artistic expression. The meaning/s that the chronotope may enable are generated only upon reading, which is what I take Bakhtin to mean when he said that the chronotope is 'almost like a metaphor (but not entirely) . . .' (1981: 84).

Fictional narratives engage in constant dialogue with actually existing time-spaces, without which the imaginary time-spaces would not have been imagined. The chronotope follows the same principle of Bakhtin's concept of 'dialogism' that recognises that there is a 'constant interaction between meanings, all of which have the potential of conditioning others.' (Bakhtin 1981: 426). Related to this mediation of reality via the chronotope is its historical nature as a textual and contextual tool. Bakhtin recognises that time and space, real or imagined, are never static. As leading Bakhtinian scholar Michael Holquist (2002: 138) explains, to view the chronotope as dialogic means that 'the time/space relation of any particular text will always be perceived in the context of a larger set of time/space relations that obtain in the social and historical environment in which it is read'. Moreover, to view chronotopes as dialogic means that their meanings can change across time (Morson and Emerson 1990: 369).

Although developed for studying the novel, a growing number of film scholars have used the chronotope in film analysis. In fact, film theorist Robert Stam (1989: 11) argued that the concept is 'ideally suited' for film analysis. After all, films literally encapsulate the taking place of time, the film-screening itself an event through which 'spatial and temporal indicators are fused into one carefully thought-out concrete whole' (Stam 1989: 11). A number of film theorists have used the chronotope in a similar way to how I formulate the slum chronotope here. Sue Vice (1997), in her introduction to Bakhtinian theories, reformulates the 'chronotope of the road' in her feminist reading of the popular Hollywood film, *Thelma and Louise* (1991), which she approaches as a road movie. Paula Massood (1998, 2011) identifies the 'antebellum chronotope', 'the black city ghetto chronotope' and the 'hood chronotope' in her study of the historical development of African American films. In a reading of lesbian spaces in cinema, Lee Wallace (2011: 11) suggests the examination of the 'apartment chronotope' in selected narrative films as 'the privileged marker of lesbian possibility'. Martin Flanagan (2009) examines classic Bakhtinian chronotopes at play in contemporary Hollywood genres.

Two works that use the chronotope in film analysis relate more closely to how I develop the slum chronotope in relation to generic and representational significance. First, I look to Vivian Sobchack's (1998) well-known essay on classic American film noir, where she identifies 'lounge time' as the genre's 'master chronotope'. The chronotope of 'lounge time' is apparent in the primacy of spaces of non-dwelling (bars, saloons, brothels, hotels) in film noir's narrative and character configuration, corresponding to the cultural anxieties of the loss of home and tradition in the historic period of post-war America. For Sobchack (1998: 150) chronotopes serve as 'the spatiotemporal currency between the two orders of existence and discourse', bridging the film text to its context, the fictional world to the 'real' world. Sobchack (1998: 151) reiterates the chronotope's generic significance as such: 'Never merely the spatiotemporal backdrop for narrative events, they provide the literal and concrete ground from which narrative and character emerge as the temporalization of human action, significant in its diacritical marking of both cultural and narrative space.'

I also draw from Hamid Naficy's (2001) use of the chronotope for textual analysis in his influential study of 'accented cinema' or films by exilic filmmakers. According to Naficy (2001: 153), the chronotope operates as the 'optics with which we may understand both the films and the historical conditions of displacement that give rise to them'. In his textual readings, Naficy reads into the 'structures of feelings' (taking after Raymond Williams) enabled by certain chronotopes which are often present in accented cinema. For example, 'open chronotopes' of nature, mountains and monuments are imbued with temporal feelings of introspection and nostalgia related to imaginaries of the homeland. In contrast, some exilic filmmakers use 'closed chronotopes' of prisons or jail cells connoting times of claustrophobia and panic. Some films under the genre of accented cinema might also use 'border chronotopes', the middle ground of open and closed chronotopes where narratives depict journeys and border crossings. In locating chronotopes in his case studies of accented cinema, Naficy (2001: 153) explains how these chronotopes are 'mutually inclusive', such that they may 'reinforce, coexist with, or contradict one another'.

While Sobchack's and Naficy's works address the chronotope's value as generic and representational tool in textual analysis, I return to the concept's literary roots to strengthen this study's aim of seeking imaginaries of spatial justice. Julian Murphet's (2001) study of representations of space in novels set in Los Angeles is useful in this regard. According to Murphet (2001: 24): 'The tradition in structuralist thought of presenting cultural forms as "imaginary resolutions to real contradictions" acquires a new potency when these contradictions are grasped as *spatial*.' This is an assertion that directly links with the perspective of spatial justice. Murphet proceeds to develop this spatial approach with Lefebvre's production of space, emphasising that Lefebvre's spatial triad 'can hardly be thought of as fitting into some agreeably harmonizing palimpsest of totality' (2001: 24). According to Murphet, Lefebvre's understanding of the production of space does away with dilemmas of authenticity in representation, with the premise that 'the "real" is always and already shot through with representationality' (2001: 28). A chronotopic approach thus means examining cultural texts 'not as mirrors held up in nature, but as acts of appropriation of social space' (Murphet 2001: 28). As Murphet (2001: 28) argues, chronotopic representations can be read 'as a series of enactments of spatial appropriation by individuals (and their group affiliations)'.

Similarly, in my own chronotopic readings of spatial justice in Philippine urban cinema, I am not out to prove authenticity, or even to evaluate filmic realism. Chronotopic readings already assume that reality is always mediated in artistic expressions. Rather, I am interested in looking at how films organised through the imaginary of the slum chronotope may enable and offer moments of spatial appropriation in the films, which is constantly in dialogue with the spaces of justice and injustice beyond the screen. A chronotopic approach to spatial justice mines texts for instances in which characters – these 'subjectivities commensurate with their social spaces and times' (Murphet 2001: 30) – struggle against modes of injustice within their milieu.[3] In seeking spatial justice in these visual narratives, emancipatory potentials can be gleaned from strategies that attempt to reveal and/or suppress modes of domination and repression through their use of space in the time of narrative unfolding. From the perspective of this socio-spatial dialectic, slum films can be more productively evaluated in terms of the ways they are able to use space towards instances of emancipatory politics. Even if the ideological closure of the film narratives may at first glance be taken to mean the absolute absence of hope, this does not mean the films do not reveal moments where the social agents enact desires toward justice configured by the slum chronotope – the specific chronotopic form that I turn to next.

The Slum Chronotope

The slum chronotope that I locate as the organising centre of Philippine urban cinema, to borrow Vice's (1997: 201) words, 'may be puzzling or hard to grasp because it seems omnipresent to the point either of invisibility or extreme obviousness'. Most of the films analysed in this study are set within, reference or dialogue with the imaginary of Manila slums. If we understand the term 'slum' as referring generally to spaces of urban poverty, it would be reasonable to expect narratives and images that revolve around the theme of poverty. As Michael Montgomery (1993: 5) puts it: 'The chronotope references real-life situations rife with everyday associations for audiences, helping to create a sense of shared place.' Beyond this commonsensical view, the slum's chronotopic function significantly locates these narratives in the here and now of Philippine urban history, emplacing the genre in both local and global urban imaginary. It is in unpacking the spatio-temporal specificities of the slum chronotope, and the meanings they generate in relation to genre, that slum spaces function beyond mere setting, that is, chronotopically. As the slum chronotope organises narrative unfolding, so too can it potentially organise our ways of thinking about the times and spaces we live in.

The slum chronotope is what I deem to be the privileged structuring artistic expression that enables narrative unfolding in Philippine urban cinema. The slum chronotope operates as the organising centre of film narratives on two levels: (1) as that which constitutes and circumscribes (taking after Sobchak) the emerging genre of Philippine urban cinema; and (2) as the mediating form that bridges the real and imaginary worlds of slums. Like the very concept of slums, what I designate as the slum chronotope as imagined in film texts takes on specific configurations only when located in historically specific urban contexts. This means that the slum chronotope can potentially be used as a tool for analysis in films in other urban contexts. The choice and/or simulation of the Philippine slums as setting and space of reference in the narrative films included in this study, is generative of particular thematic concerns and characters and is the connective thread that runs through the emerging genre of Philippine urban cinema.

The slum chronotope relates to genre in two ways. First, as a tool for identifying the generic markers of what I consider Philippine urban cinema. In doing so, I am well aware of the limiting dangers of genre analysis in that it 'attempts to reduce and to channel the free play of meanings in certain predetermined manners' (Naficy 2001: 3). However, these pitfalls can be managed if sensitive to historical and cultural specificities in classifying films especially from non-Western contexts, and with the view that genres are never static. Second, I look at how the slum chronotope dialogues with genre as a structural guide for the study's progressive chapter discussions. The slum chronotope produces and dialogues with the genres of coming of age, the modalities of melodrama and noir, the Overseas Filipino Worker genre in the fourth chapter, and the teen film genre laced with the melodramatic mode in the final chapter. Looking at how the films' plots and character configurations dialogue with established genres and modalities enriches my textual analysis as I am able to identify similar, yet culturally specific modes of representation.

I deliberately invoke the term 'slum' in my designation of the slum chronotope to enter the various discourses that this word has generated in its very usage, or the discomfort that the term invokes in both ordinary and academic terms. Alan Gilbert (2007) all but denounced the use of the term 'slums' by Davis and the UN, calling it a dangerous resuscitation of the term. Gilbert (2007: 701) argues: 'What makes the word "slum" dangerous is the series of negative associations that the term conjures up, the false hopes that a campaign against slums raises and the mischief that unscrupulous politicians, developers and planners may do with term.' Relatedly, Jeremy Seabrook (2009) argues in a *Guardian* column that the slum term is a problematic, colonial British term, saying that it assumes homogeneity of slum formation and development. For Seabrook (2009): 'the word "slum" is a treacherous term. Since slums have all but disappeared in western cities, this suggests they are an inescapable phase of progress, and will, in due course, also vanish from Kinshasa, Cairo and Nairobi.'

A number of non-Western thinkers have critically engaged with the slum imaginary, while being wary that this is a provisional term. Vyjayanthi Rao (2013) for instance, is known for proposing the 'slum as theory'. She describes 'the particular understanding of slum as theory or [slum] as imaginary, rather than merely as empirical object' (Rao 2013: 681) in figuring the emplacement of the megacity in the global city. Ananya Roy (2011: 225) has also argued, while proposing new subaltern concepts to think through the megacity, that 'it is necessary to confront how the megacity is worlded through the icon of the slum'. Although this study's theory of the slum chronotope is aligned with the slum as theory approach, I also take heed of Pushpa Arabindoo's (2011: 643) warning to 'restrain it from becoming a rhetoric linchpin that dehistorcises and depoliticises the experiences of the urban poor' – which is why I strive to contextualise the study's film texts in Philippine sociopolitical conditions.

Poverty Pornography

The unfavourable commentary surrounding slum imaginaries recalls the accusations of poverty pornography surrounding films like *City of God* (Meirelles and Lund 2004) set in the slums of Rio de Janeiro and the remarkably successful film, *Slumdog Millionaire* (Boyle 2008), set in the slums of Mumbai. Novelist Arundhati Roy's (2009) harsh critique of *Slumdog Millionaire* provides a succinct description of poverty pornography: 'Politically, the film de-contextualises poverty – by making poverty an epic prop, it disassociates poverty from the poor. It makes India's poverty a landscape, like a desert or a mountain range, an exotic beach, god-given, not man-made.'[4] Philippine urban cinema's success in the international circuit coincides with the production of these other 'slum films' – with Filipino filmmaker Brillante Mendoza's Best Director triumph at the Cannes Film Festival for the film, *Kinatay* (2009), occurring in the same year as Danny Boyle's triumph for *Slumdog Millionaire* at the Oscars.

This charge of poverty pornography ascribed to slum films is actually what piqued my own interest in this study, prompted as well by criticism of Philippine slum films by Filipino academics. In an early critique, Gary Devilles (2008) comments on the 'poverty of pornography' exhibited by Philippine independent films seemingly made for the voyeuristic consumption of an international audience. Similarly, filmmaker and academic Eulalio Guieb (2012) argues that many of these films fail to recognise and represent the political structures that produce and sustain Philippine poverty. In a critical essay that hugely informs my selection of Philippine urban cinema, Patrick Campos (2011: 13) notes the thorny issue of 'pornography' in 'new urban realist films' in terms of how they have 'capitalised on "regressive discourses" about its own culture'. Leading Filipino film scholar Rolando Tolentino (2014) calls the recognised look of Philippine independent films the new mainstream and challenges indie filmmakers to go beyond what he deems predictable representations of poverty. In a more recent article, Enzo Gonzaga (2017) argues that Philippine urban poverty films, exemplified by Mendoza's works, demonstrate excessive displays of poverty that are unnecessary to the narrative.[5]

While I do not completely disagree with the existing critique of Philippine urban cinema as poverty porn, it's worth thinking through what the category means. Otherwise, using the term risks outrightly dismissing films organised around slum imaginaries, or even limiting the question to: 'How much poverty is too much poverty?' To use the poverty porn critique is to rightfully raise questions around audience and the ethics of representation. Who are these films for?[6] How are the films' subjects portrayed? What social and political signs are the films capable of referencing? While I'm unable to engage fully with the question of audience, I attempt to wrestle with questions of representation and ethics through the tools of the slum chronotope and spatial justice in the analysis of my selected films.

I contend that Philippine urban cinema remains a productive scope of inquiry if we attempt to locate different, and hopefully supplementary, routes of reading to the poverty porn critique. Thus this study's proposal of the slum chronotope is rather like a necessary detour from poverty porn, as it attempts to track alternative routes of reading in what I argue to be productive examples of Philippine urban cinema. As a point of clarification, this study is not arguing that all films charged with poverty porn are potentially progressive; nor am I saying that the films I have chosen to examine here absolutely radical or subversive. While taking care not to overplay the political interventions of Philippine urban cinema, I am starting from the position that these films are not completely devoid of hope, dignity and imaginaries of social justice as they might initially seem. I contend that the lens of spatial justice and the concept of the slum chronotope enable a new route of approaching slum imaginaries in films that are often accused of poverty pornography, which does not discount the ethical conversations that can be brought forth by analysing narrative and subjective configurations.

On Realism and Cinematic Ethics

The charge of poverty pornography ascribed to slum films implicitly situates Philippine urban cinema within the discourse of realism and the related issue of ethics in film studies. The question of the 'real' hovers over the sinuous issue of how to represent poverty in films, with the poverty porn charge bearing with it not just a sense of inauthenticity, but more significantly, violence and exploitation of the film's marginalised subjects and subject matter. Mendoza, when asked to respond to accusations of poverty porn, has consistently argued he only seeks to show Philippine reality. In one interview, he says: 'Why are we embarrassed to show the truth, if this is really truthful, if this is what's really happening?'[7] (ABS-CBN News 2012). In a *New York Times* interview, he remarks: 'So is it poverty porn when you are telling stories of society?' (Qin 2016).

It is not difficult to see some of the elements associated with film neo-realism in Philippine urban cinema.[8] Emerging post-World War II, Italian neorealist films, primarily represented by *Rome, Open City* (Rossellini 1945) and *Bicycle Thieves* (De Sica 1948) are known for the use of location shooting, non-professional actors and documentary-style aesthetics (Fabe 2004; Shiel 2012). Italian neorealist narratives are also known to focus on working-class protagonists and their struggle against material and social conditions (Fabe 2004; Shiel 2012). In terms of setting, neorealist films are set in bleak and impoverished post-war urban spaces, with Robert Stam (2000: 73) describing post-war realism as emerging from the 'smoke and ruins of European cities'. Not limited to Italian cinema, neorealist elements have been redeployed and reconfigured in the cinematic traditions of other national contexts with more overt sociopolitical motivations, such as the Cinema Novo in Brazil and the Third Cinema movement in Latin America (Giovacchini and Sklar 2011).

Although this study does not dwell fully on the aesthetics of neorealism, the real is undoubtedly present in the films analysed here – most of which (although not all) take place on location in actual slums. As argued in the previous section, the study thinks through realism via the chronotope, which assumes that the 'real' is always mediated in artistic expressions. The theory of the chronotope acknowledges that mediated artistic expressions are derived from 'actual chronotopes of the world' (Bakhtin 1981: 235) – the slum chronotope could not have been imagined if not for the actual existence of slums. I welcome Igor Krstić's (2016) approach to neorealism as a transnational style of filmmaking that has been adapted and reconfigured in other urban centres of the world. In his work, he cites some of the Philippine films included in this study as examples of 'digital realisms' (Krstić 2016: 164), a new mode enabled by the digital turn. Echoing Lúcia Nagib (2011), who remarks that the digital medium has allowed access to locations that were once inaccessible, Krstić notes how the digital turn has enabled shooting in difficult spatial environments such as urban slums. With this new mode of production, Krstić underscores the constant shifting of fictional and factual worlds in the films, as shooting on location captures the lived reality of slum life and its inhabitants in the films' fictional narratives – an observation that closely relates to what I mean by chronotopic mediation.

As for realism and ethics, Nagib's (2011) formulation of the 'ethics of realism' is useful in thinking through the value-laden visual rendering of the slum imaginary.[9] Nagib (2011: 10) defines ethics not in the moral sense, but as 'realist modes of production and address, typical of new waves of new cinemas', and she argues: 'to choose reality instead of simulation is a moral question, but one that concerns casts and crews alone in their drive to merge with the phenomenological real' (2011: 10). She argues that when the cast and crew demonstrate fidelity to the act of capturing physical reality in films – 'this commitment translates into ethics' (2011: 32).

While this book aligns with Nagib's thoughts on physical realism in some of the ways I analyse the presentation of the built environment of slums and urban spaces (especially the kind of reality produced through and because of contingencies while filming), I approach ethics not just in the sense of presentations of physical reality, but also in the broad philosophical sense of moral codes and imaginaries of social justice visually rendered through the socio-spatial dialectic. While Nagib is careful not to define ethics in the philosophical sense, this book, with its aim of locating moments of spatial justice, aligns itself with attempts at examining 'cinematic ethics' (Sinnerbrink 2015), which recognises the value of cinema as 'a medium of ethical experience' (Sinnerbrink 2015: 3). I share the belief of philosopher Alain Badiou (2013: 211) when he argues that cinema serves a moral purpose in its capacity to represent 'great figures of humanity in action'. It is worth quoting Badiou's (2013: 232) remarks on the ethics of cinema as it can be linked to the abject realities imagined in slum films: 'Cinema . . . says in its own way: "There are victories even in the worst of worlds."' This is not to say that this study embarks on a sort of moralising quest; it does, however, raise and touch upon issues of morality in its readings of narrative and character configurations aimed at understanding attempts at representing social agency and subjective formation through spatial appropriations – attempts at seeking spatial justice in spaces of injustice.

Notes

1. Harvey (1973: 98) argues that social justice as it relates to space refers to 'a just distribution justly arrived at'. It is this formulation of space and social justice that Harvey (1997; 2000) updates, revises and expands throughout the years in order to address contemporary concerns such as environmental justice (e.g. new environmental hazards in spaces of poverty) and the politics of difference. At the same time, Harvey (1997) cautions against superficial claims to identity and difference that obscure the social processes that reinforce inequality and social exclusion.
2. See Igor Krstić's (2016) discussion of Jacob Riis's image of New York slums.
3. Murphet (1998) earlier used the theory of the chronotope in a compelling essay on film noir, where he reads the absence of the feminine and black spaces in the genre as projections of a certain racial unconscious.
4. The term 'poverty pornography' emerged fairly recently in the 1980s. According to Nandita Dogra (2013), the term was popularised by Jørgen Lissner, and later gained currency among academics and aid workers who critiqued the use of images of starving children in fundraising campaigns led by international organisations.
5. In his essay, Gonzaga proposes the concept of 'slum voyeurism' instead of poverty porn as he argues this better captures the lack of consent from those subjected to the camera's gaze, as well as how it links with poverty tourism. I'm not

opposed to the term, however, I also think the term poverty porn signals the exact same ideas, perhaps even more productively if we recall its historical emergence in the context of international aid and development work.
6. Mendoza, when asked about who his films are for replied: 'The middle class. These films might be about the lower classes, and it is their stories we are telling, but these films are not for them.'(Baumgartel 2012: 11)
7. Translation mine.
8. André Bazin's (1967; 1971) writings on film realism remain highly influential in contemporary film analysis, which endorsed the realist aesthetics of the long take and deep focus.
9. Nagib (2011) makes a distinction between presentation and representation, with her study being more aligned with presentational cinema, or what she calls 'presentational ethics'.

CHAPTER 2

The Rise of Manila Slums and Philippine Urban Cinema

This chapter introduces the theory of the slum chronotope in Philippine urban cinema. I first outline the rise of Manila slums as urban forms that reveal a history of spatial injustice. I then locate the slum chronotope alongside the development of Philippine cinema, citing earlier notable films set in Manila, leading up to the current independent wave of Manila-based films.

Metropolitan Manila ranks seventeenth in the world's most populated urban populations, with an estimated 13.5 million residents (United Nations, Department of Economic and Social Affairs, and Population Division 2019). In 2011, roughly 4 million slum-dwellers, or one out of ten people, lived in the seventeen cities and districts that comprise Metropolitan Manila (Ballesteros 2011). This figure would have grown by 3.4 per cent annually, with figures projected to reach 6.5 million in 2020, and a staggering 13 million in 2050 (Ballesteros 2011). In 2018, Manila's slum inhabitants stood at 17 million (UN-Habitat 2004).

While there is no strict definition for Philippine slums, some general markers have been identified, which essentially refer to inadequate living conditions: 'Slums are defined as buildings or areas that are deteriorated, hazardous, unsanitary or lacking in standard conveniences. These are also defined as the squalid, crowded or unsanitary conditions under which people live, irrespective of the physical state of the building or area' (UN-Habitat 2003: 215). In terms of location, Manila slum communities are 'generally dispersed, located wherever there is space and opportunity' (UN-Habitat 2004: 215).

In contrast to the *favelas* of Brazil, the *kampungs* of Malaysia and Indonesia, or the *aashwa'i* of Egypt, the most popular word for slums and slum inhabitants in the Philippines remains the English term, 'squatter', converted phonetically into Tagalog as '*iskwater*'. As Erhard Berner (2000: 556) has found in his research on Philippine slums, the terms 'slum', 'squatter' and 'urban poor' blend into each other in actual usage. More specific Tagalog words for Manila slums might refer to location or spatial description, as quoted below from the UN special report on global slums:

- *iskwater* (a physically disorganised collection of shelters made of light and often visually unappealing materials where poor people reside);
- *estero* (narrower than sewers and associated with a bad smell);
- *eskinita* (alleys that fit only one person at a time);
- *looban* (meaning inner areas where houses are built very close to each other and often in a manner not visible to the general view of the city);
- *dagat-dagatan* (areas frequently flooded);
- "*Bedspacer*" (subtenant occupants of bunk bedding rental accommodation, four or six to a small room, usually young women who have come to the city looking for work. (UN-Habitat 2003: 10)

It is important to note that not all those who live in slums in Manila can be classified as poor, especially given their inclusion in the formal and informal economy. Berner (1997) notes the diverse composition of the urban poor in Manila:

> The so-called urban poor – i.e., people living in slums and illegal settlements – include not only the unemployed, underemployed and members of the informal sector but also major sections of the middle classes, like policemen, teachers, nurses, office clerks, and sales personnel, among others. Simultaneous inclusion and exclusion characterizes the urban poor's relationship with the metropolis. (Berner 1997: 124)

The production of urban slum spaces in the Philippines reveals a history of spatial injustice with its history of colonial occupation and segregation. We can trace this development from the period of colonial occupation up to the present period of stark inequality among Manila's urban inhabitants. As with many cities in the Third World, colonial occupation is embedded in the urban development of Metropolitan Manila. As Epifanio San Juan (1990: 189) powerfully notes: 'For the truth is that it was not through the clearing of wilderness to establish guilds and market-fairs, but through organized violence and the forcible imposition of feudal Christianity and theocratic authority that the scaffolding of the Philippine cities –not just Manila – was erected.'

The construction of Manila was ushered in by the establishment of the 'walled city' of Intramuros, which became the fortress of Spanish colonial rulers from 1571. The configuration of spaces around Intramuros indicates social segregation during the colonial period (Alcazaren et al. 2011; Reed 1978). Outside the walled city – aptly called Extramuros – the *indios* (the Spanish pejorative term for Filipino natives) were segregated along with other non-European inhabitants of Manila (Lico 2003). The streets of Extramuros were racially segregated: 'Dilao for the Japanese, Parian and Binondo for the Chinese, and Arrabales for the indios' (Lico 2003: 22).

The Spanish colonial period saw the forging of Manila as the Philippine archipelago's economic and political capital, with the surrounding areas of Intramuros serving as the main port for the galleon trade (Arn 1995). As Manila became the country's entrepôt centre for economic activity and international relations, more and more people took up residence in the city (Arn 1995). A century after Spanish occupation, Manila's population rose from 2,000 to a hundred thousand residents (Arn 1995). The population of the *arrabales* (suburbs) outside the walls of Intramuros steadily grew in spaces near port and factory areas (Alcazaren et al. 2011; Doeppers 1984).

Upon American occupation in 1898 following a mock Spanish-American war, Manila remained of prime importance to the new colonisers. In 1905, American architect Daniel Burnham, with his partner Pierce Anderson, proposed to build Manila under a 'City Beautiful' plan, which 'focused on the creation of a strong central civic core, from which radiated an enlarged and ordered city linked by grand radial and axial boulevards and embellished by plazas, fountains, parks, and playgrounds' (Alcazaren et al. 2011: 5). The plan 'sought to portray the colonial capital as an ordered, hierarchical, formal, and therefore a civilized city' (Cabalfin 2014: 155).

While some aspects of the Burnham Plan for Manila were initiated such as new residential areas in the suburbs, informal settlements and crowding started building up around the port areas of Tondo. In the 1930s the American colonial government formally identified Manila slums, areas that were described in official documents as 'breeding grounds for disease, crime, and sedition' (Alcazaren et al. 2011: 9). According to Cristina Evangelista Torres (2010: 71) the Burnham plan essentially addressed the needs of Americans living in the Manila, arguing that:

> Nowhere in the plan was there mention of upgrading Manila's slums where people, living in bamboo and nipa huts, were vulnerable to fire and epidemic outbreaks. Manila's poor were to remain in their wretched homes while government funds were spent on the upgrade of infrastructure for business, improvement of government buildings, and creation of rest and recreation facilities that ordinary Filipinos were probably too poor to afford and enjoy. (Torres 2010: 71–2)

The succeeding years saw the steady rise of slum communities in Manila, which American officials and the Philippine Commonwealth responded to with slum-clearing and relocation projects, interrupted by the destruction of the capital during World War II (Alcazaren et al. 2011). The post-war years and the granting of Philippine independence from the United States in 1946 resulted in the surge of even more migrants to the capital (Alcazaren et al. 2011). The ruins of Intramuros, which were completely destroyed by bombings in the war, became a popular squatting site for rural migrants, 'which provided settlers with ready-made walls via the ruins of old Spanish-era convents and churches' (Alcazaren et al. 2011: 62).

The state of Manila slums as most residents recognise it today was profoundly shaped by the rapid urbanisation in the 1960s and the modernising projects launched under the dictatorial regime of Ferdinand Marcos (Caoili 1988; Ortega 2016a, 2016b; Pinches 1994; Shatkin 2004). It was during the Marcos regime (1965–86) that the seventeen cities and districts that now constitute Metropolitan Manila was consolidated in 1975 (Alcazaren et al. 2011; Caoili 1988). The popular slogan, 'Marcos means more roads!' captures the spatial urban development associated with the Marcos period (Alcazaren et al. 2011). Upon declaring Martial Law in 1972, Marcos railroaded urban modernising projects with the aim of attracting multinational investments (Naerssen 2003). Significantly, Marcos urban projects were supported by a huge $2.5 billion loan from the World Bank (Naerssen 2003; Ortega 2016a).

Squatting was criminalised during the Marcos period under Presidential Decree 772 (repealed in 1997), which justified the government's aggressive mass relocations and evictions (Arn 1995; Berner 2000). Davis (2006) cites the case of Manila as exemplary in the regularity and scale of squatter evictions during the Marcos period. Mass evictions were infamously carried out during international events, such as the 1974 Miss Universe pageant and 1975 World Bank (WB)–International Monetary Fund (IMF) conference (Arn 1995; Davis 2006). Compared to the $13 million spent on housing construction in 1976, the Marcos administration allotted $360 million for the World Bank–IMF conference towards the construction of new hotels for the international delegates (Arn 1995). First Lady Imelda Marcos, who became Governor of Manila, thought of squatters as eyesores and as 'plain landgrabbers' (Berner 2000: 559).

The Marcos years laid the foundations for the state of Manila at present, as well as the very configuration of the Philippine economy as oriented towards exports and dependent on foreign loans and investments (Naerssen 2003). Succeeding administrations continued to ramp up projects that aimed to make Manila a global urban centre at the expense of displacing the urban poor (Shatkin 2004). Gavin Shatkin (2004: 2479) notes the neoliberal vision that underpins the government's urban policies: 'The Philippine government has cut its budget, decentralised the provision of infrastructure and services, and focused on attracting investment through the development of trunk infrastructure.' Similarly, Arnisson Andre Ortega (2016a: 35) argues that the development of properties financed by local and international developers in recently gentrified districts of Manila is intertwined with the decline of informal communities in these areas. The global facelift of Manila, according to Ortega (2016a: 36), is inseparable from the state's 'urban warfare against informality'.

Alongside the state's violent efforts to rid Manila of slums, it is important to note that slum inhabitants constantly stake their right to the city by strongly resisting demolitions. Noteworthy anthropological and ethnographic studies (Antolihao 2004; Arcilla 2015; Berner 1997; Jocano 1975; Lagman 2012) emphasise that slum inhabitants are not just victims of the state, but consistently stake their claims to inhabit the city. In his ethnographic study of Manila's slum inhabitants and their constant struggle against dispossession, Chester Arcilla (2015) highlights subaltern practices of resistance that show how the 'urban subaltern' assert their right to the city. Barricades set up against slum demolitions, for instance, are embodied acts of resistance that show political consciousness and resourcefulness. Arcilla (2015: 25) points at how the urban poor use whatever means at their disposal to strengthen their barricades against police and demolition agents: stones, bottles, dirty water, even '*tae* bombs' (faeces).

A memorable display of the urban poor's collective force, regarded with disdain by the middle and upper classes, was the urban event called 'EDSA 3'.[1] In this 2001 uprising, the urban poor took to the streets to protest the ouster of populist and former actor President Joseph Estrada whose persona was imagined to be pro-poor (Garrido 2008). Paradoxically, the urban poor is a huge resource that politicians tap for votes during election season (Hutchison 2007), even though their land rights are largely ignored. Despite the state's efforts to eradicate squatter settlements, these spaces have become integral to Manila's urban landscape, and in fact, to its very survival. As Berner (1997: 169) puts it, Manila slums and its inhabitants are 'fundamental rather than marginal. The globalized metropolitan economy is heavily subsidised by the existence of squatter colonies, and cannot function – let alone be competitive - without this subsidy.'

Philippine Urban Cinema and Traces of the Slum Chronotope

Manila figures prominently in Philippine film history as a real and imagined setting. In an essay that outlines representative 'Manila-centric' films from 1898–2000, film historian Nick Deocampo (2009) argues that Manila has functioned as symbolic metaphor for imagining the Philippine nation, from the time it was captured in newsreels during American occupation. American filmmakers went to Manila shortly after occupation in 1898, capturing or re-enacting images that portrayed American triumph in its new territory. Footage taken by American filmmakers from that period showed American soldiers alongside Filipino 'natives' supposedly embracing the influence of the new colonisers, with footage including images of American flags hanging from windows (Deocampo 2009). During the three-year Japanese occupation in

World War II, Japanese propaganda films depicted Manila as a city 'liberated' from the Americans by its new colonisers. (Deocampo 2009). The 1940s–60s post-war era produced movies like Lamberto Avellana's *A Portrait of the Artist as Filipino* (1965) which reimagined a romanticised view of Intramuros before the war, signalling a nation struggling with its colonial past and identity construction (Deocampo 2009). Manila imaginaries in early films paved the way for the emergence of the slum imaginary in later films, running parallel to the city's modernisation and urbanisation in the post-war era.

Canonical literature on the development of Philippine cinema generally recognises two 'Golden Ages' (David 1990; Guerrero 1983b; Tiongson 1983a). The first is dated to the 1950s studio-system era that produced genre films, while the second golden age – which will be referenced often in this book – covers the period of the 1970s to the 1980s during the Marcos dictatorial regime (Tiongson 1983a; David 1990).[2] The present period that has seen the rise of digital independent cinema is what some have touted as the third golden age.

From the first golden age, Lamberto Avellana's *Anak Dalita* (*Child of Sorrow*, 1956) might be an early example of a film grounded on the slum chronotope. The film, awarded Best Film in the Asia Pacific Film Festival, is set in the ruins of Intramuros and tells the story of a prostitute and a war veteran's involvement in crime. More significant, however, are the social realist Manila-set films from the second golden age, which can be considered precursors of contemporary Philippine urban cinema. Lino Brocka's *Maynila sa mga Kuko ng Liwanag* (*Manila in the Claws of Light*, 1975) and Ishmael Bernal's *Manila By Night* (1980), also known as *City After Dark*, are regarded as some of the most significant films from that period. Brocka and Bernal's films challenged the urban imaginaries of modern development during the Marcos era. *Manila By Night*, an ensemble narrative that privileges the marginalised characters of the city at night (prostitutes, addicts, queers), changed its title because Imelda Marcos thought the film showed the capital in a bad light (David 2012). Brocka's *Manila in the Claws of Light*'s narrative is considered the prototype of the narrative of the rural migrant swallowed by the darkness of the city. The film follows the story of Julio Madiaga, a fisherman who ventures into the city in search for his beloved, Ligaya (Joy), who was forced into prostitution. It is also impossible not to mention Brocka's *Insiang* (1976) which tells the story of a young girl's suffering in the slums of Tondo – a Manila district that signifies slums in the Philippine imaginary (I discuss Tondo further in Chapter 4).

It is not difficult to glean traces of the slum chronotope in these second golden age canonical Philippine films. In Rolando Tolentino's (2014: 10) monograph on Brocka films, he analyses the use of 'squatter colonies' in Brocka's city films as 'sites of disruption in the ideal transnational space that seeks both to erase poverty as development utopia as much as it was engrossed in poverty for the continuous supply of urban surplus'. Meanwhile, film critic Patrick Campos (2011: 5) identifies *Manila in the Claws of Light* as 'the pioneer urban realist film'. Campos (2011) argues that Brocka and Bernal's urban realism – in foregrounding the slums and the urban poor – directly countered Marcosian urban posturings at the time of their release.

Among the filmmakers in the second golden age, Brocka is undoubtedly the most highly regarded, and was an active proponent of social realism (Guerrero 1983a; Tolentino 2014). Among his many accolades, Brocka was the first Filipino filmmaker to have a film screened at the Cannes Film Festival. His large body of work has set the standards by which new Philippine films are measured against in terms of subject, style and a host of other factors. Despite the difficult subject of some of his films, Brocka is lauded for his commercial success and his exceptional retooling of Hollywood genre conventions in his own films (Capino 2006; 2010). New Filipino filmmakers, Mendoza especially, are often touted as 'the next Lino Brocka'.

Although the late Brocka is revered among local and international critics, he has not escaped the charge of exoticising Philippine poverty for foreign audience consumption (Capino 2010; Tolentino 2014). I note that the first Brocka film screened at the Cannes Film Festival, *Insiang* (1976), strongly dialogues with Philippine independent urban cinema's use of the slum chronotope, given its privileging of the slums of Manila as setting. *Insiang* is a family melodrama about a young woman's struggle to escape the oppressive slums of Tondo, Manila, and might be considered Brocka's most internationally acclaimed film alongside *Manila in the Claws of Light*.

Nicanor Tiongson (2013) dates the rise of 'the new wave indie film' in 2005, citing the following reasons for its emergence: the advent of cheap digital technology, the faltering of the local film industry, the establishment of new local film festivals (particularly the Cinemalaya Film Festival), the resurgence of patronage of indie films by the 'educated middle class', and the entry of a new class of indie filmmakers. The Manila-based Cinemalaya film festival numbers indicates the gradual rise of Philippine independent cinema: from thirty features and six shorts in 2005, the festival produced seventy-five full features and 110 shorts in its tenth year (Zulueta 2014).

The rise of the digital independent wave in Philippine cinema comes at the heels of a struggling mainstream film industry (Hernandez 2014), with the steady decline of films cited as indicative of the slump. From an average of 140 local film productions annually from the 1960s to 1999, only an average of seventy-three per year were produced in the following decade (Virola 2010). The rise in ticket costs, rampant piracy, competition from foreign films, government censorship and state-imposed taxes are some of the reasons behind the decline of the Philippine film industry (Del Mundo Jr 2013; Whaley 2012). Philippine independent cinema, according to its proponents, is the local filmmaker's welcome response to the dying film industry (Del Mundo Jr 2013; N. G. Tiongson 2013; Tioseco 2007), even as the films remain limited to a middle-class audience.

While film practitioners have generally been optimistic about the new wave of Philippine indie cinema (N. G. Tiongson 2013; Tioseco 2007), some scholars approach this recent development with a grain of salt. Leading Philippine film scholar Joel David (2014) seems hesitant to dub the current period, or 'the self-valorization of independent (now synonymous with digital) contemporary film artists', as the new golden age. Since the digital wave took off, the notion of independence has become more flexible, as local networks and corporations started funding so-called independent films (Hernandez 2014; N. G. Tiongson 2013). Acclaimed film critic Rolando Tolentino (2014: 13) also harshly criticises the new breed of films for its lack of aesthetic diversity and the establishment of its own internal hierarchy, with internationally acclaimed filmmakers on top: 'Some ten years of Philippine indie cinema has achieved what probably took mainstream cinema a hundred years to develop – to become his own hegemony.'

The Philippine independent industry itself seems aware of the charges of formulaic aesthetics and subject matter in films that feature urban poverty. An interesting mode of self-criticism comes in film form, with the film *Ang Babae sa Septic Tank* (*The Woman in the Septic Tank*; Rivera 2011). The film is a satirical movie-within-a-movie that takes on the exploitative inclinations of Philippine independent cinema. A memorable scene features the fictional film crew's search for the perfect slum location for an award-winning film. Interestingly, the film won major awards in that year's Cinemalaya Film Festival, including Best Film.

While there are a number of Filipino filmmakers who are now 'regular fixtures on the foreign festival circuit' (Zafra 2011), the filmmaker that I consider to be at the forefront of contemporary Philippine urban cinema is 2009 Cannes Palm d'Or winner Brillante Mendoza. Mendoza is the first Filipino filmmaker to have been nominated in the prestigious category. He won for directing *Kinatay* (2009), one of the films that will be examined in this study. *Kinatay* opens in Manila slums and unravels to track the brutal abduction and murder of a prostitute by a gang of dirty cops. A number of Mendoza's films produced prior to and after *Kinatay* are set in or heavily feature Manila slums, while all of his films to date tackle difficult themes. As earlier noted, Mendoza consistently denies the charge of poverty porn. He also admits that while his films feature fictional characters that depict the urban poor, his films are for students and the middle class (Baumgartel 2012; Valerio 2012).[3]

In contrast to the urban imaginaries offered by representative films from the second golden age, what are the new aesthetics offered in contemporary Philippine urban cinema? Campos (2011: 9) identifies spatiotemporal markers as the distinguishing features of urban realist films from the Philippine independent wave: '1) the radical emphasis on milieu as primary locus of narrative knowing and 2) the appropriation of real-time visual narration'. For Campos (2011), while these aesthetics are not new in world cinema (comparable to Italian neorealism), they are arguably new in Philippine cinema if compared to Brocka's brand of realism. In an early appraisal, academic and filmmaker Alvin Yapan (2008) identifies three aesthetic elements of Philippine independent cinema that has to do with its mode of production: first, single location shooting (which he argues Brocka has already done); second, the 'singularity and presence of the involved camera'; and third, the use of time 'set not only in the present, but in the quotidian'.[4] These general aesthetic markers of contemporary Philippine urban cinema can certainly be gleaned from the films included in this study, set in dialogue with the genre and modalities organised by the slum chronotope.

Notes

1. EDSA is short for Epifanio delos Santos Avenue, which is known as the site for the 1986 People Power uprising that ousted Ferdinand Marcos. See Sumsky (1992).
2. David (2014) notes the inclusion of an earlier golden age in the 1930s as outlined in a government-commissioned encyclopaedia; this is not generally recognised by Filipino film scholars.
3. Mendoza became an even more troubling auteur in the year Duterte assumed office. He directed the Duterete's first State of the Nation Address and produced two pro bono short films backing the new administration's war on drugs.
4. In this short paper presentation, Yapan also cites Bakthin's essay on the chronotope, but he quotes Bakhtin's description of exoticism rather than the theory of the chronotope.

CHAPTER 3

The Slum Chronotope in Philippine Cinema Genres and Modalities

Film historian Nick Deocampo (2007a, 2007b, 2011) describes the development of Philippine cinema as taking shape through a 'trialectic of cultural influences', with the combination of Hispanic, American and Filipino influences. Motion picture was introduced in 1897 in Manila while an insurgency was being waged against the weakening Spanish forces (Del Mundo Jr 1999; Deocampo 2007b). Cinema was subsequently used for colonising purposes by the Americans (Deocampo 2007b, 2011; Flores 1998) followed by efforts by local elites to indigenise the new technology (Del Mundo Jr 1998; Lumbera 1983). This triad of influences remains evident in the films produced at present. Relatedly, Jose Capino (2006) suggests viewing Philippine films as a rich cinema of hybridity that has shown how a local industry appropriates foreign traditions in filmmaking, particularly in terms of genre films.

From this understanding of the hybridity of Philippine cinema, this chapter looks at how the slum chronotope reorganises genres and modalities situated in the Philippine context, providing the broad contours of the film analysis in Part II. I outline some elements of the coming-of-age genre and the teen/youth film genre, the modalities of melodrama and noir, and the Overseas Filipino Worker genre, and look at how these are generally retooled in Philippine urban cinema before the close analysis of films in Part II.

COMING-OF-AGE: CHILDREN AND YOUTH NARRATIVES OF DEVELOPMENT

The conventional elements of the coming-of-age genre are anchored on the choice of young characters, usually male, who undergo a significant transition from innocence to maturity. This model comes from the German literary tradition of the *Bildungsroman*, also called the novel of formation or the novel of development. Jerome Buckley (1974: 17) describes the genre's plot structure as such: 'A child of some sensibility grows up in the country or a provincial town, where he finds constraints, social and intellectual, placed upon the free imagination.'[1]

In European cinema, the coming-of-age genre emerged from the ruins of World War II, particularly in Italian neorealist films and German rubble films (Fisher 2007; Sorlin 2000; Wood 2006). Historian Pierre Sorlin (2000: 109) notes the 'invention' of childhood in European films in the 1940s, and suggests that before then, the presence of children in films were marginally used to reinforce the ideas of masculine superiority and the nuclear family. Philosopher Gilles Deleuze's (2013) notion of the child as seer in Italian neorealist films remains influential in its characterisation of the child figure's function in post-war cinema. According to Deleuze, the child as seer is a passive character whose sensory motor-skills are rendered immobile by deep trauma. For Deleuze (2013: 3): 'in the adult world, the child is affected by a certain motor helplessness, but one which makes him all the more capable of seeing and hearing'. The child seer for Deleuze is not an image of movement or action, but is an image of time that belongs to 'a cinema of the seer and no longer of the agent' (Deleuze 2013: 2).

Deleuze's foundational account of the child as seer has since been challenged for its configuration of a mere passive figure. Jaimey Fisher (2007: 33) argues against Deleuze's characterisation of the child figure as weak, saying that this 'reeks of an imaginary discourse about youth'. Fisher's account is premised on his assertion that neorealist films, or what Deleuze has characterised as the shift from movement-image to time-image signified through the emergence of the child figure, is actually more reflective of the loss of traditional male agency rather than child's weakness. This lament for weak masculinity, according to Fisher, explains why in most German rubble films and Italian neorealist films, the child figure is male. Fisher (2007: 33) argues that children in film reveal 'an oscillation of the child between active agency and passive observation'.

In her study on the figure of the child in film, Karen Lury (2010: 1) argues that the child's position as the 'other' of the rational adult often situates the figure in alternative spaces and temporalities where 'the child must work with and against their imperfect ability to speak of their experience'. Discussing the archetypal use of the setting of the forest and the fairy-tale narrative in war films, Lury (2010: 125) examines how child figures are able to provide 'for a sensual impression and response that takes the viewer beyond meaningful/meaningless silence to a more visceral or haptic confrontation with the violence of the war-time environment'. The same emphasis on the child's experience as 'other' might be said of the Philippine urban films centred on the figure of the child, although instead of the forest, the child figures are situated in the culturally and historically specific slum spaces of Manila.

Philippine urban films centred on slum children in the neoliberal era relate more closely to figures of children in neorealist world cinema. The image of 'the street kid' is a recognisable character in neorealist world cinema (Krstić 2016: 108), with Luis Buñuel's *Los Olvidados* (1950) being a pioneering example. Igor Krstić (2016) aligns world cinema's street kid with Italian neorealist films, which generally end in tragedy. An example of the street kid character is the 'street urchin film' from the cinemas of Mexico, Brazil, India and Argentina. For João Luiz Vieira (2009: 228), street urchin films 'deal with fundamentally similar situations in which youth are undervalued and, as a result, they perceive their daily lives as senseless and often engage in criminal behavior that ultimately leads to a dead-end future'. More interestingly, he cites the possibility of bringing in recent films from Philippine independent cinema into this grouping of 'a sort of genre of favela cinema' (Vieira 2009: 243).

Coming-of-age narratives organised around the slum chronotope spatialise the particular time and space of childhood traditionally associated with notions of play and innocence. However, the time-space of childhood in slums is far removed from this carefree configuration. Writing about the politics of childhood, Sharon Stephens (1995) remarks that some children, street children, are perceived to be less vulnerable than others. Children who loiter on streets, spaces considered to be outside their spheres of safe socialisation *are* the risk – these are children who are literally and symbolically 'out of place' (Stephens 1995: 13). The slum chronotope configures coming-of-age narratives that, from their very conception, already assume the formation of children that are already out of place and out of time, whether they are at risk or they *are* the risk. Because they are out of place and out of time, the slum chronotope makes possible the configurations of a space of childhood that is not aligned with the liberal formulations of innocence and play. It is in this way that we can understand the slum space to be a space of injustice particularly for children.[2]

And yet, by choosing to anchor narratives on children, coming-of-age narratives that take place in slums also inherently express a desire for the future. As Robin Wood (2006: 190) puts it in his description of neorealist cinema narratives: 'the precarious, shifting balance of despair and hope for renewal is repeatedly poised in the lives (and deaths) of children'. Children occupy a paradoxical position in slum spaces, in that their presence in such dire conditions is deemed atrociously unacceptable, and yet they also keep the slum space alive, in a manner of speaking. Mike Davis (2006: 186) for instance, has remarked that child labour in slums all over the world 'constitutes an important sector of most informal urban economies'. Studies on child poverty in the Philippines often find that children are compelled to work to help their families survive – a fact that has undoubtedly made its way in Philippine literary and visual representations. The focus on the abundance of children in slum spaces globally points to the potential of a future generation, at the same time that it suggests the precarity of that future given that their childhood is taking place in the dire conditions of the slum space.

At the heart of the coming-of-age narrative configured by the slum chronotope is the implicit desire for the future – which is why I would argue that the slum child constantly strives for a semblance of innocence even as the figure is socialised in dangerous and abject spaces. The child figures exhibit the slippage between active agency and passivity, punctuated with the hope that there are time-spaces to look forward to when they grow up and out of the time-space of childhood. The slum chronotope configures coming-of-age narratives where children set out on a journey of seeking a place for themselves in the future. To claim time, or to claim a future, the slum child must find spaces in the slums where time exists. And in attempting to appropriate spaces that are simultaneously attempts to find time, the slum child protagonist is actually engaging in spatial practices aimed towards a sense of justice. Matthew Kaiser (2011) raised a similar point in his characterisation of time-space in Victorian slum narratives:

> When people have no future, no time to call their own, space becomes all the more meaningful to them, the very foundation on which they cultivate a sense of self. If slum-dwellers seem excessively territorial, obsessed with controlling a particular street corner to the point of death, it is because the control of space provides what little ego-gratification is available within a slum. The slum intensifies the experience of space. (Kaiser 2011: 72)

The figure of the slum child as a complex figure of agency in films – as opposed to being a helpless victim – informs my analysis of selected coming-of-age Philippine urban films. In Philippine literature and cinema, the character of the orphaned child or the street urchin has been used time and again in popular works. In Lino Brocka's body of work, for instance, film historian Rafael Guerrero (1983a: 235) notes the presence of 'orphans or at least children deprived of a normal daily life …' Among the film titles Guerrero (1983a: 235) mentions, it is useful to note *Lumuha Pati Mga Anghel* (*Even Angels Wept*; 1971) which features 'a ragtag band of street urchins fending for themselves'. Guerrero also notes that this film pays tribute to another classic Philippine film centred on an abused child heroine, *Roberta* (La Torre 1951).[3]

A notable title that features a child protagonist in mainstream production is the tear-jerker *Magnifico* (de los Reyes 2003), which is about a young boy's struggle to care for his dying grandmother and disabled sister. From the independent scene, several films screened at the Cinemalaya Film Festival might be considered coming-of-age films, foremost being the whimsical musical, *Pepot Artista* (*Pepot Superstar*; Del Mundo Jr 2005) which won Best Picture in the first Cinemalaya festival the same year *Ang Pagdadalaga* was screened. Notable indie titles that feature child protagonists dealing with difficult subject matters include *Sampaguita: National Flower* (Pasion 2010) and *Children's Show* (Cabrido 2014). The first features a group of street kids who peddle garlands of *sampaguita* for their livelihood, while the latter deals with children who are forced to fight in underground wrestling.

While I have so far discussed coming-of-age films that focus on children, there is also the teen film, which I will touch upon in my final chapter. In American cinema, the formalisation of the youth film or teen film genre is dated to the 1950s, alongside the very development of youth culture itself that saw the 'invention' of the concept of adolescence and the teenager (Cruz 1988; Doherty 2002; Driscoll 2019; Shary 2002). As with all genres, the generic markers of teen films are never fixed but evolve over time in different cultural contexts, depending on perceived adolescent concerns. Early teen films, for instance, featured juvenile delinquency, while teen films in the 1980s evolved into subgenres that gave a glimpse of changing adolescent interests and concerns, as outlined by Timothy Shary (2003: 503): 'the horror film, the science fiction film, the sex comedy, the romantic melodrama, the juvenile delinquent drama, and the school picture ...'

It is difficult to specify a fixed age range for what constitutes the period of adolescence across different cultures. However, leading studies on youth culture have found it useful to approach it as a liminal period 'during which individuals break free from many of features of childhood without yet fully adopting all of the characteristics associated with being an adult' (Hodkinson 2007: 1). This time of liminality is a useful way of characterising the period in which characters are emplaced in teen films. Describing liminality in youth films, Adrian Martin (2018: 298) said: 'In this ephemeral state of suspension, everything seems eternal – and possible.' Coming-of-age in the slum space suggests being located in a space both visible and invisible to the urban economy, its youth figures located both inside and outside the modern city.

In American cinema, Philippine urban cinema's youth films can be aligned with 'hood' films. These films featured young black men in urban ghettos, making visible the experience of the city space for marginalised communities (Massood 2003). In world cinema, it is possible to align youth-centred Philippine slum films to global youth films that tackle themes beyond typical Hollywood imaginaries, such as diasporic identity formation, religion and race (Berghahn 2010; Shary and Seibel 2007).

While there is no existing comprehensive study on the youth film genre in Philippine cinema, film historians and critics have made reference to teen stars and prominent films with youth protagonists. Tiongson (1992) cites the youth film in connection with the development of the musical genre –

which he identifies as the fourth major genre in Philippine cinema (following the action, drama and comedy). Tiongson (1992) identifies the rise of film *sarswelas* in the 1940s–60s, dominated by singing young heterosexual couples, typically star-crossed lovers separated by class differences. Joven Velasco (2004) makes reference to the popularity of 'James Dean clones' in the 1950s among male teen stars, who embodied the 'misunderstood youth' and 'bad boy' image in family melodramas. The 1980s produced teen films with larger themes beyond puppy love: 'strict parents, nasty *barkadas* [cliques], mean or sex-starved teachers, and social class (Tiongson 1992: 38), typified by the ensemble youth film *Bagets* (Reyes 1984). In a more recent article, Richard Bolisay (2019) examines Twitter fandom around young Filipino loveteams who dominate Philippine mainstream media.

Filipino critic Isagani Cruz's early working paper on 'Portraits of Youth in Philippine Films' outlines some youth typologies in award-winning films, mostly from the second golden age. These categories, Cruz argues, show 'the way real-life youth believe or wish themselves to be' (1988: 2). In this brief reflection, Cruz names four types of youth portraits that may overlap: the youth as victims, villains, heroes and anti-heroes. In many of the films Cruz mentions, the youth figures are emplaced within the Filipino traditional family unit which utilises the melodramatic modality, such as the character of Brocka's *Insiang* (1976) a young girl who comes of age in the slums of Tondo. Cruz also mentions the film, *Batch '81* (De Leon 1982), which depicts male youth violence embodied and enacted through the masochistic rituals of fraternity hazing.

The children and youth protagonists in coming-of-age Philippine urban films are distinct as they move within the built environment and cultural dynamics of Manila slums, which in turn influence the visual strategies deployed. For instance, there is an obvious absence of panoramic or wide shots in the films I've chosen to discuss in Chapter 4, which focuses on the movements of children. The absence of wide shots can be linked directly with the constricting spaces of the *looban*, a kind of labyrinthian space particular to Manila slums. *Looban* is an interesting term given how it denotes literal and visual segregation. *Loob* (inside) is separated from *labas* (outside), which makes spatial sense since the expanse of most *loobans* is hidden from view to those who live in the spaces outside or surrounding them. The figure of a child navigates the *looban* in the literal sense, as children can more easily make their way through the narrow alleys (*eskinitas*) that comprise this space, signifying potential instances of spatial appropriation. In my analysis of the second film (*Tribu*) in Chapter 4 that features youth figures, as well as the final chapter that focuses on youth protagonists, I pay attention to the production of space via acts of sound and performance, grounded on the configuration of slum chronotopes that reference the histories of specific localities (Tondo and Pandacan).

Melodrama

Definitions of melodrama often begin with the seminal study of Peter Brooks (1976), which heavily influenced the recuperation of this so-called pejorative genre by the likes of Christine Gledhill (1986, 1991, 2000, 2002) and Linda Williams (1998). The way I use melodrama slides from melodrama as a genre, which is useful for categorical purposes, to melodrama as a mode of expression that manifests itself across various genres. Gledhill reconciles genre and mode when she argues that melodrama as modality:

> defines a specific mode of aesthetic articulation adaptable across a range of genres, across decades, across national cultures. It provides the genre with a mechanism of 'double articulation,' capable of generating specific and distinctively different generic formulae in particular historical conjectures, while also providing a medium of interchange and overlap between genres. (Gledhill 2000: 229)

In 'Melodrama Revised', Williams's (1998) interpretation of Brooks is a useful springboard for my aim of locating spatial justice in Philippine melodramatic urban films. Williams (1998: 52) argues that a 'quest for a hidden moral legibility is crucial to all melodrama'. This quest to surface moral legibility, which Brooks called the 'moral occult', relates to the aim of locating spatial justice if we consider the characters in melodramatic narratives as moral agents whose actions produce spaces of in/justice. Of the elements of melodramatic cinema that Williams has identified, it is the 'dialectic of pathos and action' (1998: 42) combined with the desire to return to a 'space of innocence' (1998: 42) that reveals the mode's implicit chronotopic configurations. The pathos-action dialectic, according to Williams, is a 'give and take of "too late" and 'in the nick of time' (1998: 69). In the melodramatic narratives enabled by slum chronotopes, it is the time of 'too late' that is more pronounced than 'in the nick of time', while the 'space of innocence' is not a return to an idealised space, but rather, a 'return to repression' that serves to reveal the heroine-victim's hopes and desires.

Melodramatic narratives enabled by the slum chronotope begin in a space where it is already 'too late'. In developmental theory, slum formation is underpinned with the notion that these are urban spaces that are unable to catch up with the image of the developed modern city. Slums are sometimes regarded as 'unintended cities' (Nandy 1998: 2) – they have already developed to a point that there is no ideal time or place to go back to. It is this temporal configuration of the slums being a space beyond the last-minute/nick-of-time rescue that invokes a view of pathos. As such, Gledhill's (2002: 21) identification of a 'nostalgic structure' in European nineteenth-century family melodramas does not exist in the same way in the Philippine urban films in question.

In melodramatic films set in Manila slums, that or whom must be rescued in the nick of time is already lost; there is really no last-minute rescue to be expected. In *Kubrador* (Jeturian 2007), the protagonist's son whose ghost appears at certain time-spaces within narrative time can no longer be rescued, because, after all, he is already dead. In *Foster Child* (Mendoza 2007), the 24-hour slice-of-life narrative occurs on the day her job ends – the day the foster mother has to hand over the child she reared to his rich adoptive parents. In *Lola* (Mendoza 2010), the narrative begins when the murder of one grandson by the other has already taken place. This is not to say, however, that all hope is lost in these films. Imaginaries of hope remains, as I will touch upon in my textual analysis, but these can be found not in the 'exhilaration of action', but in the 'paroxysm of pathos', to borrow Williams's (1998: 58) turn of phrase.

The time of 'too late' also takes place in slum spaces characterised by the excess of poverty. *Kubrador* and *Foster Child* are set in sprawling *loobans*, while *Lola* is set on and along the *esteros* (waterways) and shanties comprising a squatter settlement called *Sitio Ilog* (river site) in Malabon city, north of Manila. In Holywood melodrama, the 'space of innocence' to return to is often thought to be the domestic (private) space of the home, or any space that somehow suggests a restoration of order. However, in melodramatic narratives enabled by the slum chronotope, a thin line divides public and the private spheres. The porous built environment and the density of bodies that inhabit the slum space make it difficult to delineate the private from the public, which in turn makes it difficult to identify spaces of idealised virtue and innocence that belong to the private domestic sphere.

Instead of a return to idealised spaces of innocence, I borrow the idea of the 'return to the repressed' that Geoffrey Nowell-Smith (2002) used in his famous essay where he relates melodrama to Sigmund Freud's 'conversion hysteria'. For Nowell-Smith, melodrama is a genre characterised primarily by repressed emotions that the plot struggles to accommodate through action in the narrative development. Excessive emotions are thus consequently expressed in other filmic devices such as *mise en scène* and music. Nowell-Smith (2002: 73) argues that: 'The "return of the repressed" takes place, not in conscious discourse, but displaced on the body of the patient. In melodrama . . . a conversion can take place into the body of the text.'

Although Nowell-Smith's essay is brief, this is a crucial premise for my understanding of melodrama's spatial rendering as configured by the slum chronotope. My argument is that melodramatic excesses can be read in the ways the slum space dialogues with the female body, which is demonstrated exceptionally in the films I have selected. In these melodramatic films, time moves according to the embodied movements of its female protagonists, particularly through the spatial practice of walking. As with the temporal configuration of excessive urban development expressed in the notion of 'too late', excess is built into the slum's spatial configuration as containing a surplus of poverty and squalor. The melodramatic element of excess can be found in certain key moments where hysteria is converted into what I designate affective chronotopes.

Most Filipino viewers would not contest that excess is what characterises traditional Philippine melodrama. As Joven Velasco (2004: 40) has asserted, 'in the Philippines, the tendency to go overboard seems greater' than in Hollywood films. There is no existing study that focuses primarily on Philippine melodrama as a film genre, although Philippine film critics have provided useful overviews (Deocampo 2011; Reyes 1989; Velasco 2004). Most film critics relate Philippine melodrama to the perceived virtues of Catholicism, particularly the myth of suffering. Tiongson (1983b) has argued that current Philippine film genre traditions can be traced to theatre, which was introduced during Spanish occupation. He identifies five types of theatrical drama as having migrated from theatre to film: *komedya*, *sinakulo*, *sarsuwela*, *drama* and *bodabil*. Traces of all of these theatre forms have found their way into Philippine films, but perhaps it is the *sinakulo* that comes closest to the possible beginnings of Philippine melodrama (Tiongson 1983b). The *sinakulo* is a musical staging of the story of the Passion of Christ, a practice that continues today in rural and urban Philippines. According to Tiongson (1983b: 85), the lasting influence of the *sinakulo* in Philippine culture explains why 'In most Filipino movies meekness, servility and patience in suffering, coupled with the ability to shed buckets of tears, are regarded as obligatory characteristics of leading female and child characters.'

Deocampo (2011) reiterates the observation that 'melodrama is, perhaps, the most durable genre of Tagalog movies'.[4] Talking about American genres reformulated in Philippine cinema, Deocampo (2011) argues that the 'core' of most Philippine films is melodrama, because the genre draws on martyred figures from Catholicism. Like its Hollywood influences, Tagalog melodramatic tear-jerkers centre mostly on women, launching the careers of many 50s Filipina film actresses in 'roles of martyr wives, misunderstood mistresses, ever-patient mothers, understanding girlfriends, or orphaned children' (Deocampo 2011). Deocampo (2011) argues excessive emotions and sentimentality cut across all other forms of Philippine genres.[5]

While not primarily focused on melodrama, Rafael Guerrero's (1983c) commentary on the myths propagated in Tagalog cinema also addresses some of the typical character and plot lines in Philippine melodrama. He cites the enduring myth of 'machismo and masochismo' (1983c: 111–14) that relates to male- and female-driven films. According to Guerrero, machismo can be found in the realm of action films. Masochismo, on the other hand, is the virtue that the ideal female protagonist is expected to uphold, once again derived from the Catholic belief in the virtue of suffering. Guerrero (1983c: 114) explains: 'To project the desired image of Filipino womanhood on the screen, it has become necessary to beset her with every conceivable emotional, physical and spiritual dilemma so much so as to transform our heroines into veritable martyrs. Women in Tagalog movies endure much, because . . . it is their job.'

Moreover, Philippine melodramatic films engage with the myth of 'class-consciousness', played out for instance in romantic tales that dissolve 'capitalist-proletarian dichotomy' into the 'morality play' of virtues (Guerrero 1983c: 114) played out in the love stories between the landlord's son and the farmer's daughter, among other variations. Related to class representations, Emmanuel Reyes (1989: 33) also notes that in Philippine melodramas where class rivalry is a major plot line, 'those who have less in life should have more in characterisation . . . the poor are depicted as rich in spirit while the affluent are just plain mean'.

The shadow of second golden age auteur Lino Brocka looms large over Philippine melodrama. Popular film reviewer Noel Vera (2005) echoes the notion that melodrama is the Filipino genre of choice, and boldly argues that Brocka's 'melodramatic realism' contains a 'sense of realism and urgency . . . that sell these melodramas as absolute truth'. While I don't subscribe to this totalising statement, it points to the possibility of reconciling the modes of melodrama and realism that the films I examine might be said to engage with. The term 'melodramatic realism' raises a seemingly contradictory fusion, as the excesses of melodrama do not seem congruent with the sense of realism as fidelity to verisimilitude. However, it has long been argued that there is an interesting overlap between the two terms, particularly considering how melodrama has been reworked in national contexts beyond Hollywood (Dissanayake 1993). In *Global Melodrama*, Carla Marcantonio (2015) argues that melodrama and neorealism share the aims of moral legibility, paying attention to Italian neorealism's political aims of revealing the suffering of ordinary people's lives in the urban ruins of World War II. If this is the case for Italian neorealist filmmakers, for Filipino filmmakers from the second golden age, it was the repressive conditions of the Marcos dictatorial period that arguably inspired Philippine urban realism, according to film critic

Patrick Campos (2016). Against the global aspirations of former first lady Imelda Marcos's 'City of Man', filmmakers from the second golden age of Philippine cinema opted to feature the emerging slums of the capital. Describing Brocka's brand of urban realism, Campos (2016: 287) argues that: 'The credibility and political potential of his realist imagery, coupled with his keenness on melodramatic conventions, have also become discursively inseparable from the critical milieu of his time.'

Rolando Tolentino (2014) has argued for readings of Brocka's films as social realism, linked to the political goals of Third Cinema. In his analysis of two of Brocka's popular domestic melodramas, *Insiang* (1978) and *Bona* (1980), Tolentino reads the female heroine-victims as having recourse to the virtues of the Catholic configuration of martyrdom. However, they find no redemption in the narratives' closures, which Tolentino frames as the failure of the female characters to transcend class, even if they are able to subvert gender limitations. For Tolentino (2014: 145), these films are representative of how Brocka's domestic melodramas dialogue with the 'political melodramas' of the nation, with the subaltern female characters imagining a contrast to the elitism of the female political figures at the time the films were produced.

While Tolentino configures Philippine melodrama's female figures as conversing with the discourse of the nation, my reading of more recent female-centred melodramas takes a more intimate route. While framed within the context of the Philippine urban imaginary, I focus here on how, echoing Marcantonio (2015: 2): 'Melodrama's power and efficacy derive from the ways in which the body and ordinary experience – of those who would become the nation's citizens – come to bear the brunt of signification.' In my film analysis, I look at the excessive rendering of affect through and on the bodies of the female protagonists. In the melodramatic films I will discuss, suffering is redistributed (Zarzosa 2013), and made legible, through the films' affective chronotopes and production of space.

Film Noir

From female-centred narratives, I turn to male-driven films configured by the slum chronotope that can productively be framed as noir. Classic noir narratives puts its heroes to the test, where the limits of law and order signify the limits of masculine identity and desire (Krutnik 1991: 86). The embodiment of masculine anxiety in noir is the femme fatale, the 'cynosure of imperiled masculinity'(Fay and Nieland 2009: 148) who emerged in response to shifting gender roles post-World War II. Along with the femme fatale is the 'structuring absence' of home or domestic spaces (Sobchack 1998: 144) in classic noir.

To rehearse the familiar trajectory: film noir can be traced to post-World War II American crime film dramas said to be indebted to German expressionism, later on dubbed 'noir' by French critics (Luhr 2012; Silver and Ursini 2006; Spicer and Hanson 2013). What differentiates film noir from the crime film, specifically the gangster film, is that the 'ordinary citizen' as opposed to the 'professional criminal' is the one embroiled in crime (Fluck 2001: 383). Film noir enables us to understand the noir hero's guilt beyond questions of legality. As William Fluck (2001: 390) argues: 'Film noir can be seen as a genre that attempts to do justice to individuals who have become guilty.' There is a wealth of literature on the endless debate as to whether film noir is a genre, style or cycle. As James Naremore (2008: 5) has argued, noir is 'not a specifically American form'; it is an ideological concept, or a 'discursive construct' (2008: 6) whose meanings change over time. It is useful to cite some of the works that pay attention to noir elements that enable a reconfiguration of 'darkness' in narratives organised by the slum chronotope.

What prompts my noir framing of selected Philippine urban films is the idea of the city as crime scene. Indeed, criminality is a thematic preoccupation of the genre, if we look back at the foundational essays from the noir French critics. Nino Frank (1946: 15), who coined the term itself, underlines the subjective nature of crime in film noir compared to traditional crime narratives: 'They belong to a class that we used to call the crime film, but that would best be described from this point on by a term such as criminal adventures or, better yet, as criminal psychology.' Taking after Frank, Raymond Borde and Etienne Chaumeton (2012: 19) argue that: 'It is the presence of crime which give *film noir* its most constant characteristic.' They distinguish film noir from the 'crime-documentary', saying that the former privileges the point-of-view of the criminal rather than the police. Undoubtedly, however, the theme of crime in film noir is wide-ranging. Willam Luhr's (2012: 6) description provides a concise generalisation, which raises the related notion of crime and injustice: 'Film noir invoked dark forces, from within individuals or from criminal conspiracies or social injustices, but rooted those forces in the everyday contemporary world of domestic or business antagonisms, psychic disturbances, criminal schemes, and political machinations.'

Most studies agree that the city is film noir's setting of choice. The city in film noir is often characterised as a 'vortex of corruption' (Naremore 2005: 87), its mean streets and alleys filled with smoke and shadows. In noir, the city is a space of darkness, which can mean 'alienation, isolation, danger, moral decay, and a suppressed but very present sexuality' (Mennel 2008: 49). Now, the darkness ascribed to the urban space is no longer limited to the mean streets of American cities. Critics have expanded the term to register noir as a global concept (Broe 2014; Fay and Nieland 2009; Pettey and Palmer 2014).

David Desser (2003: 531) makes a case for 'global noir' as he argues that 'we need not debate the existence of film noir, its purity, or its hybridity, but rather admit that both filmmakers and film consumers have acknowledged a kind of "noir" and that this noir has a global dimension and impact'. An expanded view of noir can lead to more productive lines of inquiry beyond iconographies of fedoras and femme fatales (Shin and Gallagher 2015: 6).

If American noir is invested in returns to the past, Manila noir's darkness is derived from the fear underlying representations of slum cities as cities of the future. I take my cue from Gyan Prakash (2010) who suggests in *Noir Urbanisms* that the phenomenon of slumification across the globe has added a dystopic dimension to the imaginaries of urbanisation in the Third World. Prakash (2010: 2) borrows the cinematic concept of noir, recognising how 'the practitioners in other disciplines deploy it metaphorically to refer to a grim, dystopic reality'.

The 'noir-ness' of the urban space in slum cities like Manila can be configured along the lines of urban dystopia, which puts emphasis on the future rather than the past. Jennifer Robinson (2010) criticises the way thinkers in urban studies, particularly Mike Davis and architect Rem Koolhaas, have framed the process of slumification as narratives of urban dystopia, arguing that: 'The urban dystopia genre depends on recounting the characteristic (stereotypical) features of "Third World cities" as indicators of this futuristic present – features such as extensive poverty, informality, economic decline, infrastructural decay, and failures of collective provisioning.' I posit that slum noirs are the flipside of industrial urban dystopias, like *Blade Runner* (Scott 1982) in reverse. In slum noirs, the darkness of the future is not cast by imposing skyscrapers or flying cars as signs of extreme urban modernity; instead, the darkness of slum noirs comes from the overwhelming presence of slums. As writer Rana Dasgupta (2006) has exclaimed following the success of *Slumdog Millionaire*: 'Perhaps the Third-World city is more than simply the *source* of the things that will define the future, but actually *is* the future of the western city.'

The characterisation of slum cities as urban dystopia is supported by an understanding of dystopia as 'a utopia that has gone wrong, or a utopia that functions only for a particular segment of society' (Gordin et al. 2010: 1). A similar notion of 'dystopic modernism' runs through American noir and neo-noir, which Luhr (2012: 15), citing Raymond Chandler, relates to 'a world gone wrong'. In elaborating the relationship between the ideas of utopia and dystopia, Gordin et al. (2010: 2) argue that dystopia 'bears the aspect of lived experience' because it is much more frequently imagined: 'Whereas utopia takes us into a future and serves to indict the present, dystopia places us directly in a dark and depressing reality, conjuring up a terrifying future if we do not recognize and treat its symptoms in the here and now' (Gordin et al. 2010: 2).

How can we understand this notion of the 'futuristic present' in urban noir narratives organised by the slum chronotope? If in American noir, the narrative is disrupted by returns to the past in order to resolve narrative crisis, in Manila noir, the slum chronotope enables narratives, and protagonists, that are heavily invested in changing their conditions *in the present* as they strive towards a better future. Let me explain this further by returning to classical film noir's spatio-temporal configurations and its reworkings in Manila noir.

R. Barton Palmer (2004) offers a useful sketch of noir's temporal configurations in his reconsideration of Vivienne Sobchack's (1998) lounge time. Through his analysis of *Out of the Past* (Tourneur 1947), Palmer argues that noir's heroes are characterised as having dark pasts 'which are frequently explored in some form of backward turning that is motivated by a present crisis'. This crisis in noir is disrupted and resolved by frequent returns to the past. Palmer thus argues that the noir narrative is temporally configured by contingencies.[6] According to Palmer, film noir:

> juxtaposes the false promise of a future with the reality of a present that, instead, turns back to the past, trapping the protagonist 'between times' and in a multiplicity of irreconcilable spaces . . . such protagonists ordinarily come to their end 'in transit,' attempting to save what they never can, which is themselves. (Palmer 2004: 63)

Like coming-of-age and melodrama, there is no existing literature that focuses specifically on the concept of noir in Philippine cinema. However, some elements of film noir fall under the genre of Philippine action films, also called *bakbakan* (fighting) films. According to Deocampo (2011): 'Almost any film that depicted strong male characters and a lot of action (such as warring tribes, war scenes, high-speed chase, bloody murders and sinister plots) were lumped together as action films.' Agustin Sotto (1987: 2) contrasts American film noir with the emergence of the Tagalog action film, listing 'the strict form of morality, the idealism of the honor code, the set attitudes, the traditional values and the folk thinking' as what makes action films 'very Filipino in character' (Sotto 1987: 2). Sotto (1987) suggests that Filipino action films might be traced to the themes of the *moro-moro* play during the Spanish period, a 'morality play' that pitted Christians against Muslims featuring battle scenes where Christian characters emerged victorious. The action film led to the emergence of the male 'action stars' in the late 50s: from the gun-slinging local version of the Western hero (Fernando Poe Jr), the working class hero who hails from the slums (Jose 'Erap' Estrada), and the criminal-hero (Ramon Revilla).[7]

Not unlike melodramatic films that are marked with excess, the typical Philippine action film is known for hyperbolic displays of masculinity through violence. Reyes (1989: 52) echoes Sotto, describing the typical action film as 'an ultraviolent genre that dwells on stories of revenge, insurgency, gangland mayhem and police operations'. Action films showcase distrust of figures of law and authority, with a male protagonist who 'believes in dispensing his own brand of justice in the bloodiest manner imaginable' (Reyes 1989: 52). Guerrero (1983c) similarly identifies the action film as a genre centred on the theme of vengeance that serves to project the Filipino myth of 'machismo' in response to the emasculation of Filipino men by colonisers during Spanish occupation.

From the above description of Philippine action films, I derive a strand that might be called Manila noir: male-centred crime films set in the urban space, which are configured by the slum chronotope. If American film noir sensibilities emerged post-World War II, it is possible to argue as well that the post-war period in the Philippines saw the emergence of Manila noir, given the heightened visibility of slums in the ruins of the capital. Although there are similarities in subject matter between American film noir and the Philippine action film, there are obvious aesthetic differences. In a brief description of the action film, Joel David (1995) comments on the absence of the typical noir look in Philippine cinema. Referring to Schrader's noir aesthetics of darkness and shadows, David (1995: 13) explains: 'Essential to this definition is the climatic properties of the temperate countries where film noir flourished – the misty atmosphere and grimy surfaces caused by fog and pollution that tended to acquire brightness and sharper detail in tropical settings.' David (1995: 13) also credits Brocka for bringing film noir to Philippine cinema, saying that the filmmaker who adapted noir aesthetics to his own, setting the standard for gangster films in Philippine local industry. Brocka's film *Jaguar* (1979) is an example of early Manila noir from the second golden age, a film about a poor male security guard who is exploited and drawn into the world of crime and gangsters by his wealthy boss.

In the films I approach as Manila noir, the city in the shadow of the slum chronotope is configured as a space where crime lurks at every corner, at any given time. While it might have been possible to group these films according to the genre of crime films, to approach them as noir highlights the dystopic 'darkness' offered by the use of the slum chronotope, at the same time that noir puts emphasis on the films' urban context. It is useful to recall that in the Philippines, the term *ikswater* is widely used to refer to slum inhabitants regardless of technical differences between squatters and slums, emphasising the discourse of criminality that is associated with slum dwelling. The criminal discourse of squatting and slum-dwelling in the Philippines provides the state with the legal and moral justification to enact laws and policies that continue to dispossess the urban poor of their right to the city. The precarious practice and experience of squatting lies not just in the location and dangerous conditions of the spaces they occupy – it is also because as illegal occupants of urban space, squatters are always in danger of eviction. According to geographer Erhard Berner (1997: 171): 'For the squatters, renters and sidewalk dwellers who are the majority of Manila's population, eviction is a permanent threat and insecurity of tenure the most severe problem.' This 'permanent threat and insecurity of tenure' that underpins the criminal discourse of slum dwelling relates directly to the slum chronotope's configuration of Manila noir narratives with an overall sense of impermanence and insecurity.

While there are similarities to classic noir's configuration of its male characters as always looking to the past, slum noir's anti-heroes are heavily invested in the futuristic present. The narratives in Manila noir do not return obsessively to the past; what matters is the present moment that looks to the future. Instead of a return to the past, Manila noir's characters labour heavily in the present, with a view to the future. What frequently occurs are 'returns to the present' rather than returns the past. This is different from the configuration of what we might refer to as a 'vicious cycle' as I will discuss in my textual analysis of Manila noir representative films. They do not simply go full circle but actually suggest a degree of striving towards the future. To read noir figures as constantly returning to the present with a view of a better future is a more productive way of interpreting Manila noir narratives as embroiled in the day-to-day, even minute-to-minute politics of survival, despite its often fatalistic projection of the future. If film noir's basic structure 'is like a labyrinth with the hero as the thread running through it' (Dyer 1993: 53), Manila noir's heroes constantly, at all times, attempt to locate the labyrinth's exits, even though these attempts prove futile.

THE OVERSEAS FILIPINO WORKER (OFW) GENRE

The OFW genre is unique to Philippine cinema, emerging from the Philippine state's aggressive neoliberal labour export policy that has seen one in ten Filipinos working abroad. I will historicise this period in more detail in my film discussion in Chapter 7; the purpose of this section is to introduce the general markers of this specifically Filipino film genre. In general terms, the OFW genre narrativises the struggle of Filipino migrants abroad and usually uses melodramatic elements. These films typically present the OFW as a heroic figure who is willing to suffer in the foreign land not just for their families but also for the good of the nation. Underlying the typical OFW film narrative is the migrant's desire to go home once they earn enough money to do so.

While there is massive scholarly work on the OFW phenomenon in the area of social sciences both from Philippine and international scholars, there remains a need to consolidate research on the OFW genre in Philippine cinema studies.[8] Selected works by leading Filipino cinema scholars have certainly touched upon the subject of the OFW diaspora in critical essays, which I draw from in the succeeding overview of the OFW genre in Philippine films.

As a genre, Campos (2016: 532) views the OFW narrative as something 'that should never have existed, but does'. It is a genre that relies heavily, and problematically, on the suffering of Filipino migrant workers in the homeland and in the host country. Many of these films are titled with the names of the cities/countries of destination, as if these are enough to signify the OFW's global distribution. Some of these films include *Milan* (Lamasan 2004), *Dubai* (Quintos 2005), *Barcelona* (Portes 2006), *Katas Ng Saudi* (Reyes 2007), and *Barcelona: A Love Untold* (Lamasan 2016). If the earliest examples of OFW films – such as *'Merika* (Portes 1984) and *Sana Maulit Muli* (Lamasan 1995) – portray migrant subjects wanting to return, later films portray subjects striving to stay permanently in their countries of destination, or at least struggling to stay until they have earned enough to go back permanently. The sustained popularity of the OFW genre among Filipino viewers is apparent in the success of the most recent blockbuster OFW film *Hello, Love, Goodbye* (Garcia-Molina 2019) – now considered the highest-grossing Filipino film of all time. The film is a romantic drama between two Filipino migrant workers in Hong Kong.

Campos's (2016) overview of the OFW film is a useful take-off point to identify the typical space and time markers of the genre. He dates the genre's emergence from the 1990s to the 2000s, describing the OFW film as generally a tragic narrative of migrant workers 'before, during, or after their stay in another country' (Campos 2016: 528). He further argues that 'The OFW film is a uniquely Filipino (i.e. national) genre, unlike films that have been categorized as "cross-culture," "accented," "exilic," or even "diasporic" . . . With very few exceptions, the OFW film is a national assemblage: produced by the local industry . . .' The studio-backed OFW films, particularly the remarkably successful Rory Quintos film, *Anak* (*Child*; 2000) proved so successful in the domestic and international market that they arguably served 'another lifeline for the dying industry of the late 1900s' (Campos 2016).

The OFW genre has since expanded to include international films that feature OFW figures. In 2013, Joel David edited a special issue of international journal *Kritika Kultura* (2013) which focused on 'OFWs in Foreign Cinema'. The essays included in this issue approach the OFW diaspora from different perspectives, but they all highlight that the OFW figure, whether in international films or locally produced films, is almost always the female/feminised domestic helper. For instance, David (2013b) examines the figure of the 'diasporic helper' in the American queer film, *Reflections in a Golden Eye* (Huston 1967) in his absorbing essay, 'Panthoms in Paradise: A Philippine presence in Hollywood Cinema'. The film includes in its cast an almost forgettable Filipino character who plays 'the effeminate and unruly domestic helper that a homecoming American military couple would bring from the Philippines' (David 2013a: 566). David (2013a: 575) offers a radical reading of the Filipino diasporic figure as a 'resistant subject' who initially surrenders (or disappears, in spectral terms) for survival, but resurfaces when it is tactical to act against the hostile foreign space. Also included in David's edited journal is the earlier published version of Campos's (2013) essay titled 'Ghostly Allegories: Haunting as Constitution of (Trans)National (Cinema) History' which was expanded into a more comprehensive book chapter in 2016. Campos examines the ghostly presence of Filipina domestic helpers in two internationally circulated horror films that 'in the process of haunting the transnational screen, illuminates the modern drive to maintain state sovereignty . . . Eminently, the ghost in the midst of transnational exchanges embodies the ideals that nation-formation ought to aspire for' (2016: 541–2).

While David and Campos focus on the Filipino migrant's spectral representation in films circulated overseas, Rolando Tolentino (Tolentino 2009a) examines Overseas Contractual Worker (OCW) films produced by female filmmakers in 'Globalizing National Domesticity Female Work and Representation in Contemporary Women's Films'. Opting to use the term Overseas Contractual Worker (OCW) over OFW, Tolentino (2009b: 426) identifies the OCW film as a 'sub-genre of Philippine melodrama that deals with the social anxiety of the female OCW'. He traces the OCW genre from the immensely successful film, *The Flor Contemplacion Story* (Lamangan 1995), based on the infamous case of an OFW accused of murdering her employer and fellow OFW in Singapore – a case that yielded four other films.[9] Tolentino (2009b: 426) argues that the 'OCW film was the female response to biographical movies typified by male heroism'. He further argues that the OCW film can be approached as feminist texts in terms of subject matter, as well as the fact that the three most successful studio-backed OCW films were directed by the 'three out of thirteen female directors in the entire history of Philippine cinema' (Tolentino 2009b: 426). In his readings of *Anak* (2000) and *Milan* (2014), Tolentino argues (2009b: 439) that these films are ultimately 'in dialogue with the official experience of the nation-state, echoing and humanizing its rhetoric for the contemporary audience'. The films do this by utilising the mode of melodrama and using the iconic 'star power' of its female stars. Tolentino argues:

Melodrama echoes the centrality of the family unit, the sacrificing mode of the OCW character, the reiterative scope of overseas contract work, and the spectacularization of domestic work. Iconic stars act out OCW characters, invigorating the reproduceability of OCW in audiences – themselves potential OCWs – witnessing their future foretold and unfolding. (Tolentino 2009b: 439)

All of the above accounts strongly point to the chronotopic configurations of the OFW genre where space and time are fleeting, which in turn enable the creation of an OFW feminised mobile figure whose positioning can only be described as neither here nor there. Moreover, the use of the melodramatic mode in the OFW feminised genre configures the OFW figures as moral agents, with the genre working towards uncovering 'a hidden moral legibility' (Williams 1998: 52) through its narratives laced with the affects of female suffering.[10] The contradictory location of the OFW as a mobile figure and the genre's melodramatic mode informs my examination of chronotopes of in/visibility in representative OFW film, *Transit*, in Chapter 7.

Notes

1. Bakhtin (2010) is also known for an unfinished essay on the *Bildungsroman*. On the *Bildungsroman* as symbol of modernity, see Moretti (2000). For criticism of *Bildungsroman* as European and male-centric genre, see Gairola (2005), Feng (1998) and McWilliams (2009).
2. Vieira's (2009) description cites the significance of the future in street urchin films, which can also be said of the Dickensian tradition of slum narratives in the Victorian age. Writing about conventions in slum narratives in English literature, Kaiser (2011: 64) remarks that these stories show 'the political fantasy of the child as a redemptive agent, a symbol of possibility'.
3. Interestingly, both *Lumuha Pati mga Anghel* and *Roberta* were based on the stories of Mars Ravelo, a popular comic book cartoonist. He is perhaps best known for creating the character of the Philippine female superhero Darna, also an urban poor figure, which has also been adapted into several films.
4. Deocampo (2011) references are cited from the official Kindle ebook format, which does not have fixed pages.
5. Deocampo's claim of melodrama being the dominant genre in Philippine films extends to other kinds of popular media, such as television and local advertisements. While Philippine melodramas are 'women's films' in that they have women protagonists, these are not solely marketed to female viewers. As cultural critic Vicente Rafael (2000: 181) remarks: 'Within the Philippines itself, the practices of film going have long been class rather than gender specific.' In the 70s, there was a certain demographic of the lower class, the *bakya* crowd, who were assumed to be the patrons of melodrama. For more on the *bakya* crowd, see Lacaba (1983).

6. Palmer's idea is not far from Paul Schrader's (1972: 58) thoughts in 'Notes on Film Noir', where he argues that 'the noir hero dreads to look ahead, but instead tries to survive by the day, and if unsuccessful at that, he retreats to the past'.
7. All three of these action film heroes became politicians. Revilla served in the Senate, Estrada became president (and was later on ousted), while Poe Jr ran for the presidency.
8. In Philippine literature, the OFW figure has appeared in a number of notable novels, although not necessarily as the main protagonist. A recent example is *Ilustrado* by Miguel Syjuco (2010), which won the Man Asian Literary Prize in 2010 (a first for the Philippines). In the novel, the protagonist speaks with an OFW in a plane ride back to the Philippines. Historian Caroline Hau (2011) has explored the representation of the OFW in the novel.
9. See Alice Guillermo (2000) for more on the four versions of the Contemplacion story.
10. Carlos Piocos III (2016) examines the affect of suffering, sacrifice and mourning that are at play in configuring the OFW imaginary through his study of filmic and literary representations.

Part II

*Routes of Reading Philippine
Urban Cinema*

CHAPTER 4

Kids in the Hood: Chronotopes of Passage in Ang Pagdadalaga ni Maximo Oliveros *and* Tribu

> The street is the heart of slum life. The common expression *anak ka ng kalye* (child of the street) metaphorically exemplifies the importance of the street to the lives of the people in Looban. (Jocano 1975: 37)

This chapter examines the slum chronotope and its configurations of spatial justice in two exemplary coming-of-age films from contemporary Philippine urban cinema: *Ang Pagdadalaga ni Maximo Oliveros* (*Ang Pagdadalaga of Maximo Oliveros*) (Solito 2006) and *Tribu (Tribe)* (Libiran 2007).[1] I argue that these two films bring to light the complexities of spatial justice in the time-space of childhood in the slums, with one suggesting a narrative of escape and the other suggesting a narrative of entrapment. The chronotopes of passage I identify in the films reveal narrative instances where the child figures stake their claims to space. Although through limited means, the child protagonists in these films are complex social agents who have the capacity to participate in the production of space, and consequently, their futures.

Ang Pagdadalaga (henceforth *Ang Pagdadalaga*) and *Tribu* came out at the time that the government launched the 'Metro Gwapo' (Handsome City) urban beautification project under then Metro Manila Development Authority (MMDA) chairperson Bayani Fernando, known for his strongman urban policing strategies. 'Metro Gwapo' enforced squatter evictions, sidewalk clearance of street vendors, urban graffiti removal and other means of urban 'beautification' that sought to instil discipline among the urban poor. According to Boris Michel (2010), Metro Gwapo was a neoliberal urban campaign ultimately aimed at procuring foreign investments. In fact, Metro Gwapo was also called 'Investor's Route', which referred to both the physical infrastructure that foreign investors should see en route to the capital, as well as the routes through which the urban campaign could spur investment (Michel 2010: 394). Michel (2010: 293) explains: 'Metro Gwapo's stated aim was to erase what might contradict the image of a promising site for investment and, like street vendors, what do not fit the image of a modern and successful global city.' Positioned at a time that actively sought to hide the urban poor from sight, *Ang Pagdadalaga* and *Tribu*, set in *loobans* or sprawling slum communities often not visible from the larger urban space, are assertions of visibility in light of the state's attempts to eradicate the urban poor from globalising visions of the city's future.

The chronotopes of passage I locate in *Ang Pagdadalaga* and *Tribu* are time-spaces within the narratives that facilitate the child figures' coming-of-age within the slum space. I use the term 'passage' as it denotes time and space related to the notion of 'rites of passage'. Chronotopes of passage are times and spaces in the narrative that literally and symbolically channel the characters' coming-of-age. Elizabeth Kenworthy Teather (1999) notes how the body inhabits space in undergoing rites of passage. Teather (1999) further notes that rites of passage are linked with thresholds and crisis, which I take after in suggesting that the films' chronotopes of passage lead to threshold chronotopes: the crucial moments where the characters transition into maturity (not necessarily adulthood). Bakhtin describes threshold chronotopes as the 'places where crisis events occur, the falls, resurrections, renewals, epiphanies, decisions that determine the whole life of a man' (1981: 284). All the while, chronotopes of passage and threshold chronotopes dialogue with the slum chronotope as the films' organising centre of narrative and character development.

Ang Pagdadalaga and Queer Coming-of-Age

In the spirit of coming-of-age narratives, *Ang Pagdadalaga* is anchored on an important 'first' for the young protagonist – Maxi's first love. The film narrates how Maxi becomes enamoured with Victor, a police officer. Maxi's attraction to a police officer becomes the film's source of conflict, as Maxi's family make their living as petty thieves. The conflict thickens when Maxi accidentally discovers that his older brother, Boy, has killed someone while stealing a mobile phone. As Maxi becomes closer to Victor, Maxi is faced with the dilemma of choosing between his love for his family, or his affection for Victor. Maxi's 'blossoming' takes place in his immediate *looban*, with brief moments where he ventures outside, leading up to the film's memorable ending which I discuss in detail later.[2]

While the slum child is not new in Philippine cultural imagination, *Ang Pagdadalaga* is the first Philippine feature film centred on the story of a young queer protagonist growing up in the slums. The novelty and value of *Ang Pagdadalaga* lies in its depiction of queer childhood set specifically and almost entirely in the imaginary of Manila's urban slums.[3] The slum chronotope in *Ang Pagdadalaga* thus dialogues with a culturally specific queer coming-of-age narrative different from popular Hollywood queer cinema's preoccupation with the theme of 'coming out'.[4] In fact, a number of international reviews expressed surprise at how Maxi's father and brothers take no issue with Maxi's queerness, which in the film includes effeminate gestures, cross-dressing, wearing make-up, performing domestic chores.[5] Rather, *Ang Pagdadalaga*'s queer theme is much more in line with the politics of survival.

Ang Pagdadalaga configures Maxi's queer character as *bakla* (or *kabaklaan*), the term used for male homosexuality specific to Tagalog gay culture, a figure immediately recognisable to a Filipino viewer.[6] *Bakla* is a term that 'conflates the categories of effeminacy, transvestism and homosexuality' (Manalansan 2003: 25), predicated on the notion of interiorised femininity or the misguided notion of a man with the heart of a woman (Garcia 2008; Inton 2018; Manalansan 2003). The stereotypical *bakla*, moreover, often signifies lower-class status, embodied in the caricatures of *parlorista* or even *baklang squatter/talipapa* (from the slums/fishmarket) (Manalansan 2003: 55). While the *bakla* concept is admittedly limited and problematic, Filipino queer critics have used the term critically as the most widely used 'enduring social category' for Filipino male homosexuality (Manalansan 2003: 24) and remains a 'powerful discourse' (Garcia 2013: 61) through which queer identities can be viewed. The term carries with it the potential for queer creative practices that the *bakla* uses to navigate and survive the exigencies of daily life (Diaz 2018; Manalansan 2003).

Ang Pagdadalaga configures Maxi as a young *bakla* figure from the very beginning, the opening sequence endowing him with what Robert Diaz (2018: 406) has called '*byuti* from below', or 'performances of fierceness that economically marginalized trans subjects in the Philippines willfully enact amid the realities of pleasure and pain'.[7] The film opens with a series of images signifying squalor: plastic floating along an *estero* (open sewer) lined with a mountain of garbage, kids mindlessly playing with dirty water, a jeepney passing through the facade of a derelict house. These images are contrasted with images of *byuti*: a flower among the rubbish, Maxi's clean feet, an immaculate pink dress hanging next to tattered clothes hung to dry. The final cut of the opening montage is of Maxi flashing a smile directly at the camera, with a flower he picked up from among the rubbish tucked behind his ear.[8] The film's exposition thus configures Maxi as a distinctively queer figure in the slums.

The opening sequence queers the production of the heteronormative spaces of the *looban* throughout the film. If in popular imagination the *looban* is a dangerous space, Maxi's opening saunter destabilises this preconception. His *byutiful*, effeminate, almost pageant-like walk facilitates our entry into the *looban*, the tracking shot inviting us to follow Maxi's delicate footsteps as he takes us further inside his slum community. Shortly after Maxi's opening walk, the film shows us other scenes of *kabaklaan* through the beauty pageant that Maxi stages with his friends. The pageant can be viewed as a queer form of play that the film's child figures enact, creative practices of *kabaklaan* that destabilise the heteronormative slum space.

Throughout, *Ang Pagdadalaga* demonstrates an ethics of realism, or the film cast and crew's realism commitment to physical realism as its mode of address (Nagib 2011). The use of real footage of everyday life in the capital locates the narrative in the lived reality of Manila's inhabitants, at the same time that it signals the beginning of the film's fictional narrative. Maxi's gaze in the final shot of the opening sequence momentarily breaks the artifice of the film world as it beckons the audience to pay attention to both the real and imagined world of the slums.[9] The film's ethics of realism can be combined productively with the film's queer production of space, which Judith Halberstam defines as 'place making practices by queer people' and 'new understandings of space enabled by the creation of queer counterpublics' (2005: 6). The chronotopes of passage that I discuss in the next section show the ways in which Maxi navigates the heteronormative configuration of the *looban* as the narrative unfolds.

Chronotopes of Passage in *Ang Pagdadalaga*

The chronotopes of passage in *Pagdadalaga* are moments in which Maxi finds himself troubled, in a sense, to borrow from the queer notion of troubling gender. These are key scenes that take place in the alley in the film's opening sequence, the staircase leading up to his home, and the makeshift cinema space Maxi frequents with other children in the neighbourhood. These spaces produce moments of negotiation for the film's queer child figure, between what I deem to be a heteronormative versus queer childhood and coming-of-age, as represented respectively by Victor and Maxi's family.

The alley I locate as chronotope of passage is used in the beginning as well as towards the end of the film. It is just a bit wider than an *eskinita* as it can fit slightly more than one person. The alley is of prime importance to Maxi's mobility in his slum community, as it functions as the entrance and exit to the *looban*. Moreover, it is the alley that leads to other key spots inside the *looban*, such as the stretch of neighbourhood *sari-sari* (variety) stores that contain other alleys, where Maxi interacts with other members of his community. This alley is the space that divides the *loob* (interior) from *labas* (exterior), at the same time that it signals tension between the real and imaginary in the film's ethics of realism. As discussed earlier, Maxi effectively queers this alley through his opening walk as *bakla* figure. His careful movement from *labas* to *loob* also captures the dialectic tension of *kabaklaan* that Maxi has to constantly negotiate: (female) interiority and (male) exteriority (Figure 4.1).[10]

Figure 4.1 *Maximo walking into a* looban *in an early scene of* Ang Pagdadalaga ni Maximo Oliveros.

More crucial to the narrative, this is the alley where Maxi first encounters the rookie cop, Victor, who becomes the object of Maxi's affection. While walking home, Maxi is assaulted by two men who tease him for 'looking pretty'. Victor dramatically interrupts the assault, his deep voice and silhouette breaking through the alley's darkness under the light of a lamp post. It is clear from Victor's manner of entry in the narrative that he is supposed to function as the beacon of light in the darkness of the slums in the eyes of Maxi. Following Maxi's rescue, Victor carries Maxi on his back and takes him home, where the film makes use of the chronotope of the staircase.

The form of the staircase in just about any narrative derives its symbolic function from its literal function, that is, as a spatial form that serves to connect opposing levels of space. The staircase that serves as chronotope of passage in *Ang Pagdadalaga* is the one that leads up to Maxi's home, which is framed from below or above in different instances of the narrative. Maxi's home is located on the upper floor of closely built shanties, which is portrayed to be the safe space Maxi shares with his father and two brothers. Their home space is on higher ground from the dangers of the streets, another space that Maxi effectively queers throughout the narrative. In the absence of a mother figure in the film, Maxi, the youngest among three brothers, takes on the feminine roles in their home: he cooks, cleans and mends clothes for his family.

Like the contrast between darkness/light and interior/exterior in the alley, each time Maxi inhabits the staircase, he is caught in between a duality of moral choices. A key scene that takes place on the staircase is an instance that Maxi finds himself having to choose between his family and Victor. Maxi, standing on top of the staircase, looks down at his father who tells him Victor has sold them out to the police. The dialogue that ensues between Maxi and his father is powerful as it captures the ambiguities of morality that play out differently in Maxi's immediate slum space. Leading up to this confrontation, Maxi's other brother decides to take the heat for the oldest brother, who is charged with murder. Maxi's father, Paco, wants to send Maxi away to protect him while the situation remains unresolved. They have a heated exchange that ends with Maxi beginning to comprehend that his family are complicit with the violence surrounding him. '*You're going to kill him, aren't you?*' Maxi says to his father, who was rebuking Maxi for wanting to protect Victor. The scene ends with Maxi ascending the staircase, symbolically choosing Victor over his family, at least at this point in the narrative.

Another chronotope of passage in the film is the makeshift cinema space, a small ground-floor room run as informal/illegal screening space by a neighbour. The cinema space is a space of leisure as well as learning for Maxi and the other queer kids in the *looban*. In the instances the space is shown in the film, the audience is comprised of children. The chronotope of the makeshift cinema space dialogues with an earlier scene that reveals Maxi's lack of formal schooling, where Maxi struggles to read the English title on the cover of a pirated DVD case. In another scene, Maxi exits the cinema space and encounters peers coming home from school. One of the kids insults Maxi, but he immediately responds by asserting his monetary capital, offering to buy water for all the other kids. Maxi retorts: '*Schoolboy can't afford water.*' Although not featured heavily in the film, this cinema space enables Maxi to imagine his future, when he projects himself on to the characters on screen. In one cut, for instance, the film frames Maxi's face next to a close-up of a Filipina actress, Claudine Barretto, in a poster for the film *Anak* (*Child*), suggesting *Ang Pagdadalaga*'s preoccupation with the theme of family, but one that is queered by Maximo's non-normative configuration as queer child.

The film's chronotopes of passage reveal Maxi's struggle between his desire to integrate with heteronormative spaces versus non-normative and potentially queer spaces, the former symbolised by Victor, the other by his family. Victor polices Maxi literally and symbolically: he coaxes Maxi to follow the law and give up his brother to the cops, just as he teases him about why he doesn't have a girlfriend. For Victor, who is removed from the production of space in the *looban* which Maxi and his family are embedded in, the slum space should be subjected to governmental notions of law and order. Meanwhile, Maxi's family enables the production of non-normative spaces through their involvement in illegal trade, as well as the production of queer spaces, (albeit within the bounds of femininity). At one point, Maxi's father hands him money and teases him about purchasing sanitary napkins. Maxi's brothers engage in feminine play without judgement, for instance, when one of them allows Maxi to braid his hair. This is not to say that the Oliveros family portrays a kind of queer family; it does suggest, however, a departure from the traditional heteronormative family institution.

PASSING THROUGH THE THRESHOLD

From chronotopes of passage, I turn to the film's threshold chronotope – the sequence that culminates in the death of Maxi's father. This confrontation scene between Maxi's father and the new police chief, facilitated by Victor, stands out in terms of style, from camera movement to music. Stylistically, this is the only time that the camera movement departs from the aesthetics of realism applied for over a third of the film. This scene governed by threshold time gives pause as it confuses who among the two stands as the film's moral figure, blurring the lines between cop and criminal. The beginning of the encounter establishes just that, with alternating close-ups of Paco and Dominguez. At one point, the camera dramatically zooms out to a shot from behind the police chief that now includes Victor in the frame. Although visibly surprised by the police chief's actions, it is at this precise point that the film turns Victor from a figure of justice to one who is complicit with injustice.

Accompanied by intense guitar acoustics, the camera moves to a close-up of Paco's face, cut abruptly with a rapid sequence of Maxi running towards the scene, shrouded in the darkness of the slum space. Maxi arrives at the scene at the sound of gunshot, with the camera behind him. The scene is rendered in a deep focus frame that places Maxi and Victor in each other's direct view, just as Maxi's father falls to the ground. This shot, by capturing all the characters involved and showing their positions in space, facilitates symbolic lines of intersection, suggesting a crossing-over of the figures of justice and injustice (Figure 4.2). A second and final gunshot is followed by close-up shots of Maxi and Victor looking at each other from across the distance, with Maxi looking stunned and Victor looking forlorn. Victor then exits the scene into the shadows. The scene ends with the image of Paco's dead body in the foreground, and the camera slowly tilting up towards the night sky, in the process catching a view of Maxi's silhouette blending into the backdrop of the slum space. This traumatic encounter that results in the death of his father and the death of his lofty notions of love prompts Maxi's movement away from the space of childhood.

Figure 4.2 A scene that depicts symbolic lines of intersection among the figures of justice and injustice in Ang Pagdadalaga ni Maximo Oliveros.

Following the intense gaze captured by the close-ups of Maxi and Victor, Victor moves into the shadows while Maxi remains transfixed. The close-up of Maxi's face in this traumatic scene dialogues powerfully with his close-up in the film's opening sequence where he invites us to follow his tracks inside the *looban*. In contrast to his smile in the opening sequence, his facial expression here is almost blank, devoid of joy, a challenge to the audience to behold the violence of the scene that just transpired through Maxi's perspective. The pause provided by Maxi's close-up lends this scene to a reading of Gilles Deleuze's 'any-space-whatever' – 'where space becomes divorced from the defining coordinates of action' (Martin-Jones 2011: 135). This does not of course mean that the space suddenly loses any meaning, but that in this scene the space becomes open to other meanings. Read alongside affect-images (the close-ups of Maxi and Victor looking at each other from a distance), this any-space-whatever can 'express powers or qualities, existing as pure potentiality, rather than end results of actions' (Martin-Jones 2011: 135).

Understanding the threshold chronotope as producing 'any-space-whatever' carves out a time for Maxi to appropriate spatial justice, revealed in the film's resolution. A compression of time occurs following the threshold scene: Maxi grieves, Victor broods, the brother who is in jail is released. This series of images lead to a loaded exchange between Maxi and Victor where the film offers a nuanced understanding of justice, within the imagined world of the narrative. Space plays a crucial role in this post-death encounter. Maxi foregrounds the frame, his figure caught in sunlight as he turns his back on Victor, prompting this exchange:

> **Victor**: *This world is full of evil men, Maxi. Sometimes you have to play their game. Or else nothing will change. Do you understand?*
> **Maxi**: *Yes. There are many evil men. But I only had one father.*

This is Maxi's strongest articulation of his stakes in what Victor calls the world of evil men, which is also Maxi's strongest articulation of agency. Maxi's response is powerful in its complexity – a statement that is both an acknowledgement that 'evil' exists, at the same time that it displaces the definition of 'evil' according to his own social positioning. I take this as Maxi's demonstration of his newfound access to a level of maturity and capacity to negotiate and stake his claims in the production of the space of childhood. The visual rendering of the scene shows empathy towards Maxi as the film's protagonist, who has a stronger claim to justice compared to the figure of state authority, the figure framed in the shadows in this scene.

MAXI'S QUEER EXIT

The film's final scene reinforces the above reading of Maxi's coming-of-age as marked by the recognition of his own agency. The way the final scene plays out suggests that leaving the slums is *Ang Pagdadalaga*'s imagined resolution for Maxi. In contrast to the opening sequence, this time Maxi exits the *looban* at daybreak in his school uniform, walking at a slow and even pace, suggesting a claim to space outside the crime and violence of the slums. Victor, driving his police jeep, spots Maxi and steps out of the jeep to stage an encounter.[11] Maxi's figure emerges from afar while Victor leans on his car in anticipation. But Maxi pays no attention to Victor as he walks steadily towards the screen. Maxi pauses slightly, but he smiles as he keeps walking until he exits the frame.

I read this final scene as Maxi's queer exit from the slum space, illustrating his constant struggle through the in-between spaces of *labas* and *loob* that constitute his queer childhood. While wearing his school uniform, he proudly carries a pink rucksack, earlier handed to him by his brother who compliments his *byuti*. Maxi's slow and steady pace while walking past Victor, much like his strut in the film's opening, affirms that it is his queerness that enables him to walk away from the slums as well as from Victor's embodiment of heteronormative policing. Interestingly, when the film rolls into credits, *Ang Pagdadalaga* takes us back to the *looban*, showing Maxi gently folding and putting aside his late mother's clothes. Read alongside the final scene of Maxi's queer exit, the film's final images of Maxi affirm the new phase of his coming-of-age where Maxi defines queerness in his own terms, divorced from the mimicry of the roles his late mother performed for the family. Ultimately, *Ang Pagdadalaga* offers a narrative of escape from the slums, but a queer one at that, as its imaginary of spatial justice.

TRIBU AND TONDO

From the tender story of *Ang Pagdadalaga* that offers a coming-of-age narrative of escape from the slums, I turn to *Tribu* as an example of a narrative of entrapment. The film, mostly told through the perspective of ten-year-old Ebet, revolves around the cycle of gang wars in the notorious district of Tondo, the largest and most densely populated district in the City of Manila.

Tribu's success in local and international festivals trailed the momentum that Philippine independent cinema sparked in the year that *Ang Pagdadalaga* made waves.[12] Like *Ang Pagdadalaga*, *Tribu* mostly used tracking shots to follow its characters around the *eskinitas* that make up selected areas of Tondo. On occasion, wide establishing shots were used to signal shifts from day to night, or shifts in location within the immediate slum community.

Written and directed by broadcast journalist Jim Libiran, who himself grew up in Tondo, the film boasts of casting real-life gang members as its fictional characters. Part of the intrigue and appeal of the film is its 'real' actors. Six 'Tondo Tribes' put their differences aside while the film was being made, with Libiran calling the film a 'tool for conflict resolution' (Conde 2007). Libiran has always been outspoken about his pedagogic motives behind the making of the film, even screening it in a number of public schools. In his acceptance speech at the Cinemalaya awards, he said: 'To the Manila police, the kids you regularly round up are now Best Actor awardees. There are other ways to stop riots in Tondo and other Tondos in the Philippines. Please don't kill these kids. They might be future National Artists' (Atanacio 2007).

Tribu's narrative tracks the intersections of three Tondo Tribes: Thugs Angelz, Sacred Brown Tribe (S.B.T.) and the Diablos (Figure 4.3). The film's narrative is spurred by the murder of an S.B.T. member supposedly carried out by the Diablos. Members of Thugs Angelz come across the dead body while roaming the streets one night, just as police officers arrive at the scene. Predictably enough, the narrative is propelled by S.B.T.'s desire to avenge the death of their member. A member of the Thugs Angelz is mistaken for the murderer, leading to an alliance between S.B.T. and Thugs Angelz. The lead child figure, Ebet, becomes involved in the gang wars as he is tasked to spy on the Diablos, while the other gangs plan the big hit. Everything comes to a head in the bloody ambush that S.B.T. wages against the Diablos. The film's events take place over the course of two nights: it begins on the night the dead body was discovered, and ends on the night of the gang war.

Figure 4.3 *A clash between the Tondo gangs in* Tribu.

Tribu showcases the culture of Pinoy rap that these gangs have embraced, an aspect that some reviewers have highlighted as the film's unique offering.[13] In addition to the rap performances, interspersed with the general narrative are performative scenes of ordinary slum life in Tondo: the sudden outburst of a wife threatening a cheating husband with a knife along a narrow street for all the neighbours to see; an electricity inspector being heckled by residents; a street corner vendor breaking into poetry. These scenes that take place during daytime interrupt the violence of the film's narrative of gang wars that are captured at night. I will have more to say about the function of these scenes later, as they dialogue usefully with the film's chronotopes of passage.

Before proceeding further, it is worth describing Tondo as a specific locality in Manila's urban context. In the Philippine imagination, 'Tondo denotes slums, squatters, gang wars, and crime' (Hollnsteiner 1972: 31). In the 90s, Tondo was the location for what was then called 'Smokey Mountain', an urban landfill that remains a powerful symbol of Manila's poverty and squalor. Although the landfill has since been relocated to another area of the capital, and while the expanse of Tondo is not entirely comprised of slums and squatters, the notion of Tondo as *the* definitive squatters district in Manila remains strong in popular imagination.

Tondo's development into a slum district arguably peaked in the 1960s with the Marcos dictatorial regime's urban modernisation projects. In a 1968 government report, Tondo is unequivocally identified as being the 'biggest problem' (Special Committee Report 1968: 94) in the matter of slums and squatting in Manila: 'The physical conditions in Tondo are especially bad. Many squatters live along the district's many esteros [open sewers] ... The streets in the district are small, winding and narrow, with numerous pockets (*looban*) not accessible to motorized vehicles.' The report also notes the economic reasons behind the concentration of the urban population in Tondo as it is located near other areas where unskilled jobs are available:

> Squatters and slum dwellers congregate in the Tondo district because there are job opportunities there for unskilled and uneducated people. North Harbor employs many stevedores and laborers. Divisoria and other markets in the area provide livelihood to many kargadores and small vendors. The thousands of factories and little shops also provide job opportunities. The district's proximity to the Sta. Cruz and Quiapo downtown sections, coupled with the cheapness of jeepney transportation, also encourages many poor people who live off the commercial bustle of downtown (sidewalk vendors, scavengers, watch-your-car boys) to live in. (Special Committee Report 1968: 94)

Researchers have pointed out that Tondo has always had a significant role in the development of Manila. Mary R. Hollnsteiner (1972) notes that the Tondo Parish was the most populated Catholic church in the world at the time of its establishment by Spanish colonisers in 1574. She further notes the significance of Tondo as the point of arrival in the capital: 'Serving as the debarkation point of inter-island ships, the railroad line, and almost all provincial buses, Tondo has absorbed large numbers of Manila based migrants' (Hollnsteiner 1972: 31).

Because of its strong significance in the national economic and geographical context, it comes as no surprise that Tondo has often been used as a location for national literature and cinema that thematise Philippine urban poverty. Foremost among the films from the second golden age is Lino Brocka's *Insiang*, a stark melodrama about a young woman struggling to escape her harsh life in Tondo, which also became the Philippines' first entry to the Cannes Film Festival in 1978. Apart from Brocka's well-known melodramas that mark Tondo as a site of moral decay, Tondo has also been portrayed as a site for stereotypical 'tough men', especially at the time that the action genre was quite popular in the local scene. The late Fernando Poe Jr, who was an immensely popular action star and was known as the 'King of Philippine Movies', starred in a number of popular films where he plays the tough guy from Tondo (Flores 2005).

While *Ang Pagdadalaga* leads us into its unnamed *looban*, *Tribu* immediately situates its story at the heart of Tondo slums. Much like in *Ang Pagdadalaga*, the productive tension between the real Tondo and the fictional Tondo is established from the film's introductory images, potent markers that this fictional narrative dialogues with the actually existing communities that inhabit and produce the spaces of Tondo. *Tribu* opens with a series of black-and-white stills featuring images of poverty and squalor around the slums of Tondo, as well as images of residents who will later appear as the film's main characters. The stills are accompanied with the voice-over of Ebet who introduces the world of Tondo, privileging the figure of the child within this space: '*Here, a child can be tough. Here, a child can be a big shot. A child can even be God. The God of Tondo is a child.*'

The series of images is set to foreboding opening music with lyrics that repeat a common Filipino idiom, '*Matira matibay,*' roughly equivalent to the notion of 'survival of the fittest'. The stills are then interrupted with video footage of The Feast of Santo Niño, an annual Catholic festivity held in the district of Tondo, which pays tribute to the virtues of the Child Jesus. It is widely believed that participating in this festivity where statues of the Santo Niño are paraded around the district will result in good fortune. The murder that sets off the film takes place on the night of the feast, which also sets the stage for the film's focus on its young characters. This choice of festivity also suggests that the child-as-god state of affairs in Tondo is not the exception but the rule.

The film's framing of Ebet as growing up in a violent environment is not at all lacking in subtlety. It is not easy to sympathise with Ebet compared with Maxi given that he is not portrayed to be completely disentangled from the violence around him. If *Ang Pagdadalaga* introduces an endearing approach to coming-of-age through the somewhat naive character of Maxi, *Tribu*'s Ebet, as indicated in the opening, is the kid who is alert to the dangers in his community, which is not to say that he is portrayed to completely comprehend what's going on. The symbolic distinction between Maxi and Ebet is obvious: if in *Ang Pagdadalaga* Maximo picks up a flower in the opening sequence, Ebet carries a toy gun as he goes on his neighbourhood exploits (Figure 4.4).

There is a scene where Ebet plays *baril-barilan* (pretending to play with guns) with other kids in the neighbourhood, which ends with a shot of Ebet aiming the toy gun at his mother's lover. This shot is framed in such a way that he is looking straight at the camera, daring the viewers to look directly at this portrait of childhood violence. This shot of Ebet breaking the fourth wall is comparable to Maxi's close-up in the opening of *Ang Pagdadalaga* in terms of allowing the real and the imaginary to productively overlap in a way that calls attention to the ethics of realism as the film's mode address. The pretend game of *baril-barilan* in this scene adds another layer to the constant blurring of the real and the imaginary in *Tribu*, reminding us that the film is a

Figure 4.4 *Ebet holding a toy gun while spying for a Tondo gang in* Tribu.

mediation of the threat of violence surrounding the lived reality of children who reside in Tondo.

Chronotopes of Passage in *Tribu*

Ebet is a child of the streets. The *eskinitas*, streets, walls and corners that lead in and out of Tondo constitute Ebet's chronotopes of passage through the space of childhood. However, unlike *Ang Pagdadalaga* where Maxi is afforded moments of individual spatial appropriation, the spaces of Tondo are free to be claimed and contested by any and all of the characters in the film. Moreover, the moments in which Ebet is shown to inhabit spaces are not configured to be moments of moral crisis, but are everyday, habitual spaces. There is a sense of singularity in the passing of events in *Tribu* despite the ensemble cast, in that the death in the beginning must naturally beget another death (or deaths). As earlier discussed, *Ang Pagdadalaga*'s chronotopes of passage give pause – they are ethically charged moments that 'trouble' Maxi, enabling him to grapple with moral choices. The chronotopes of passage in *Tribu*, on the other hand, function as channels of violence for its young figures. Ebet's opening lines are reinforced in the previously mentioned rap song reasserted during the credits: '*Matira matibay*' – only tough children can survive in Tondo. In stark contrast to the queer potentials of childhood in *Ang Pagdadalaga*, the chronotopes of passage in *Tribu* can thus be said to facilitate Ebet's transition from a child into a man, specifically his transition into a tough man of Tondo.

It is clear that Ebet is more at home in the streets rather than the small bare room he shares with his mother. Even in terms of screen time, Ebet spends more time on the streets rather than at home. In the few instances that he is at home, he is frequently framed in tight shots and close-ups denoting a sense of unfamiliarity and unease. In these scenes, Ebet is never portrayed to be fully at home in terms of spatial occupation – he leans on corners, he peers through the cloth that serves as the door of the bedroom. Ebet is portrayed to be an outsider in his own home, always standing at a distance, observing his mother sleeping, or sleeping with someone who is clearly not his father.

Although Ebet is not exactly the embodiment of childhood innocence and purity, he is still the film's figure of whatever future is left for the child of Tondo. The distinction between child and adult is still asserted in the characters of Ebet and his unnamed mother. The only instance where Ebet is shown to enter the bedroom was upon the beckoning of his mother. Unmoving from her bed and naked under the sheets, perhaps still high from *shabu* (meth), she berates Ebet for always being out, then softens, asking him to come inside to prepare her food. Without hesitation, Ebet complies. His mother falls asleep again, and Ebet opts to snuggle up to her in what we can consider the film's most tender scene that serves to delineate the child from the adult, a scene that suggests that the child is hungry for his mother's attention.

In the absence of a traditional home, Ebet appropriates the spaces outside the tiny upstairs room as his own, where he freely wanders without any adult supervision. In an early scene, the same night he sees his mother having sex with a man who is not his father (a man we find out is connected with the Diablos), Ebet is shown darting away from their house in the middle of the night. The camera captures his feet as he runs along the streets, panning up to a wider shot as he moves away from the camera to reveal the narrow spaces he navigates in the darkness – a series of images that exemplify the spaces of Tondo operating as chronotopes of passage. It turns out that Ebet is on his way to watch initiation rites being held by Thugs Angelz. Ebet's familiarity with the Tondo Tribes is apparent in the warm welcome he receives from the gang. Ebet sits amongst the older gang members, and he even raps a little bit, mimicking the words of one of the members. He is coaxed to taste beer for the first time to the delight of the teenagers around him. In this scene, the film is clearly indicating that while Ebet does not undergo physical hazing like the new gang members, he is already partaking in his own mode of initiation.

The spaces that constitute the sprawl of the Tondo slums are not just Ebet's chronotopes of passage – these are the very same routes that earlier generations have walked through and occupied. The camera tracks Ebet tracking the gang members as they walk through the streets of Tondo. The camera is positioned behind Ebet, who in these tracking scenes is always shown to be lagging behind, literally following in the gang members' footsteps. In these tracking scenes where the camera tracks Ebet following the older gang members, the film captures intersections of Tondo children's past and present, spaces of childhood that continuously fold into each other, trapped in the cycle of the Tondo slum chronotope.

That the narrative of *Tribu* is mostly framed from Ebet's line of vision can be linked to the figure of the child seer that Deleuze (2013) has identified in post-World War II neorealist films (mentioned in Chapter 3), a passive character whose sensory motor-skills are rendered immobile by deep trauma. However, the child-as-god theme that runs through *Tribu* reformulates the child-as-seer figure in interesting ways. Ebet is clearly the opposite of immobility, but he does function as seer who is capable of enhanced seeing and hearing. This is not even just a symbolic function in *Tribu*, given that Ebet acts as a spy for Thugs Angelz and S.B.T. in preparation for the final ambush. His effectiveness in this role as spy cannot be attributed to a specific instance of trauma, but to his everyday immersion in the slum chronotope where potentially traumatic moments can erupt at any moment. Hence, Ebet is not the traumatised Deleuzan child seer; he is the desensitised child seer. Ebet's lack of affect combined with his physical smallness allows him to roam the slum streets in a rather carefree, childlike manner – although his motives run counter to this childlike image.

Apart from growing up in the everydayness of violence, it is striking that Ebet is virtually silent in most of the film, even though his voice-over is what opens and closes the narrative. It is not just that Ebet is physically small that allows him to remain unseen in the slums; it is that he is silent. His silence is a stark contrast to the noise created by the Tondo Tribes with their brand of Pinoy gangster rap. Ebet's silence throughout the film is the symbolic threshold that separates his time of childhood from manhood. The 'noise' of rap functions as the distinguishing element of *Tribu* as it invests enactments of spatial justice with the rich dimension of sound. It is in this way that we can understand the explosive ending of the film. Through the rap performances offered in the narrative – a mode of address that relates to the ethics of realism – the film is able to reveal moments of spatial justice, which I turn to in the next section.

SEEKING SPATIAL JUSTICE IN *TRIBU*'S NARRATIVE OF ENTRAPMENT

Although *Tribu* grounds itself firmly in Tondo, the film's engagement with the culture of rap simultaneously expands the scope of the social issues the film can be said to converse with. The most obvious would be the film's similarities with African American 'hood films' that became popular in the 90s at the same time that its distinct brand of gangster music was becoming more and more commercially viable. These films generally 'detail the hardships of coming of age for their young protagonists' (Massood 1996: 85) as well as 'place their narratives within the specific geographic boundaries of the hood' (Massood 1996: 85). With its strong resonance with rap and hip-hop culture, it can be argued that *Tribu* is imbricated in what Halifu Osumare (2001: 171) has called the 'connective marginalities' enabled by hip-hop, which refers to 'social resonances between black expressive culture within its contextual political history and similar dynamics in other nations'. Rap music, recognised to have emerged from the Black and Latino youth of the post-industrial impoverished spaces of South Bronx and New York in the mid-1970s has since exploded globally, resonating more powerfully with marginalised youth who infused rap with local inflections (Osumare 2001; Rose 1994).

Rap's global reach easily expanded to the Philippines, given the flow of migrant workers to and from the United States. Today, there is a strong Filipino-American presence in American hip-hop culture particularly in the Bay Area (A. T. Tiongson 2013; Wang 2015) and the West Coast (Harrison 2012; Weiss 2015). In the Philippines, Pinoy rap slowly began to take root with the breakthrough of the 'Father of Philippine rap', Francis Magalona, whose first rap album showcased nationalist and anti-colonial themes. Although rap in the Philippine context is not as dominant (or commercially successful) compared to its position in the American music industry, it remains a persistent part of the local music industry. As everywhere, rap in the Philippine context isn't wholly progressive and is often charged with misogynistic tendencies, however it continues to lend itself to the possibility of aligning with emancipatory politics. In the past two decades, the most popular commercial Filipino rapper has been Gloc-9, whose lyrics have gradually taken on a radical edge with songs that overtly tackle themes of poverty, nation and migrancy. In 2010, shortly after *Tribu* was released, the Fliptop Rap Battle League gained popularity – which sets the scene for the 2016 film *Respeto* that I discuss in the book's final chapter.

In *Tribu*, Pinoy rap as performed by the real/imagined characters of *Tribu* is a powerful means by which the marginalised male youth characters enact appropriations of spatial justice. It is in this way that they make noise, so to speak, as a way to assert power within their immediate community as they articulate their territorial stakes. The distinct brand of Pinoy rap that is showcased in *Tribu* flows through the film's chronotopes of passage, that is, the concrete spaces that constitute Tondo. Mostly written in Tagalog with a smattering of '*tagalised*' English words, the three gangs in the fictional world of *Tribu* are given space to perform, with each gang asserting itself as the strongest in Tondo. These assertions function much in the same manner as what Tricia Rose (1994: 2) has described as rap music's dynamics in the US context: 'Rappers speak with the voice of personal experience, taking on the identity of the observer or narrator. Male rappers often speak from the perspective of a young man who wants social status in a locally meaningful way.'

Of course, the lyrics are undoubtedly violent given the nature of the film's narrative, and I am not saying that the songs showcased in the films are progressive given their extremely violent lyrics. But while watching, there is a sense of energy and spontaneity in these rap performances that makes them powerful assertions of identity through the creation of noise. As George Attali (1985) has put it, the creation of noise relates to assertions of power. Noise is 'Equivalent to the articulation of a space, it [noise] indicates the limits of a territory and the way to make oneself heard within it, how to survive by drawing one's sustenance from it' (Attali 1985: 6). In *Tribu*, sound is another means through which the gangs both produce and appropriate space as their own. A powerful example would be the scene at the wake where S.B.T. members break into a spontaneous rap performance where they articulate their grief, as well as the desire to avenge the loss of one of their members.

One can also not completely divorce these diegetic performances from the fact that these songs were written and performed by the 'real' gangsters of Tondo, who in subsequent interviews articulate their sense of pride in being *taga-Tondo* (from Tondo). As OG Sacred, one of the gang leaders in *Tribu* said in an interview: 'We want to represent Tondo [through rapping], that we're not killers or thieves, we have talent' (ABS-CBN News 2010). He continues: 'I want to show people that someone from Tondo can get ahead in life, I want to be an example to kids growing up in my community' (ABS-CBN News 2010). So while the closure of the film narrative is that of entrapment in the slums, the story of the film as a cultural product does not stop there, sustaining productive tension between the imaginary and the actual grounds of the slum chronotope. In fact, the making of *Tribu* became a springboard for transnational connections for Tondo Tribes through rap. The group and Libiran became involved in a social project called 'Rap in Tondo' which allowed them to collaborate with other rappers from Germany, France and Japan. Although I am wary of how the film's extra-diegetic story can be peddled uncritically as an example of how poverty can be transcended, it would be a disservice as well not to recognise how participating in the making of *Tribu* might have actually bettered the lives of the gang members involved in the production.

The sinister rap songs, all performed at night, can be contrasted to the film's other performances that take place during the day that I have earlier mentioned in passing: the couple fighting on the streets for all their neighbours to witness; the electricity inspector arguing with residents over their bills; the chicken '*pagpag*' vendor breaking into poetry.[14] These are moments in the film in which the camera departs from Ebet's point of view and focuses on these other moments of 'noise' created by Tondo inhabitants. Actual Tondo inhabitants participated in the making of these scenes, particularly the one where the residents are heckling an inspector about expensive electricity rates.

One Filipino reviewer thought that: 'the presentation of these vignettes ... while documenting the social realities of Tondo, distracts from the dramatization of the flesh-and-blood stories of the characters. The connection between the social and the personal is not expounded' (Austria Jr 2009: 160). The reviewer ends by saying that the film, while exposing gang wars, 'begs for an in-depth investigative report to make sense and give meaning to the complexity that Libiran represents in his film' (Austria Jr 2009: 160). I find this demand from a film like *Tribu* unwarranted, as this desire for a more in-depth understanding of gang wars is precisely the productive value of the film. The vignettes that the reviewer thought 'interrupted' the narrative are positive interruptions, as we are provided with scenes where the inhabitants of Tondo produce noise, in the same manner that the youth of Tondo produce noise through rapping. These are the moments in which the film reminds us that the imaginary Tondo cannot be reduced to the violence that takes place at night; it is also kept alive day by day by its inhabitants who fill Tondo's spaces with signs of life. Rather than detracting from the narrative, these performative interruptions provide time for assertions of spatial justice by its real/imagined Tondo inhabitants.

PASSING THROUGH THE THRESHOLD

To return to Ebet. The significance of rap as a means to assert power and identity in a space of injustice that is Tondo becomes clear when considered alongside Ebet's silence in the film, and what he ultimately does to break this silence. Although the violent sequence of stabbing and shooting between S.B.T. and the Diablos is what the narrative sets up to be the film's climax, there is more meaning to be derived from the scenes that follow, leading up to film's ending.

There are casualties for both S.B.T. and the Diablos, but tragically, the S.B.T. members for whom the film shows more sympathy are shot and stabbed to death. The Diablos run after a random S.B.T. member fleeing the encounter. As the Diablos turn a random corner in pursuit, the unwitting brother (who is not even a gang member) of the leaders of Thugs Angelz is fatally stabbed by the Diablos. Presumably on his way back home, Ebet encounters Pongke, the leader of Thugs Angelz, who learns from Ebet that his brother is dead. In a rage, Pongke runs through a random street only to crash into the Diablo members who killed his brother. Another bout of violent stabbing ensues, this time even more disturbing as it occurs without the non-diegetic rock music that was used in the earlier clash.

These final scenes occur in the narrowest of *eskinitas*, the most effective cut being a long shot that frames the scene as though it is happening in the deepest spaces of the *looban*. The shot is locked from the entrance of the *eskinita*, its foreground the corners of the alley from which the camera peers through to see the shadows and hear the sounds of stabbing. The camera remains transfixed until the gangsters exit the *eskinita* as they move casually towards the direction of the screen. As they exit the alley, Pongke, the leader of Thugz Angels whose brother was killed says to another member: '*Come on, let's go see Dennis at the morgue. He hates being left alone.*'

The irony of this final statement is obvious, especially considering that Dennis represents a figure who could have escaped the slums. He was not a gang member and he went to school; in fact, he was killed while wearing his school uniform. What his death does is reinforce the randomness of the everyday violence of the slums and its streets. The streets that constitute Tondo's chronotopes of passage in *Tribu* might be viewed as any-space-whatevers, in that each corner can become a potentially fatal or liberating turn, depending on where one is coming from.

The series of murders lead up to *Tribu*'s threshold chronotope, which occurs right after the fatal *eskinita* scene. Ebet is framed as if he were just standing outside the *eskinita*, watching the murder. He is not on the streets, but back at home. The camera frames his face as he looks at the direction of the street in a medium tight shot. His face is a bit out of focus, caught in the darkness of night, while the interior of the small space leading to his mother's room is sharpened and well lit. In this scene, Ebet finds his voice – produces noise – and takes action.

Ebet's movement into his mother's room is paced by his voice-over and symbolic lighting. His face is in darkness when this voice-over is heard: '*This is no place for cowards. Only the tough survive.*' Red light and the sound of a police siren break the scene, just as Ebet says: '*Tondo is only for the brave and tough.*' Ebet then turns to walk towards the bedroom, each pause in the voice-over building up to the intense final scene: '*Here a child can be bad-ass. Here a child can fight.*' Now Ebet's back is turned against the camera, and he is preparing to go inside the room where we hear his mother and her lover in the act of having sex. Ebet reaches for the real gun he picked up from that night's gang war and enters the room with the final line – '*Here, a child can even be God.*' The film fades to black and erupts into a rap song as the credits roll, which suggests that Ebet fired the gun, even though the act of killing is not actually shown.

The rendering of *Tribu*'s final scene where the young Ebet takes matters into his own hands recalls the chilling effect of the scene in the famous Italian neorealist film, *Germany Year Zero* (Rossellini 1948), where the child, Edmund, poisons his father. Describing the calm manner in which Edmund prepares the poisoned tea and brings it to his father from the kitchen to the bedroom, Pierre Sorlin (2000: 121) remarks: 'There is something very chilling in the simplicity of a domestic routine which is also an execution.' Sorlin (2000: 120) reads this scene as an example of the ambivalence of youth – youth abandoned by adults in post-war Europe: 'the boy is able to define his private law, which makes him as powerful as an adult, and allows him to murder his father'. This sense of ambivalence can also be said of the character of Ebet in *Tribu*. In spatial terms, the domestic space and the streets of Tondo fold into each other in this final scene as spaces of violence for the young Ebet.

Tribu's final scene functions as Ebet's threshold chronotope. The moment he enters the room with the gun is the moment he transitions from a child into one of the 'gods' of Tondo. The moment he finds his voice is signalled by the voice-over and gunshot/rap. Of course, Ebet finding his voice in the narrative of *Tribu* means getting deeper inside the slum chronotope rather than stepping outside of it, a resolution that suggests that *Tribu* imagines a narrative of entrapment for its child protagonist.

Conclusion

Ang Pagdadalaga and *Tribu* are valuable examples of films that approach spatial in/justice in Manila slums from different routes, with one moving away and the other moving deeper into the slum spaces. Both films reveal significant moments in which its child protagonists stake their claims in configuring their futures through acts of spatial appropriation. In *Ang Pagdadalaga*, spatial justice is found in the negotiation between *loob* and *labas* enabled by the production of queer spaces in and outside the slums as signified by the film's closure. In contrast, *Tribu* reveals the brutality of injustice that compels children to take matters into their own hands, at the same time that it shows how the youth struggle against being silenced.

In this chapter, I have argued that framing the narratives through the lens of the coming-of-age genre and the ways the narratives dialogue with the slum chronotope enable the location of chronotopes of passage and threshold chronotopes. The productive dialogue amongst these chronotopes reveals how the films are able to raise ethical issues – in terms of the choice of realism as the films' mode of address, as well as in the philosophical or moral sense – through the means by which the child protagonists configure and are configured by their immediate slum spaces. Locating the slum chronotope more specifically in the context of Manila's *loobans*, *eskinitas* and the slums of Tondo enables a more critical reading of the films that takes into account the means by which the child protagonists struggle to become active participants in the production of space.

Finally, this chapter has argued that these two exemplary coming-of-age films, while located in the confines of *loobans*, implicitly dialogue with spaces beyond the slum chronotope. Maxi's manner of exiting the frame in the final scene encourages viewers to ask what the world outside the *looban* holds for him. Meanwhile, *Tribu*'s use of rap, as well as its mode of production that developed into a kind of community project involving Tondo's young inhabitants, reveal the dynamic potentials of the production of spatial justice within and outside the films.

Notes

1. Filmmaker Aureus Solito is also known by his indigenous name, Kanakan-Balintagos.
2. The metaphor of blossoming is apt not just for the subject of the film, but for what *Ang Pagdadalaga* signalled in Philippine independent filmmaking. It is considered a breakthrough film in the rise of the independent new wave, not just for the numerous international laurels it garnered, but more so for how it gained an audience beyond local cinephiles (N. G. Tiongson 2013; Tioseco 2007). It competed and won the Special Jury prize at the first Cinemalaya Film Festival, the local festival that eventually became the go-to space for aspiring independent filmmakers. The film also made waves at the Berlin Film Festival, and garnered nods in international festivals located in Spain, Canada and Singapore, to name a few.
3. For more on the representation of the *bakla* figure in Philippine cinema, see Diaz (2018), Inton (2015, 2017, 2018), Baytan (2008). For a postcolonial perspective of the *bakla* figure, see the pioneering work of Garcia (2008).
4. When I taught *Ang Pagdadalaga* in a UK university, my British students were astonished that the theme of coming out was absent in the film.
5. For critical articles on *Ang Pagdadalaga*, see Lim (2016), De Chavez (2016), Garcia (2006).
6. Tagalog is the Philippine national language. *Bakla* combines the Tagalog words *babae* (woman) and *lalaki* (man). There are certainly other queer terms used in Philippine regional languages. For instance, Garcia (2000: 279) mentions *bayot* in Cebuano, *agi* in Illongo and *bantut* in Tausug.
7. *Byuti* is a play on the word beauty, and is also used as a critical queer concept by Manalansan (2003).
8. The image of the miserable street kid selling garlands of sampaguita for measly change, risking life and limb on the busy highways of Manila, is quite popular in Philippine literary and visual imagination.

9. *Ang Pagdadalaga* was shot in the filmmaker Aureus Solito's own neighbourhood, with some of the scenes shot in Solito's own home. Explaining the film's location, Solito remarks: 'You're entering now into a place that you couldn't enter before. I can also film in a more intimate community. Like when we shot Maximo in my street, it was very easy. The people weren't even looking. Versus a big crew and a 35mm camera and you couldn't get in the neighbourhood' (De La Cruz 2010).
10. See Garcia (2008).
11. Solito purposefully framed this scene in the same manner as in *The Third Man*'s final sequence.
12. *Tribu* won in the Best Film, Best Actor (ensemble), and Best Music categories of the 2007 Cinemalaya Film Festival, and is heralded as the first non-European film to win in the Festival Paris Cinema. A foreign reviewer aligns *Tribu* with earlier examples of Philippine urban cinema in terms of its stylistic depiction of the slums: 'If you've seen the recent spate of Philippine indies doing their festival rounds, you might walk into "Tribe" (Tribu) wondering if you're still navigating the set of "Kubrador," "Slingshot" or even "Ang Pagdadalaga of Maximo Oliveros"' (Lee 2007).
13. 'Pinoy' means Filipino in Tagalog slang.
14. '*Pagpag*' which translates into the act of dusting off, refers to scavenged meat. It is well-known practice in urban poor communities where people deep-fry meat scavenged from dumpsters.

CHAPTER 5

Women Walking: Affective Chronotopes in the Melodramatic Imaginaries of Kubrador, Foster Child and Lola

> In a post sacred world, melodrama represents one of the most significant, and deeply symptomatic, ways we negotiate moral feeling. (Williams 1998: 61)

From the previous chapter that examines films focused on children, this chapter examines the configurations of spatial justice in narratives driven by female protagonists. The films *Kubrador* (*Bet Collector*, Jeturian 2007), *Foster Child* (Mendoza 2007) and *Lola* (*Grandmother*, Mendoza 2010) are about 'affected' women who are on the move – their physical movement structures narrative unfolding, mapping the urban space in dynamic ways as they move within, away and back to the slum spaces they inhabit.

In these melodramatic films, the slum chronotope enables the production of what I call affective chronotopes. The films in this chapter easily lend themselves to readings of spatial in/justice: *Kubrador*[1] situates its female protagonist in the grey zone of ethics with her involvement in illegal gambling; *Foster Child* lays bare ethical tensions behind the monetary value attached to the act of fostering; *Lola* complicates the question of justice in the exchange that occurs between the two women seeking to protect their grandchildren, with one having killed the other. The connective thread that weaves through the narratives' affective chronotopes is the spatial practice of walking, a device that the films use in different ways. In each film I examine how affective chronotopes dialogue with the spatial practice of walking, producing different imaginaries of spatial in/justice.

Like chronotopes of passage in the previous chapter, affective chronotopes move the melodramatic narratives of *Kubrador*, *Foster Child* and *Lola* in order to reveal moments of spatial in/justice. I take my cue from studies in human geography that incorporate theories of affect and embodiment with the production of space and subjectivities (Paterson 2009; Pile 2010; Thrift 2004). Affect, according to Brian Massumi (explaining Gilles Deleuze and Félix Guattari) is the body's 'ability to affect and be affected' (Deleuze and Guattari 2004: xvii). Affect is an abstraction that may find specific, subjective expressions in embodied emotions or feelings. From this, I suggest that affective chronotopes are the key instances in the narratives where melodrama's pathos-action dialectics are registered.

In the films I examine, the spatial practice of walking is an affective ability that enables the production of space and subjective formation. Walking, in its enactment and duration, invests space with potentially affective meaning/s. To quote Michel De Certeau (2011: 99): 'Walking affirms, suspects, tries out, transgresses, respects, etc., the trajectories it "speaks."' Walking is also a mode of experience highly charged with emotions and thought (Tuan 2014; Wunderlich 2008). It is in this way that the walking is an affective experience, produced through sensorial and emotional encounters. Finally, it is important to remember that walking is 'an irreducibly social and cultural practice that is learned, regulated, stylised, communicative and productive of culturally oriented experiences' (Edensor 2010: 74) – prompting the contextualisation of the films I examine here in the experience of Manila's urban spaces.[2]

WALKING IN *KUBRADOR*

Kubrador follows the movements of middle-aged Amy as she goes around her slum community taking bets for the illegal numbers game, *jueteng*.[3] As Amy walks through her neighbourhood coaxing acquaintances to place their *kubra* (bets), the film also provides glimpses of everyday life in the slum community. Shot on location in a slum community within Barangay Botocan in Diliman, Quezon City, the film covers three days – the third being All Soul's Day, which in the Philippine context marks an event when people flock to the cemeteries to honour family who have passed away. That the film ends on the day of the dead relates to the haunting presence of the ghost of Amy's son, Eric, throughout the film. Eric, who was a member of the Armed Forces of the Philippines and presumably died in combat, appears in uniform in the film's spectral instances.

Aesthetically, *Kubrador* is mostly comprised of shaky tracking shots characteristic of hand-held camera shooting.[4] In the walking scenes, the camera often begins by following Amy from behind, establishing real-time pace, turning slowly to the side or the front of Amy, pausing to listen and observe whenever Amy encounters someone familiar. It is also worth pointing out that the film is almost entirely devoid of a musical score, except for the instances in which the ghost of Amy's son appears – which are the key points I will examine later as the film's affective chronotopes.

In *Kubrador*, walking is fundamental to Amy's capacity to labour. To walk is to labour, in a literal sense, given that a *kubrador* has to wander the streets of his/her assigned territory, or 'cell' in order to find potential bettors. That walking is crucial to her as means of production is contrasted to Amy's husband who walks with a limp, which is why he has been relegated to manning the family's store at home. The slum chronotope dialogues with walking in *Kubrador* by producing times and spaces that correspond to *jueteng*'s demands. By this I mean that Amy's working hours and routes, which the film narrative tracks, are constituted by the structure of the game itself. As *kubrador*, Amy's walking has a clear purpose (to collect bets and deliver them to the *cabo*) and operates within the hours before the daily *bolahans* (which in most cases takes place three times a day).

Amy's walking, while structured by *jueteng*, is also laden with contingencies. Her route within her territory also has a dimension of day-by-day randomness as she scours the streets for potential bettors. Moreover, her senses are almost always heightened through corporeal expressions remarkably acted out by the lead actress. There are times when Amy's body becomes tense, at moments when she is on the lookout for the police. Her generally jovial facial expression and demeanour changes into nervous glances and calculated steps when she feels the enemy might be near. In terms of spatial manoeuvrings, Amy avoids larger streets that can accommodate police vehicles, or spaces that make her trade more visible. At one point, another *kubrador* warns Amy to steer clear of the highway: '*May kalaban*' (The enemy is here), the man warns; to which Amy scoffs in what can be taken as an expression of nervous defiance: '*Palagi naman eh*' (That's always the case, anyway). Thus, like the principle of *jueteng*, Amy's daily walks are laced with a strong element of chance.

Amy is not the sturdiest of walkers, due to age and her incessant smoking. Occasionally, she uses her umbrella as a cane. As she sets off to work following an early morning spat with her husband and a tender moment with her grandchild, she walks like someone who knows the streets and its inhabitants by heart, but her pace denotes a sense of caution. Because of the element of chance that governs her walk as a *kubrador*, the rhythm of Amy's walk is infused with the twin affects of fear and familiarity.[5] Although Amy knows her territory, there is always a chance that something will turn awry. This is foreshadowed just a few minutes into the film. She begins her day on a happy note as she takes her first bet of the day, even expressing her gratitude out loud as she walks on. But just seconds after her *buena mano* (lucky first customer) Amy unfortunately steps on shit. The camera follows her walk at eye level, but she suddenly stops, looks down (the camera follows) and exclaims displeasure at her early morning misfortune. The camera lingers a bit on this shot of Amy's feet, capturing her footsteps as she walks to the corner to wipe the shit off her slipper on the pavement.

The overall rhythm of Amy's walking in *kubrador* expresses a steady 'expenditure of energy' (Lefebvre [1992] 2013: 30) which is what I deem to be a key element in *Kubrador*'s understated melodrama.[6] The same can be argued for the other films included in this chapter, given the dominance of long takes and tracking shots that constitute the narrative development. The absence of explosive bursts of energetic movement (brisk walking, or running such as in the previous chapter), and the domination of the monotonous rhythm of the steady practice of walking gives the impression that *Kubrador* leans more towards the expression of realism over melodrama. I am inclined to agree with Patrick Campos's (2016: 292) observation that *Kubrador*, unlike typical Philippine melodramas from the second golden age, shows 'resistance to the affect of melodrama', as it does away with the tropes of hysteria (screaming, hair-pulling).[7] This is not to say that elements of melodrama are absolutely absent; rather they are more strategically deployed. To borrow from Agustín Zarzosa (2013: 14), melodrama can show the 'redistribution of suffering; its modal existence refers to the infinite instantiations of this distribution'. In these contemporary melodramas of Philippine urban cinema, what we see are tactical implosions of affect rather than explosions of hysteria, manifested in the films' affective chronotopes.

Affective Chronotopes and Spatial In/Justice in *Kubrador*

I locate *Kubrador*'s affective chronotopes in the four instances of the film in which the ghost of Amy's son, Eric, appears within the frame. These are the only instances in the film where a musical score is used, which harks back to the understanding of melodrama as 'a dramatic narrative in which musical accompaniment marks the emotional effects' (Elsaesser 2002: 50). While classic melodrama might have used music throughout the film to heighten emotion, music is used sparingly in *Kubrador*. This film tempers melodramatic hysteria throughout, until it reaches a crescendo in the film's final scene, which is also the ghost's final appearance.

The musical score that accompanies Eric's appearances can be described as soft, haunting music; almost like the opening notes of a police siren. The music is a combination of organ and guitar music beginning at a slow tempo that becomes slightly faster the longer it plays out. The spectral appearances progressively become longer, just as the musical accompaniment is played longer, spilling into the credits after the final scene. The first time Eric's ghost appears is the morning of the first day, where he is shown shaking his head and smiling fondly at Amy's morning spat with her husband. This scene lasts a little over ten seconds, and introduces the spectral presence that will run through the narrative. This music signals Eric's spectral appearance, denoting that he is a disjointed presence in the film. This music alerts us to Eric's ghostly presence, which could have otherwise blended in as just another body among the throng of slum inhabitants.

The second instance lasts longer, a tender moment that is preceded by the sound of Amy's heavy breathing overlaying a shot of Eric's framed photo. Having come home from a long day of walking, Amy is exhausted and feverish. From Eric's picture the film pans to a medium close-up of Amy being comforted by Eric who massages her forehead. From Amy's close-up the camera pans to the face of Eric affectionately looking at his mother. In this scene, the film suggests that Eric is a constant presence and source of comfort for Amy. Once again, the scene is accompanied by the same ghostly music, only this time playing longer, just as the scene with Eric's ghost lasts longer than the first.

These first two instances of Eric's appearance take place in the immediate vicinity or inside Amy's home, with each appearance breaking through the time-space that Amy inhabits with the spectral time-space that Eric's ghost inhabits. Each spectral appearance creates affective chronotopes in the narrative as a product of the encounter of different time-spaces, and as moments in between the film's walking scenes. The first two instances can be described as affective chronotopes that produce emotions related to feelings of sadness and longing, especially if we are to consider that Eric's ghost is a projection of Amy's desire to see her son. It is as if the memory of Eric is what keeps her going and what gives her strength. This is reinforced by the shot of Eric's picture before his ghost appears in the second spectral scene. Amy refuses to eat upon returning home, rejecting her husband's suggestion, and goes to sleep instead, turning to the ghost of her son for comfort.

The third and final spectral appearances in *Kubrador* convey the affective chronotope of fear, produced in the act of getting lost while walking. The affect of fear, according to Sarah Ahmed (2014) is an experience in the present that inherently points to a future in which one anticipates harm. Although the subject of her analysis relates to the politics of racial affects, Ahmed's description of fear as embodied experience can be seen in Amy's character: 'One sweats, one's heart races, one's whole body becomes a space of unpleasant intensity, an impression that overwhelms us and pushes us back with the force of its negation, which may sometimes involve taking flight, and other times may involve paralysis' (Ahmed 2014: 65).

Fear is especially manifested in Amy's embodied experience in the affective chronotope of Eric's third spectral appearance. This occurs in a labyrinth of *eskinitas* that Amy gets lost in. The scene takes up over three minutes of screen time. Amy departs from her house, absent-mindedly calculating the amount of bets on a piece of paper she holds as she walks. She takes a wrong turn and reaches a dead end, but manages to go back to the alley's entrance as the first turn only covered a short distance. She resumes her calculations and absent-minded walking and takes another turn, which brings her to another dead end. It is here that the music turns up gradually, which effectively projects the state of fear that is beginning to grip Amy. She turns around and hurriedly enters another *eskinita* as the music keeps with the pace of her panicked walking. Here is where we see the silhouette of Eric enter the frame, shot from behind as Amy scampers away to enter another *eskinita*. The camera follows with tight medium shots that span the width of the *eskinitas* Amy treads, alternating shots from the front or from behind, or encircling her in continuous shaky takes.

The same haunting music continues to play as Amy encounters one dead end after another. She is completely unfamiliar in the space she finds herself in, where not a soul in the otherwise dense slum community can be found. It is as if the spaces encapsulated by the *eskinitas* Amy loses herself in have been transformed into a ghost town. This phrase bears metaphoric weight when Eric reappears in the frame at the point when Amy hits yet another dead end. In a memorable tight long shot, the camera captures Amy's anxious expression as she looks straight at the dead end, while Eric enters the scene behind her, moving from the shadows from one *eskinita* to another (Figure 5.1). Amy's change in expression indicates that she might have sensed this spectral presence, which is expressed through the relatively faster tempo of the music. The guitar accompaniment becomes faster and more urgent as she moves swiftly to follow through the *eskinita* that Eric's ghost walked into. The camera moves to the front of Amy, capturing the intensity of this walking scene as though Amy were walking out of a tunnel. The music stops as Amy

Figure 5.1 *The ghost of Amy's son walks behind her in a scene where she gets lost in a* looban. *A scene from* Kubrador.

reaches the end of the *eskinita*, the camera moving out of its claustrophobic gaze.

This scene is a powerful visual and aural rendering of Amy's enactment of spatial appropriation. It is a scene that layers multiple chronotopes: the time-spaces of *jueteng* fold into the time-spaces of Amy's personal life, which folds into the time-spaces of memory and haunting expressed through the son's ghostly presence. In doing so, the scene is ripe for reading as the unfurling of affective chronotopicity embodied in Amy's drive to re-appropriate the claustrophobic labyrinth of *eskinitas* that engulfs her. It is a scene in which conversion hysteria takes place, not overtly, but by means of spectral haunting and aural accompaniment. It is telling that this scene occurs shortly after Amy visited the wake of a neighbour's son who died in a random hit-and-run, triggering the memory of Eric. The weight of her son's death is what Amy has been repressing throughout the film, which is what the film ushers in through the affective chronotopes of Eric's spectral appearances. Whether Eric is a projection of Amy's memory or whether it is a 'real' ghost in the world of the film does not change the reading of Amy's agency, given that the overlapping times and spaces rendered in this affective chronotope were conjured through the mode of walking enacted by Amy. This is perhaps the most powerful scene in the entirety of *Kubrador*, even more so than the final scene, because it is able to capture the socio-spatial dialectic that Amy navigates on a daily basis, and how she wills herself to push through the fear of losing her footing in the face of poverty, sickness and death.

The final spectral appearance occurs in the larger space of the cemetery where Amy joins the throng of people commemorating All Soul's Day. The sea of bodies surrounding and occupying the cemetery space is in itself the film's assertion of life in the midst of a space of death. When the rest of her family joins Amy near Eric's tombstone, Amy moves away to have time for herself. This solitary move was also prompted by her annoyance at her husband's major blunder the night before, which resulted in Amy having to bury herself in further debt. Tania Modleski's (1984: 24) remarks fits Amy's role in the family, at the same time that it points to the emotions that Amy has had to carry throughout: 'Women in melodrama almost always suffer the pains of love and even death . . . while husbands, lovers, and children, remain partly or totally unaware of their experience. Women carry the burden of feeling for everyone.'

Alone, Amy gets caught in a random altercation where she is grazed by gunshot. When she realises that there is blood on her shoulder, the haunting music turns up again, with the camera zooming out to include Eric's spectre in the frame. He watches as Amy stares fearfully at her bloodied hand. Her heavy breathing and moaning overlay the music. Once again, the affect of

Figure 5.2 The ghost of Amy's son watches her just before she exits the film screen in Kubrador.

fear surfaces in this scene, with Amy realising in that very instance that she narrowly escaped death. As Bliss Cua Lim (2011: 295) has put it: '*Kubrador*'s penultimate scene thus drives home what we know to have been true all along: Amy's precarious life is constantly grazed by death.'

From this near-death scene, the film offers what can be deemed the narrative's open closure. While still visibly shaken and caught up in the throng of people descending upon the man with the gun, Amy picks up her umbrella and her hand towel, and walks away, exiting the frame. The film then briefly lingers on Eric, who follows Amy's exit from the screen (Figure 5.2). The film ends with a shot of bodies whose backs are turned to the camera, as they watch the police car drive away with the suspect in custody, just as the film fades to black and the same haunting music is played throughout the credits. I want to emphasise that Amy's final act is to pick herself up and walk away; and this time, it is the ghost of her son that follows in her tracks. In this final scene she demonstrates how in the face of death, she chooses to just keep walking. By locating *Kubrador*'s affective chronotopes in the spectral appearances in the narrative, the film opens itself up to a reading of spatial justice where walking becomes a means of spatial appropriation. Amy walks away from death, presumably to return to the tombstone where her family is honouring the life of her son, where she will once again manage her emotions, or 'take up the challenge of loss' (Modleski 1984: 24) in order to keep on living.

WALKING IN *FOSTER CHILD*

Like in *Kubrador*, an overall sense of emotional restraint runs through the melodramatic narrative of *Foster Child*.[8] The film tracks a day in the life of Thelma, a foster mother living in the slums of Manila. The narrative takes place on the day she is set to 'discharge' her three-year-old foster child, John-John, for formal adoption to an American couple. Like *Kubrador*, the film is built through and around the movements of Thelma in the final hours she spends with her latest ward who has been under her care for three years. The narrative reveals that Thelma has been in the business of fostering for eight years – pictures of different children adorn a wall in the shanty house she shares with her family. More than half of the film takes place in Thelma's slum community, while roughly a third of the film takes place in the commercial district of the capital where John-John's discharge takes place. In what follows, I explore how walking is used in the film, and later examine how this spatial practice dialogues with the affective chronotopes that take place in 'pissing' scenes that recur throughout the narrative.

The act of walking is used to reveal the production of space in *Foster Child*. It is the spatial practice that introduces the labyrinthian space of Thelma's *looban*. In an early scene, the film follows the social worker, Bianca, as she ventures inside the slum community. The camera follows Bianca through the sprawl of *eskinitas* where she encounters mothers and children at just about every turn. Via Bianca's walking, the film introduces this slum community as brimming with the energy of mothers and children. While Bianca's walking scenes map the slum space as a figure from outside, Thelma's walking scenes enacts movement away from the *looban*. The film follows Thelma walking towards the narrow opening that serves as the *looban*'s portal to Manila's outside urban space, where they step out to flag public transportation.

The shift in the rhythm of Thelma's walking is evident in the film's shift from the slum space to the commercial district. If she walks confidently in the seemingly confusing maze of the slums, her disorientation is palpable in the uncertainty of her steps when she enters the commercial district where the American couple's hotel is located. She nervously tugs at her shirt as she follows Bianca who leads the way to the hotel entrance ridiculously guarded by SWAT police. When Yuri, Thelma's son, says he will wait in the lobby, Thelma, in mild panic, says he has to come up with them.

Thelma's walk through the *looban* is the opposite of her walk into the interiors of the posh hotel space. She holds the hand of her foster child for comfort. The camera follows Thelma as she marvels at the grandeur of the hotel lobby and glances at its inhabitants who are completely foreign to her. If in her *looban*, with its unpaved and uneven surfaces, Thelma walks with complete ease greeting friends stationed at familiar corners, the situation is clearly reversed in the hotel space where security is tight. She self-consciously tugs at her clothes and tries to fix her hair. From the hotel entrance to the reception area, it is Bianca, in her capacity as middle-class middlewoman, who leads the way, speaking and gesturing on behalf of Thelma's odd presence. '*The Stewarts are expecting us*,' Bianca tells the woman at reception. In this hotel-interior walking sequence, Thelma's gestures reveal that she feels out of place.

AFFECTIVE CHRONOTOPES AND SPATIAL IN/JUSTICE IN *FOSTER CHILD*

While more than half of *Foster Child*'s screen time offers scenes that take place in *looban* spaces, the scenes outside the *looban* demonstrate the film's gradual affective build-up. I locate the film's affective chronotopes in the spaces outside the *looban* that offer glimpses into Thelma's repressed shame, and the emotions this affect generates. These affective chronotopes build up towards the powerful affective walking scenes that take place in the last few minutes of the film.

Elspeth Probyn (2004: 330–1) has explored the affect of shame as existing in the everyday intersections of public and private spaces: 'It is perhaps the most intimate of feelings but seemingly must be brought into being by an intimate proximity to others.' Probyn (2004: 221) quotes Walter Benjamin's concept of shame: 'Shame is not only shame in the presence of others, but can also be shame one feels for them.' *Foster Child* makes legible the affect of shame. The practice of foster care itself is laden with the dual aspect of shame: there is immense dignity in caring for a child not your own; at the same time that the practice exposes the shameful reality of the existence of abandoned children. There is immense unqualified dignity in the foster care practice, even though the act of caring for a child is uncomfortably tinged with monetary value.

The affect of shame plays out in interesting ways in *Foster Child*'s affective chronotopes, which can be understood more fully along the lines of the Philippine values *hiya* and *amor propio* (self-esteem). An oft-cited study on the notion of social acceptance in the Philippine context (Lynch 1962), while suspect to blanket generalisations, cites *hiya* and *amor propio* as twin values that many Filipinos consider necessary for maintaining smooth personal relations. Between the two values, *hiya* roughly translates to shame, which refers to feelings of inadequacy and 'awareness of being in a socially unacceptable position, or performing a socially unacceptable action' (Lynch 1962: 97). To be accused of being *walang hiya* (having no shame) is to step outside one's place, or social position. *Amor propio*, on the other hand, 'is not aroused by every insult, slighting remark, or offensive gesture. The stimuli that set it off are only those that strike at the individual's most highly valued attributes' (Lynch 1962: 97). What needs to be stressed is how shame in the Philippine context is strongly tied to one's class or social standing, and is further configured by social relations. In another study, for instance, *hiya* is defined as: 'a painful emotion arising from a relationship with an authority figure or with society, inhibiting self-assertion in a situation which is perceived as dangerous to one's ego . . .' (Bulatao 1964: 428).

The ways that *Foster Child* proffers and engages with the affect of shame can be read in its affective chronotopes, captured in the film's 'pissing' scenes. In earlier scenes set in the slums, it is implied that John-John has no comprehension of what it means to piss in public – he has not developed a sense of shame when it comes to this private act. John-John pisses when his foster father tries to stop him from crying that morning. John-John does the same thing when Bianca holds him. In the scene where Thelma washes him in the slum's public bathing area, there is a rather humorous moment when John-John playfully urinates, completely unmindful of the fact that he is in a public space. In all of these scenes, Thelma and her family react with fondness or laughter; they don't really find the childish act of pissing in public obscene, in the same way that there is no shame in bathing in public if the only source of water is in a public space. In these scenes where John-John pisses in the presence of his foster family, the film suggests that there is no shame in how John-John has been socialised in impoverished conditions.

When the narrative shifts to the space of the foundation centre, Yuri takes John-John to the lavatory where they pass by a foster mother about to hand over an infant to a Caucasian couple. The camera lingers on this scene for a moment, temporarily losing sight of tracking Yuri and John-John, in order to capture the performance of discharge between a Filipina foster mother and foreign adoptive parents. As the white male figure speaks, the camera cuts to a medium shot of Yuri and John-John in the lavatory where they take turns to piss with the door open. The camera captures this pissing scene from a safe, unobtrusive distance in real time, keeping the audio of the discharge process overlaid while Yuri helps his foster brother with washing his hands. This whole scene functions like a split-screen, establishing a parallelism between the act of pissing and the performance of discharging a foster child, surfacing a sense of the perceived discomfort and impropriety of both acts.

In *Foster Child*, pissing scenes are affective chronotopes that stand for John-John's socialisation – the ways of slum life that he has learned under Thelma's care (Figure 5.3). Pissing in public spaces, divorced from an understanding of slum practices, recalls the perception of slum inhabitants as having no regard for privacy, hygiene and cleanliness. It is a misconception that can also be linked to the false dichotomy of the civilised coloniser and the

Figure 5.3 *John-John takes a piss just after bathing. A scene from* Foster Child.

barbaric native. Dipesh Chakrabarty (2002) points out, for instance, that dirt has served as a metonym for the perceived backwardness of the colonised, with colonisers citing images of garbage and open sewers lining streets where natives walk barefoot. In Philippine colonial history, American colonisers institutionalised new measures of hygiene for the 'dirty' native, including the instalment of toilets in every home (Planta 2008).[9] The same perception of the dirty native applies to the slum inhabitants of Manila, where open defecation is often identified as a pressing problem by government institutions and international organisations (Ballesteros 2010). These are the perceived dirty practices that John-John has to unlearn when he is discharged to his adoptive American parents.

The most uncomfortable affective chronotopes in *Foster Child* are located in the hotel suite where John-John's transfer takes place. In this space of affluence, the contradictions of class, race and gender erupt in silent gestures, such as Thelma's slightly hunched back, her incessant nodding, and the embarrassed smile she displays in order to compensate for her inability to communicate in fluent English. Bianca zealously compliments Thelma when she is introduced to Mr and Mrs Stewart, saying Thelma is the foundation's best foster mother. The Stewarts are portrayed as well meaning, but they are also unapologetic about this shift in venue, completely uninformed and disinterested in the time and effort it took for Thelma to even be there.

It is in the last few minutes of the film that take place in the oppressive time-space of the hotel suite that Thelma's movements begin to reveal the workings of the affect of shame. When Thelma enters the affective chronotope of the hotel suite's bathroom, which is more spacious and luxurious than her house in the slums, Thelma's shame begins to surface, initiated by her hesitation to even step inside the pristine bathroom. Her facial expression conveys a mix of awe and embarrassment – a perfect illustration of *hiya* and *amor proprio* based on a sense of class deference prompted by the encounter with the rich American couple who will take her place in John-John's life. The whole scene lasts over three minutes, the real-time rendering adding more depth to the surfacing of shame. Thelma scratches her head before entering the toilet space, where she pisses with the door ajar, all the while still marvelling at the luxury around her. She makes herself up as best she can by washing her face and fixing her hair, and stares at herself in the bathroom mirror with the same mixture of expressions before the film cuts away to a view of the city skyline at night that implies she is really out of her comfort zone.

In the next few minutes, the narrative allows for an exchange of pleasantries, both endearing and unsettling in their over-politeness. Thelma tries to feed John-John while he sits on his new father's lap on the dining table. While Thelma shows pictures of John-John growing up, the inevitable happens: John-John pisses on Mr Stewart's lap. Thelma immediately apologises and scrambles to the bathroom to clean up her ward where once again, she is confounded by the space in which she doesn't know how to operate. She laughs embarrassingly at her own ignorance as she asks the social worker for help when she accidentally turns on the shower. Although a seemingly light-hearted scene, it is actually loaded, once again, with the affect of shame as it puts Thelma in a position where she knows nothing. The affect of shame is reinforced in Thelma's final moments with John-John, whom she cradles while Bianca gently bids her to leave: '*Let's go, or you might cause a scene.*'

The affective chronotopes of pissing in *Foster Child* recall the unsettling scene in Luis Buñuel's *Le Fantôme de la liberté* (The Phantom of Liberty; 1974) where the acts of dining and defecation are turned over. In the film, eating is portrayed as a shameful act that one should do in private, while defecating is a perfectly acceptable social act enacted with dining chairs replaced with toilet seats. Placed in dialogue with *Foster Child*, the scene helps explain the unease conveyed by the scenes that take place in the hotel suite – that all the pleasantries exchanged is a farce that conceals the real exchange that will take place by the end of that night: the transfer of the child from a space of poverty to affluence. As one reviewer puts it: 'All this civilization and order and sense, says Foster Child, so that men can piss in dignity' (Phelps 2008).

That the whole thing is really a polite business transaction makes itself apparent in the scene where the American father leads Thelma and her son out of the suite. Mr Stewart tells Thelma to get in touch if she needs anything, not directly, but through the social worker. Before Thelma steps into the elevator, Mr. Stewart hands Thelma some money which she tries to refuse, but ultimately accepts. In response to Thelma's initial refusal to take the money, Mr Stewart's parting words convey that Thelma is no longer needed: '*Not another word. Ok. Have a great life.*'

Foster Child does not rid Thelma of dignity, even though it also does not completely grant her a full sense of agency. Despite the sense of shame that runs through hotel suite scenes, the film also shows how Thelma strives to hold her own against John-John's adoptive parents. The film manages to depict how Thelma is aware that her strength lies in her ability to care. Caring is her labour capital and her subjective power. There are moments when Thelma asserts herself through her knowledge of caring for John-John that the adoptive parents have no access to, like when she shows them John-John's early photographs. In another scene that confuses the American couple, Thelma affectionately speaks to John-John in Tagalog, asking if he is enjoying the food.

Thelma clearly recognises that caring is the best labour she can offer. Bianca asks Thelma, in a poignant scene where she is cradling John-John for the last time: '*If you can relive your life, will you choose to become a foster mother?*' Thelma replies, smiling, and with no semblance of apprehension or irony: '*Yes of course, Ms Bianca. That's all I know how to do.*' And while this scene takes place in the hotel suite, Thelma can productively be situated as a local articulation of the global network of feminised labour of care embodied by thousands of women who work in the care industry as nannies and caregivers overseas (addressed more thoroughly in Chapter 7). Thelma's work as foster mother negotiates and even elides the operations of global capital. As Neferti Tadiar (2009) argues in her reading of poetry about the labour of care by Overseas Filipina ('Pinay') workers:

> Pinay's ability to care and extend herself in fact does constitute her labour-power as a yaya [nanny], one of her functions as a domestic helper, and thus from the standpoint of her buyers/employers she can be seen to be already commodified. However, it is also subjectively (from her standpoint as living labour) the activity that remains beyond the purview of exchange. As this uncommodified activity, Pinay's experience is a power of her own ... (Tadiar 2009: 139–40)

Thelma's moral agency is rendered in the final sequences where the film redeploys the spatial practice of walking, this time to reinforce Thelma's alienation in the time-space of the commercial district that is a world away from the slums. The loss of her latest foster child is translated into the literal state of Thelma getting lost. With her son, Yuri, Thelma walks aimlessly along the

Figure 5.4 *Thelma and her son walk aimlessly in Manila's commercial district after John-John's discharge. A scene from* Foster Child.

pavements of the commercial district, walking by massive posters displayed on the windows of malls, advertising products Thelma would not be able to afford. In the walk past these billboards with the silhouette of mother and son, the film briefly turns up a few notes of a lullaby, revealing the sorrow repressed by this act of walking (Figure 5.4). The music abruptly stops, and when Yuri finally asks where they are going, Thelma's emotions break into her mask of control as she insists on going back to see John-John. When Yuri pleads with her to stop, Thelma's repressed affect of shame finally erupts when she exclaims she does not know where they are going. She stops at a corner in a fit of hysterical sobbing.

The power of this melodramatic scene is precisely in its delayed eruption and its overall restraint. Here, the film closes firmly on Thelma's side as the film's unquestionable protagonist, who, in the face of injustice, wills herself to move forward. At the same time, the closing of *Foster Child* subtly credits Yuri, Thelma's son, for being his mother's inspiration for her affective labour. Thelma wills herself to stop crying upon Yuri's gentle prodding. The young man takes his mother's hand and leads her up to the train station, which will take them away from the oppressive spaces of the commercial capital, back to the space of the slums heavily invested with Thelma's subjective labour power of care.

WALKING IN *LOLA*

The last film included in this chapter is *Lola*, another Brillante Mendoza film released two years after *Foster Child*.[10] The film follows the movements of two elderly women both intent on seeking justice for their grandchildren, but whose aims are at opposing ends. Lola Puring's grandson was killed in a mobile-phone theft by the grandson of Lola Sepa. As Puring collects money for her grandson's burial, Sepa collects money in the hope that she can negotiate a settlement for her grandson's release from jail.

Coincidentally, *Lola* premiered at the Venice Film Festival, conversing with the film's use of a location that is also submerged in water. Lola Puring resides with her family, comprised of her daughter and two young grandsons, in a perpetually flooded area called *Sitio Ilog* (river site). The flooded area is in one of the barangays of Malabon City, an area known to most Manila residents as one of the capital's most flood-prone cities. In contrast to Venice, the spaces of *Sitio Ilog* offer images of squalor floating along its murky waters. In place of gondolas are small, rickety wooden boats; in place of majestic cathedrals is the sorry arch of a forgotten church; and instead of quaint residential houses, there are images of dilapidated two-storey houses, their ground floors submerged in water.

Although it is not specifically referenced in the film, the flooded site that contains the submerged houses and buildings used as setting in the film is the Artex Compound, which stretches up to a thousand hectares, located in Barangay Panghulo, Malabon. The Artex Compound is known to some as 'The Venice of Malabon' or the 'Venice of the North' (of Manila), precisely because of its flooded state that became permanent when floodwaters did not recede following a typhoon in 2004 (Moya 2014; Villegas 2010). The compound is inhabited by families of former workers who staged strikes over low wages against the Artex Yupangco Textile Mills Corporation in 1984 (Moya 2014; Villegas 2010). As flooding in Malabon got worse, the company shut down in 1989, with workers opting to continue occupying the compound as part of ongoing demands for back wages (Moya 2014; Villegas 2010). This labour dispute remains unresolved, with families choosing to stay in the seemingly uninhabitable compound, partly because they cannot afford to move elsewhere (Moya 2014; Villegas 2010).

If Lola Puring, grandmother of the deceased grandson, struggles with the murky waters of *Sitio Ilog*, Lola Sepa resides in an ageing, run-down house in a bustling, dense area of the city, presumably also within Malabon. During the day, Sepa sells various vegetables on the city's sidewalks along with another grandson. They do this without a permit, at the risk of being caught in random police raids. This happens once in the film narrative, with Sepa struggling to collect the coins scattered all over the street. At night, Sepa and her grandson return home where Sepa's disabled husband is waiting to be fed.

Mendoza's penchant for laborious, unstable tracking shots runs throughout the film. The camera patiently follows the grandmothers as they move around the urban space. Relative to the films already discussed, *Lola* makes heavy use of facial close-ups, paying close attention to all the signs of ageing conveyed by the grandmothers. The overall pace of the film is also slow compared to *Foster Child* and *Kubrador*, as it keeps with the slow pace of walking by the two *lolas* who are often assisted by their younger relatives.[11]

More than anything, it is the choice of ageing female bodies as bearers of the burden of justice – which to them means saving their grandchildren – that lends *Lola* to chronotopic affective readings. There is something excessive about the choice to dramatise the frailty of the criminal justice system through the frail bodies of ageing women, with the almost invasive facial close-ups that reveal the marks of struggle and pain in the eyes of old women, combined with the overemphasis of their inability to move at a fast pace. The film's melodramatic agenda of moral legibility is written on the faces of the ageing female characters, and tracked with their slow movements that map spaces of in/justice in the urban space. The spatial practice of walking takes on an extremely slow and laboured rhythm in the ageing female bodies of Lola Puring and Lola Sepa in distinct but ultimately similar ways.

While the rhythm of walking in *Lola* is slow and laborious, it is also very careful and calculated. More importantly, walking is never without a sense of direction, or a sense of purpose. The frailty of the women's bodies is of equal measure to the strength of their resolve to redeem their grandchildren. The strength of their determination is tested against the containment of the spatial construction of the urban space, compounded by the force of nature. As they walk, the grandmothers face the overwhelming expanse, noise, density and chaos of the urban space in the midst of monsoon season, with water serving as a recurring motif throughout the narrative.

Typhoons are a way of life in the Philippines, but the situation becomes more urgent when they affect the capital. In September 2009, the same year *Lola* was released, Typhoon Ketsana struck Manila hard enough to cause national uproar, as even the affluent residents of gated communities were affected by flooding (Tharoor 2009). A state of calamity was declared in the whole of Metropolitan Manila and surrounding provinces (Olan 2014). National media was keen to point out that this particular typhoon had an 'equalising' effect, highlighting the acts of heroism that were documented during the storm, and even in its aftermath (Boehringer 2009). But despite the heart-warming stories that took place spurred by the shock of Ketsana, compassion for those who were truly affected quickly dissipated, when the national government pointed to slum-dwellers and squatter communities along *esteros* as the source of flood congestion.

Arnisson Andre Ortega (2016b: 237–8) points out that: 'The knee-jerk public reaction was to blame slum dwellers for the metropolis' environmental issues.' Citing subsequent government demolitions of slum communities targeted at those along river banks, Ortega (2016b) notes the elitist discourse that the typhoon prompted, which resulted in the forced eviction of thousands of informal settlers boosted by World Bank support of up to $1.5 million. This bourgeoise discourse has, to my mind, evolved into a narrative of 'resilience' that simultaneously praises those most vulnerable to disaster at the same time as it keeps them at bay. Resilience, while a positive value, also serves to justify the lack of action by authorities even after the devastating effects of natural calamities. Resilience is a concept that has been used and abused in recent years to describe how Filipinos survive typhoons, particularly the most recent devastation wrought on the city of Tacloban by Typhoon Haiyan in 2012. One of the most circulated tag lines at that time promotes the notion of resilience in the face of typhoons: 'The Filipino spirit is water proof!' – a statement that while well-meaning glosses over the long-lasting effects of disasters especially to the most vulnerable members of Philippine society.

The spatial practice of walking in *Lola* embodies resilience, but not along the lines of banal nationalism and celebration. It is clear that water is used in the film as a dual symbol.[12] But when juxtaposed with the narrative of 'resilience' in the wake of national calamities, the use of water in *Lola*'s walking scenes bears more meaning; the surfaces of the city, its gutters and sewers, are battered by typhoons in the same way that the ageing women brave wind and water for the sake of their grandchildren. The concept of resilience is not taken at all lightly in the film given its patient and careful tracking of the grandmother's movements during the time of a storm.

Against torrential rain and murky floodwaters, the spatial practice of walking in *Lola* is a means of survival that, because it is embodied in the frail bodies of elderly women, takes on a more intense sense of urgency compared to the two other films discussed in this chapter. These *lolas* are women who are running out of time. Lola Sepa, in appealing for her grandson, does not justify the crime, but wagers her limited time as appeal for her grandson's future: '*I'm already old. I would like to see my grandson set his life straight before I die.*' The poignance of an early sequence where Lola Puring is presented with a choice of caskets for her grandson resounds throughout the film; that the grandson ran out of time earlier than the grandmother is a reversal of fates that is cruel in its randomness. It is this tension between running out of time and the glacial rhythm of the act of walking across the urban space that gives this film its affective potentials. And like Amy in *Kubrador* and Thelma in

Foster Child, Puring and Sepa's spatial practice of walking serves as means of production and affective labour. They walk to collect money, no matter how little, in order to give their grandsons a shot at dignity: a burial for one, and another shot at a future for another.

Affective Chronotopes and Spatial In/Justice in *Lola*

If in *Kubrador* and *Foster Child*, affective chronotopes gradually surface repressed emotions, the key moments I locate in *Lola* harness the mixed affects of grief, rage, regret and love embodied by the parallel movements of the grandmothers. The melodramatic moments in *Lola* quieten down as the narrative unravels, but not because affect dissipates; rather, they are tactically managed to meet the ends of survival.

While the film initially privileges Lola Puring in her pursuit of justice for her grandson who is murdered, it unravels to provide almost equal screen time and space for Lola Sepa's struggles to earn money for her grandson's release. Their aims, while indeed opposed, are both subject to the demands of monetary capital, which is their shared struggle that ultimately compels the kind of justice offered in the narrative's resolution. In what follows, I locate the film's affective chronotopes in the scenes where the grandmothers' struggles are rendered through space, leading up to the film's concluding scenes where justice is served through the containment of affect.

The film opens by tracking Lola Puring's movements, devoting almost twenty minutes to her quiet grief at the death of her grandson. The opening scene shows Puring's struggle against strong winds and rain just to be able to light a candle at the random street corner where the murder took place (Figure 5.5). In these establishing sequences, I locate two staircase scenes that function as affective chronotopes, which warrant ascending movement through a flight of stairs to highlight Puring's struggles to contain her grief.

The first scene takes place after she places a candle at the street corner. Accompanied by her young grandson, she motions upwards and articulates her choice to take the concrete stairs leading up to a bridge. The view is menacing, with the camera capturing a wide shot of the height that Puring has to scale. But with the aid of her grandson, she persists and makes her way up, struggling to hold open a flimsy umbrella against wind and rain. They make their way to the funeral parlour where the second affective chronotope is materialised in a staircase leading up to the cheaper set of caskets. On the ground floor, the funeral director leads Puring, her daughter and two kids to a room where expensive caskets line the walls. The director rattles off the cost of caskets in a businesslike tone, the camera framed to offer glimpses of Puring's anxious expression at being unable to afford them. The funeral

Figure 5.5 *Lola Puring battles wind and rain as she ascends concrete stairs, having just lit candles on the site where her grandson was murdered. A scene from* Lola.

director, without pausing to consult the group, then proceeds to lead them upstairs where the cheaper caskets are located. As they carefully make their way upstairs, Puring's daughter articulates her anxiety at how expensive everything is.

The stairs in both scenes are symbolic of the struggles that Puring sets out to overcome in order to come to terms with her grandson's untimely death. Her movement in the act of climbing, although slow, is resolute as she voices no complaints. The staircase scenes are characteristic of the overall restraint of affect that Puring manages through movement. Shortly after Puring gives a meagre reservation payment for the funeral, the narrative provides space for her grief to emerge in a walking scene towards the back of the funeral parlour where she catches a glimpse of a cadaver. The scene is briefly accompanied by haunting music that punctures her sense of control over her emotions. She backs away from the view of the corpse, and steadies herself on a concrete wall as she tries not to weep. Her daughter comes to her aid and leads her back through the same dark passage, until they emerge into the brightness of the streets. The camera, all the while following Puring from behind through the dark passageway, turns to close in on Puring's face that by now reveals a more controlled and resolute expression following the brief traumatic encounter inside the funeral home. This is the only scene in which Puring overtly expresses grief and sorrow, but even here she demonstrates restraint.

Like Puring, Lola Sepa only overtly demonstrates excessive sorrow when she is first introduced by the film in the space of the police station. She urgently asks the policeman at the desk about her grandson, and when she is taken to see him behind bars, Lola Sepa's voice cracks as she speaks. This scene is brief and cuts abruptly to a wide shot outside the police station, with Lola Sepa's small figure making her way through torrential rain. It is as if the sorrow she expressed at the police station for her grandson is displaced and expressed through the downpour.

The staircase also functions as affective chronotope for Lola Sepa, with a recurring scene of her climb to her second-storey run-down home. As the staircase that leads her home, it is an affective chronotope that serves to temper her grief at the plight of her grandson, because she has to be level-headed in order to care for her disabled husband. On her return from the police station and after a failed attempt to get help from a local official, she proceeds to prepare vegetables for selling the next day.

The film demonstrates how the grandmothers show control over their respective spaces, which is also how they manage the affects of grief and mourning. The film unravels slowly to track the grandmothers' resolute spatial movements aimed at their respective missions to save their grandsons. Lola Puring is shown to supervise the setting up of the wake on the second floor of her home, the ground floor being submerged in water. Later, she climbs another flight of stairs on the way to an office where she sells her pension for credit. Similarly, in a demonstration of strength, Lola Sepa carries an old television set through the neighbourhood streets for pawning, as part of her efforts to raise money towards a settlement with Lola Puring.

The grandmothers' struggle over space, moreover, parallels their struggle over their ageing bodies. Their bodies falter in two instances that symbolically take place in the vicinity of the courthouse. Lola Puring soils herself when she cannot find a working toilet; in another scene, Lola Sepa massages her foot during a bout of rheumatism. These scenes suggest that the court cannot accommodate their quest for justice, as it is a space that is not equipped to welcome the demands of these poor, elderly women.

And so, these women find respite elsewhere, in spaces of poverty that are rich in community spirit. This is captured by the picturesque funeral procession of small wooden boats floating on murky floodwaters, foregrounded by the boat occupied by Lola Puring, the matriarch at the head of it all. The members of the community of ageing shanties submerged in water contribute whatever amount they can when Lola Puring goes from house to house asking for *abuloy* (donations) in a scene that is devoid of shame. Similarly, when Lola Sepa visits distant relatives in a rural town on the outskirts of the city to ask for help, her relatives welcome her kindly and give her food and poultry to take home as a gesture of support.

After the funeral procession, the film cuts to Lola Sepa visiting her

Figure 5.6 Lola Sepa descends a prison staircase to visit her grandson, who has been charged with murder. A scene from Lola.

grandson in jail. Here I locate a final staircase scene that functions as affective chronotope, which I read as the direct inverse of Lola Puring's affective chronotope in the film's opening sequence. In a brief visit, Sepa assures her grandson that she is doing everything she can to get him out. The film then tracks Sepa's departure from the visit in a locked frame shot of the staircase, depicting her laborious descent in the shadows of the prison staircase (Figure 5.6). Lola Sepa's descent of this particular staircase towards the end of the film dialogues with Lola Puring's ascent in earlier scenes, suggesting an intersection of struggles. This staircase scene that channels Sepa's descending movement signifies her encounter with Puring's ascending movements in the concrete staircase near the scene of the murder, the event that prompted the unfortunate meeting of the grandmothers. This scene signals that whatever justice the narrative offers will be arrived at by the grandmothers themselves, not by the state's figures of justice. Sepa's descent is followed by her decisive move to put up the land her derelict house stands on for credit – her land in exchange for her grandson's life.

The closing sequences of *Lola* show a compassionate, yet unromanticised, final encounter between the grandmothers that is almost completely stripped of melodramatic affect. After much contemplation, Lola Puring decides to drop the case against Lola Sepa's grandson, not so much out of a whimsical notion of forgiveness, but because it is the only option left in a country where justice is rarely granted to the poor. In their final encounter, the grandmothers calmly talk about the physical pains of ageing, and after Lola Sepa casually hands over the small sum of money she struggled to collect as a gesture of contrition, there is nothing left to be said. This scene calls to mind the classic characterisation of indifference, or blasé mentality, for the way city dwellers protect themselves from the chaos of metropolitan life (Simmel 2014). The exchange of money depicted in *Lola*, however, demonstrates a kind of indifference infused with class consciousness – the knowledge that the grandmothers and their grandchildren come from the same class of the urban poor, and the only way to survive the city is to try to keep on living. The film ends with the grandmothers parting ways as though they had never met.

Conclusion

In this chapter I have argued that the dialogue between the slum chronotope and the melodramatic mode enables affective chronotopes, configured through the spatial practice of walking. The films offer explorations of spatial justice through careful and laborious tracking of how the female protagonists move within, through, away and back to the slum spaces they produce and inhabit.

Like the films in the previous chapters, these melodramatic films are able to move beyond the fictional worlds configured by the slum chronotope. The chapter contextualised the slum chronotope in socio-spatial conditions particular to Manila slums, allowing a more critical understanding of the spatial meanings that can be derived from these films. In *Kubrador*, the politics of *jueteng* configures Amy's daily movements; in *Foster Child*, the ethical dilemma that underpins the affective labour of care drives Thelma's movements in the city's spaces of poverty and spaces of affluence; and in *Lola*, the grandmothers' laboured movements parallel the resilience of slum communities struggling to stay above water.

Read as contemporary expressions of Philippine melodrama that exercise restraint in depicting excessive emotions, I have argued that these films enact the tactical distribution and displacement of the affect of suffering through the spatial practice of walking that configures distinctive affective chronotopes. Walking in these films becomes a means of producing space, justice and survival, no matter how limited. In *Kubrador*, the affective power of grief, manifested in spectral encounters, compels Amy to continue living. In *Foster Child*, the affect of shame is countered by the subjective power that Thelma derives from her affective labour of care. And in *Lola*, the mixed affects of grief, suffering, mourning and love are tempered by the grandmothers' persistence in trying to find a semblance of dignity for themselves, and for their family. Ultimately, in this chapter, I have argued that these contemporary examples of Philippine urban melodrama are valuable in their rendering of women who wield subjective power through affective labour in the abject spaces of Manila slums.

Notes

1. *Kubrador* was well received in international festivals, including the critic's award from the International Federation of Film Critics and Best Film in the Moscow Film Festival. In the Rome Asiatic Film Mediale Competition, the film won a special jury prize and was lauded for 'the extraordinary and seismographic capacity of portraying a social situation through the suffering of one woman' (GMA News Online 2006). While it proved commercially unsuccessful on the local front, *Kubrador* was received well among critics and won top awards at the *Gawad Urian Awards*, considered a critical award-giving body in the Philippine context. Another notable award that *Kubrador* received was the Gawad Lino Brocka award, which aligns Jeffrey Jeturian's work with socially and politically conscious filmmaking.
2. The act of walking along urban spaces can no doubt be linked to the nineteenth-century *flâneur* (Benjamin [1982] 2002), its early formulations undoubtedly modelled after the privileged European male. In the Philippine urban context, Rolando Tolentino (2001) has argued that *flâneuring* takes place not in the uninhabitable highways of Metropolitan Manila, but inside the air-conditioned spaces of Manila malls where the act of window-shopping means being unable to actually purchase the phantasmagoric commodities on display.
3. As indicated in Kubrador's epigraph, *jueteng* involvement can be traced all the way to the Philippine presidency. In recent national history, which informs the film's very emergence, then President Joseph Estrada (1998–2001) was accused of being on the payroll of the top *jueteng* lords of the country at his impeachment trial, which spurred a massive uprising resulting in his ouster. His successor, then President Gloria Macapagal-Arroyo (2001–10) was also implicated as having close ties with one of the country's top *jueteng* lords; her husband and son were said to be regular beneficiaries of *jueteng* payouts. *Jueteng* has long been known as the poor man's game of choice in the Philippines. It is popular among the poor because even a peso is enough to place a bet. The game dates back to the Spanish colonial period, possibly influenced by Chinese traders. For more about *jueteng*, see Dychiu (2010b, 2010a)
4. Bliss Cua Lim (2011: 292) observes that: '*Kubrador* is distinguished by the revelation of space through camera movement.'
5. Lefebvre ([1992] 2013) suggests that rhythm can be found in gestures and patterns of movement, such as the repetitive movement of walking.
6. Rhythm is expressed 'everywhere where there is an interaction between a place, a time, and an expenditure of energy' (Lefebvre [1992] 2013: 30).
7. Patrick Campos (2016) argues that *Kubrador* marked the advent of new urban realist films in Philippine independent cinema.
8. There was much fanfare surrounding the release of *Foster Child* given its premier

at the Cannes Film Festival's Director's Fortnight. With *Foster Child*, Brillante Mendoza joined the prestigious list of only four Filipinos to have screened their works in the category, a list which includes Lino Brocka, Mike De Leon and Mario O'Hara. In an interview, the film producer Robbie Tan articulated that they made the film with Cannes in mind (Cruz and San Diego Jr 2007) – the festival that would in 2009 herald Mendoza as the first Filipino filmmaker to receive the Best Director award for a full feature film. As part of its international success, national press articles pointed out that *Foster Child* received a five-minute standing ovation from the Cannes Film Festival audience (Carballo 2007; Dimaculangan 2007). The film was also generally received warmly by local critics (Flores 2007; Franciso 2007).

9. Some examples of health and hygiene practices imposed during the American period in the Philippines include the use of utensils instead of hands for eating, as well as the discouragement of the sharing of plates and glasses. According to Planta (2008: 131): 'Most importantly, every home was to have a toilet. These new and proper ways of hygiene, sanitation, better diet, and good behavior were to be enacted through the guidance of teachers and health officials who were considered role models.'

10. Fresh from the buzz generated by Mendoza's 2009 Cannes Film Festival win, *Lola* competed in the Golden Lion category of the Venice Film Festival in the same year. It later won awards in other international festivals, such as festivals in Dubai, Fribourg and Sydney. In the Philippines, like previous Mendoza films, *Lola* was received warmly by film critics even as it was unable to generate local box-office success (Alfonso 2009; Bolisay 2009; Medel 2009)

11. For critical essays on *Lola*, see Tadiar (2013) and Beller (2012).

12. Mendoza himself said as much in explaining the symbol in *Lola*: 'Rain is a metaphor for life and for death. It is the source of life but at the same time it can be the source of destruction and catastrophe' (Phillips 2010).

CHAPTER 6

Men on the Move: Chronotopes of Mobility in the Noir Imaginaries of Kinatay, Metro Manila *and* On the Job

> Manila is where I was born, a city of heat and shadow and secrets, perfect for this genre we call noir. (Hagedorn 2013: 9)

This chapter explores the movements of male characters and their struggle for spatial justice in three films: Brillante Mendoza's *Kinatay* (*Butchered*; 2009), British filmmaker Sean Ellis's *Metro Manila* (2013), and Erik Matti's *On the Job* (2013). Unlike the films in the previous chapters, these noir films cover more ground in the urban space, as the characters move into, away from and around the slum chronotope, mapping other 'dark' spaces in the city through what I designate as 'chronotopes of mobility'.

I frame these films as noir to surface the films' parallel configurations of the 'darkness' of urban spaces and the masculine anxieties of their male protagonists. *Kinatay*'s literal and figurative darkness is a visual rendering of the protagonist's descent into criminality; *Metro Manila* shows how the city tests a man's virtues in desperate times; *On the Job* attempts to map the spaces of power and corruption in the capital through the intersections of prison inmates and law authorities. In these examples of Manila noir, the slum chronotope dialogues with other 'dark' spaces of the city through chronotopes of mobility that facilitate narrative unfolding.

These chronotopes of mobility materialise in vehicles that function as significant kernels of action in each film: In *Kinatay*, the van that takes the protagonist to the scene of murder; in *Metro Manila*, the armoured truck that is used for the heist-gone-wrong; in *On the Job*, the chase scenes that lead to collisions among the narrative's male noir figures. These chronotopes of mobility become the means of producing moments that threaten the configurations of masculinity embodied in the movements of the films' anti-heroes through urban space. These are moments in which the sense of law and order of the urban space are challenged, revealing negotiations of spatial in/justice in the struggle over spatial occupation and appropriation.

CHRONOTOPES OF MOBILITY AND NOIR'S MASCULINE SUBJECTIVITIES

While I focus on masculine subjectivities in Manila noir, this is not to say that these films are essentially masculine in orientation. I am careful not to make the false assumption that film noir is the 'antithesis of the "woman's film"' that Elizabeth Cowie (1993: 126) has warned against. My framing of Manila noir as focused on masculinities does not seek to endorse the myth of masculinity, but to uncover the gendered dimension of the production of urban space that these male-centred films are able to map.

By mobility, I refer to geographer Tim Cresswell's (2012) argument that movement is part of the production of space. If movement refers to the abstract notion of getting from point A to B, mobility refers to the representational potentials of movement. Cresswell (2012: 165) points out that mobility, or the lack of it, reveals 'uneven geographies of oppression'. Mobility, like space, is 'gendered through and through' (Massey 1994: 186), illustrated in classic film noir, where the act of driving is considered a masculine act and experience. For instance, Mark Osteen (2008: 184) explores how vehicles in classic film noir function as 'alternative homes' and 'amoral spaces where laws and social arrangements – marriage, class hierarchies – are suspended'. The car is where the 'crisis of masculinity' (Osteen 2008: 189) occurs when someone else other than the male lead takes over the wheel. Similarly, Erik Dussere (2013: 66) argues that symbolic mobility is offered by the space of the American gas station where 'male bonding' takes place.

In Manila noir, the politics of mobility play out in similar but culturally specific ways, where the experience of travelling and modes of transit reveal stark socio-economic and gendered distinctions. The capital is infamous for heavy traffic with commuters taking hours to travel relatively short distances, such as through the 23-kilometre main thoroughfare called EDSA (Epifanio De los Santos Avenue). Public transportation in Manila is inefficient even as different modes of transportation are available, from tricycles, jeepneys and coaches. The outdated trains have limited stops and get terribly crowded during rush hour. Among all modes of transportation, the private car is arguably the king of the road, its occupants setting themselves apart in terms of monetary capital from those who can only afford the dismal services of public transportation. A report in *The Economist* (2016) suggests that the increase of car ownership, interpreted as middle-class aspiration, can be blamed for the increase in Manila traffic in recent years.

The social values ascribed to transportation can be traced as far back as the history of colonial occupation and the rise of motorisation in Manila. Michael Pante (2014) argues that the introduction of the electric streetcar and the automobile by American colonisers in 1905 gave rise to a 'collision of masculinities' in urbanising Manila. Pante (2014) explains that becoming a driver or working for the transportation system enabled the public display of masculinity, with car-ownership and driving a means of subscribing to the white male construct of modern masculinity. The masculine performances among Filipinos were varied, with a marked difference between Filipino male elites, drivers and transport workers (Pante 2014).

Contemporary urban policies aimed at instilling law and order are enacted through masculine rhetoric, such as through the 2006 *Metro Gwapo* campaign (Handsome City, mentioned in Chapter 4), which saw violent squatter demolitions and street-vendor dispersals (Michel 2010). While the masculine permutations of urban policies in Manila are apparent, these masculinities are also regularly put to the test. Neferti Tadiar (2004) has argued that state policies aimed at regulating movements within the informal urban economy vacillate between masculine and feminine sexualisation. Writing at the time of Manila Mayor Alfredo Lim's (2007–13) anti-prostitution drive that targeted feminised labour, Tadiar (2004: 96) explains the 'gender trouble' in the state's neoliberal urban policies: 'while capital demands an "open-economy" – meaning a feminine, permissive and porous metropolitan body, a national identity based on masculine ideals of power and selfhood demands a centrally-controlled, self-protective economy – meaning a contained and disciplined metropolitan body'.

In tracking the chronotopes of mobility of male characters in Manila noir, I am interested in the ways the films simultaneously reinforce and problematise the configuration of male subjectivities, particularly in the films' key instances of transit. While I focus on male subjectivities here, this is not to say that increased mobility is an inherently masculine capacity, but that the films in question expose and dramatise this assumption. These chronotopes of mobility literally and symbolically drive narrative development and reveal critical moments where the male subjects of Manila noir are put to the test, revealing different negotiations and imaginaries of spatial in/justice.

Kinatay as Manila Noir

I begin with my analysis of *Kinatay* as a prime example of Manila noir, with more than half of its screen time taking place in the darkness of a van that takes the main character from the city to its outskirts, like a road movie shrouded in the darkness of murder.[1] *Kinatay* follows the 24-hour ordeal of a young criminology student who finds himself participating in the violent murder of a prostitute by a gang of dirty cops. While not wholly set in the slums, *Kinatay* begins and ends in the slums, in this sense a literal deployment of the slum chronotope constituting and circumscribing the narrative. *Kinatay* opens with establishing scenes of the slum community where the main character, Peping, resides. The film then moves through and away from the city with a long driving scene, which ultimately leads to Peping witnessing the horrific slaughter and dismemberment of the prostitute.

Kinatay's opening is deliberately deceptive, comprised of a montage of images of life. It is morning, the city's inhabitants are bustling to begin the day's work: the wet market is open, sidewalk vendors abound, commuters set off to work. The scene cuts to the main character, Peping, as he comes down from his house in the slums with his wife-to-be and newborn child. Through a window, the audience is offered a view of the crudely constructed houses that line the urban poor community. Peping and his partner leave their child with an aunt for the day and board a jeepney, where the dialogue reveals that they are on their way to civil court to get married.

The slum chronotope configures Peping as a slum inhabitant, first by showing him inside his community, followed by the camera's tracking gaze as he descends to join the throng of other inhabitants who comprise the city. The choice of daytime images is significant in the configuration of the slum chronotope as the narrative's organising centre, and already plays with generic expectations from a narrative set in such a context of poverty: crowds, garbage, noise, traffic – all signifiers of the abject conditions in the Philippine capital. Although the film's period is not actually specified, there are signs that it is contemporary: billboards, buildings and, of course, the very look of the slum space itself.[2]

Kinatay makes use of different modes of transit to literally move the narrative, with spatial mobility signifying social mobility. From their home in the slum community, the couple board a *pedicab* that takes them to a wider street where they hail a jeepney. While in the jeepney on their way to court, 20-year-old Peping excitedly tells his 18-year-old fiancée that their *ninong* (wedding sponsor) might gift him with a motorcycle, which he intends to use for extra money. After the wedding, Peping and his family board the *ninong*'s van on their way to the mall, where they are treated to lunch. Peping marvels at the newly purchased van, saying in half-jest that he would gladly take the van if his *ninong* ever gets tired of it. This bright scene in the *ninong*'s van would later serve as stark contrast to the utter darkness in the other van that Peping boards, not knowing that the night of his wedding day will initiate him into the darker facets of manhood.

The daytime scenes paint a bright picture of Peping entering manhood as a new father and husband. But the narrative shifts gear when night falls and *Kinatay* shifts to the darkness of film noir. Peping, who is studying to be a cop, meets up with a friend in a public park in the heart of Manila, where he collects drug money from street vendors to earn small change. When Peping hands over the money, his friend, Abyong, tells him that 'Kap' wants him for a 'job' that night. Peping agrees jovially, upon the promise of easy money. However, once Peping mounts the van, the film's mood turns sinister, conveyed immediately through darker lighting and soft foreboding score. Peping's figure dissolves into a shadow in the back of the van. What follows is an uneasy silence as the van moves through the dark streets leading to the red-light district where the group of men pick up the prostitute, Madonna, who owes Kap a huge sum of drug money. From this point, the van that becomes the vehicle of murder functions as *Kinatay*'s most prominent chronotope of mobility that puts Peping's sense of masculinity to the test.

CHRONOTOPES OF MOBILITY AND SPATIAL INJUSTICE IN *KINATAY*

The time of the futuristic-present governs the testing of Peping's masculinity as the van moves through the city streets. What I mean is that the van, and the violence it channels through its movement along the city's main artery, is in these moments traversing the path towards Peping's projected future as a corrupt figure of authority. It is no coincidence that Peping is studying to be a cop and that the men in charge of this operation are referred to by their roles in the police force, 'Kap' and 'Sarge'. Later dialogue reveals that Peping's father was also a cop. The historian Alfred McCoy (2000) has argued that the Philippine action film draws heavily from military configurations as the ideal model of masculinity, which extends to political figures who have either military or police backgrounds. McCoy (2000) also notes that the Philippine Military Academy is known for initiation rites such as physical hazing, an open secret that is not condemned but rather considered a valuable test of one's worth in joining the ranks of the military. This idealisation of the man with the gun as masculine figure runs through *Kinatay* and the other films in this noir chapter.

The dialogue in *Kinatay* suggests that the authority figures targeted Peping as someone worthy of recruiting into the operation, which means that this particular night serves as Peping's initiation into the world of corruption within the police force. This is a world that is hypermasculine. Misogynist jokes regularly creep into the dialogue, which Peping at some point also participates in to prove that he belongs. It is not that Peping is wholly innocent – this is established in the daytime scenes where he takes the tip left at the food court and in the scene where he expresses his desire to have a gun. So it is not that Peping is innocent; it is that he is not *yet* that corrupt. This time of 'yet' is the time that hovers in the narrative's futuristic present, rendered through the unfolding of the narrative as Peping is gradually shrouded in the darkness of the impending murder.

In a way, *Kinatay*'s long driving scene makes use of the classic chronotope of the road, where space covered equates to time spent.[3] The tough men in charge of the operation are literally taking Peping on a road test. Each second in the van is part of the test of Peping's masculinity, which in this narrative is measured by his participation in the crime of murder. He survives most of the transit scene by hiding in the darkness and by keeping silent. More significantly, Peping is alert to his testing. When 'Kap' suddenly clobbers Madonna, he demands that someone hand him a handkerchief to stuff in her mouth. Peping complies immediately. At some point, Peping looks at his phone – then catches himself and quickly says out loud that he was just checking the time even when nobody calls him out. To the tough guys in the van, the horror in Peping's eyes is not visible; to the camera, however, Peping's panic is slightly more apparent as it moves into close-ups of Peping's face in the claustrophobic space of the tinted vehicle (Figure 6.1).

The transit through the city accommodates and is accommodated by the disruptions of the actual built environment of Manila traffic, prolonging the time of transit, which drives home the notion that this time on the road is the time of the present. The disruptions throughout the time of passage are what can be deemed 'returns to the present', according to the demands of the urban experience through the traffic of EDSA. At one point, the driver comments: '*Traffic is always so heavy here in Cubao, no matter what time it is*' – referring to a node at EDSA that is notoriously known for bottleneck traffic due to the convergence of smaller streets and flyovers. While the van is stuck in traffic,

Figure 6.1 *Peping's masculinity is put to the test inside the van that traverses the city in* Kinatay.

the camera captures views of the billboards that line the highway. Kap and Sarge talk about Kap's son, who works at a call centre where fluent English is required. These casual comments serve to make the experience of the drive all the more disturbing, as if having a woman tied up and gagged in the van is but an everyday occurrence. At the same time, the call-centre comment and the billboard views that disrupt the long driving scene make the van a chronotope of mobility that channels global time-spaces through the spatial practice of driving, as it reveals the commodified urban space lined with 24/7 advertisements, the highway functioning like an outdoor mall.[4]

In terms of framing, the camera shifts from darkly lit tight shots of the van's passengers and a view of the road from the back of the van, suggesting that we are seeing the road from Peping's perspective. Peping's driving views are fleeting images that convey his detachment from urban space.[5] His views are limited because, after all, he is not the one behind the wheel. In fact, at this point in the narrative, he doesn't even know where the journey will take him. His select views of the cityscape are not just signs of ambivalence, but of exclusion from the mastery of urban space that the senior figures of masculinity exhibit.

The views of the road from Peping's seat in the van can also be invested with the affects of fear and panic, as each mile away from the city centre means Peping becomes more and more trapped in the operation he unwittingly became part of. These affects are conveyed in Peping's furtive glances at the men around him, his brows furrowed, as though searching for some sign that these men are not as tough as they seem. A sense of entrapment is indeed revealed through Peping's journey in the van.[6] The growing sense of fear and panic is further conveyed in Peping's selected driving views such as road signs that signal departure from the city centre.

However, there is a scene that momentarily provides a degree of choice for Peping and the viewers. This is the scene at the bus terminal where Peping is tasked to run an errand before going back to the house where the murder takes place. In the terminal, Peping actually boards a bus with the intention of leaving. In this scene, we realise that Peping has a choice. The exact moment when Peping makes the difficult decision to stay with the group is depicted in a deep focus shot, his face blurred in the foreground while the van is sharply in sight through the bus window (Figure 6.2). His phone rings, which he picks up to say: '*I just took a piss. I'm on my way back.*' With that, he gets off the bus and makes his way back to the van.

If the film's scenes of transit are chronotopes of mobility, this particular scene in the liminal space of the bus terminal, and inside the unmoving bus itself, might be read as a chronotope of immobility. Peping's inability to literally drive away is what made him decide to become accomplice to the crime.

Figure 6.2 *Peping's moment of indecision in the bus that can take him back home. A scene from* Kinatay.

His inability to move is what compelled him to decide to return to the van. I am not saying that Peping made this choice without difficulty, but that in this scene the film demonstrates Peping's comprehension of the difficulty of this choice. In this brief moment, Peping realises that his life depends on the death of the prostitute. The film's framing of the scene in deep focus further invites the film's audience to view this decision from Peping's perspective – his guilt becomes our guilt, his decision our decision.

The graphic scenes of sexual abuse, murder and the chopping up of the woman's body that occur in roughly fifteen minutes of screen time is interspersed with Peping bearing witness through a window from outside the house, his facial expression and heavy breathing conveying utter horror and disbelief. There is clear parallelism between the complete desacralisation of the woman's body and Peping's symbolic castration in these 'chop-chop' scenes.[7] In an earlier scene, Peping and Madonna stare at each other in the basement, both bearing expressions of terror at the violence of it all. In the entire film, Madonna is the only character who bears witness to Peping's castration, or his inability to measure up to masculine violence. Contrary to the pleasure derived through the male gaze, Peping does not witness the spectacle of murder from a position of male power, but from a position of castration anxiety. During the actual murder, Peping's spatial position of bearing witness to Madonna's murder from outside the house masks his fear from his male superiors, while at the same time his experience of terror is visible to the viewers. He scrambles to regain composure when Sarge asks for bags for the severed body parts, and acts swiftly during the clean-up.

The final scene of transit reinforces Peping's descent into corruption. He hails a taxi after collecting his money. It is dawn, and traffic is already starting to build up. Just as Peping closes his eyes, the taxi's tyre bursts. He opens his eyes in mild panic and checks if the gun he received as a gift from Kap is still in his bag, afraid that the sound of the burst tyre was gunshot. He gets out of the taxi in the middle of the highway, trying in vain to flag another one. When the driver manages to replace the tyre and motions for him to get back in, Peping, after a moment's hesitation, complies. This scene that takes place at daybreak is a clearer signal of his decision to take the ride, as it were, not because he wants to, and not even because there are no other options. He takes the ride because it guarantees a safe journey home – just as staying to finish the job in the company of tough men guarantees his survival. There are no grey zones in *Kinatay*, but there is no 'right' way either. For Peping, the only clear way through the test is the one that will get him home.

In *Kinatay*, the slum space serves to bookend the narrative, but its significance in the beginning is different from its meaning at the end of the film. In the opening sequence, Peping is tracked for the duration of the day, moving away from the slums on a hopeful note. In the final sequence, Peping is returning home to the slums, bearing the knowledge of violence required for him and his family to survive. There are many instances when Peping looks at his wedding ring, such as the scene in the toilet of the food place the group stops at before Peping decides to head home. He stares at himself in the mirror, then looks at his wedding ring as he aggressively washes his hands as though trying to rub away the violence of the night, lest his new wife see through him. Each scene where he looks at his wedding ring is a reminder that he has a family to return to, which is why he must survive. If there is a sliver of justice to be found in *Kinatay*, it can perhaps be gleaned from Peping's return to the slums in the film's final scene, with his wife holding their child while cooking breakfast as a new day breaks. This final scene, sans Peping, denotes what I have earlier referred to as the structuring presence of home in Manila noir, in that Peping's descent into darkness can only be explained – if not justified – by his desire to ensure a future for his family. Peping's immersion in the violence of the city is the cost of keeping his wife and child away from it.

METRO MANILA AS MANILA NOIR

Metro Manila tells the story of a peasant family trying their luck in the big city, only to find themselves ensnared by crime and corruption. The main character, Oscar Ramirez, takes a job in security as an armoured truck driver tasked with transporting money within the city. He is later forced by his partner, Ong, to carry out a heist to ensure his family's survival. *Metro Manila* opens and ends with a sub-story that parallels the themes of survival and desperation that Oscar encounters in the city, told through his own voice-over. The sub-story is about a man who jumps off a plane mid-flight, having robbed the plane's passengers. I will return to this curious story-within-a-story later, as it adds another layer to Oscar's configuration as a criminal in the film's closure.

Admittedly, I include *Metro Manila* with caution in the emerging genre of Philippine urban cinema, given that it was directed by British filmmaker Sean Ellis. Any reading of the film is informed by the fact that it was directed by a foreign filmmaker, which makes the film even more suspect to the charge of poverty pornography.[8] However, I think it is worth including here as a British-Filipino film, since the film's cast is comprised entirely of Filipino actors who had a hand in the film's production. Ellis wrote the script in English, while the task of translating it into Tagalog was in the hands of the cast (Wise 2013). It is also to Ellis's credit that he attempted to immerse himself in the slum spaces of Manila as part of the process of filming.[9]

In what follows, it is not my intention to fully absolve *Metro Manila* of exploitative tendencies. However, I don't think it is productive to dismiss the film outright. Even though it is not the most radical representation of the urban underclass, *Metro Manila* is not entirely devoid of imaginaries of spatial justice, especially in its configuration of the male protagonist.

First, the primary narrative: *Metro Manila* can be approached as a migrant tale of survival in the city, with the Ramirez family's transit from rural to urban space setting off the narrative. The film tracks the family's departure from the idyllic mountain province of Benguet, prompted by insufficient funds for harvest. The act of departure from the countryside is captured with remarkably picturesque wide and medium shots, dwarfing the family as they make their way through the rice paddies to a dirt road where they embark upon an uncomfortable journey to Manila via jeepney.

The first quarter of the film establishes how *Metro Manila* attempts to follow in the footsteps of the second golden age of Philippine social realism in its use of the narrative trope of the rural migrant chasing a better life in the big city. The stark contrast between the rural and the urban space is apparent once the family arrives in the city. The camera moves frantically, darting to and from the bewildered and awestruck faces of the Ramirez family. In contrast to the panoramic shots of the rural space, the camera introduces the city through a montage of modern images: billboards, footbridges, skyscrapers, all surrounded by a steady stream of bodies.

Men on the Move   117

The hapless family, homeless and penniless after being conned shortly after arriving in the city, find themselves seeking shelter in the slums lining the waterways of Tondo. Even as the film does not linger in the slums in terms of screen time, the scenes of the family's entry into Tondo is more than enough to ground the narrative in the slum chronotope (recalling the significance of Tondo in Manila's urban imaginary discussed in Chapter 4). This shift from rural to urban space signals the arrival of the time of the futuristic present in this urban noir that configures the narrative once the family find themselves without dwelling. The slum chronotope hovers throughout *Metro Manila* as the time-space that the family struggles to escape from, or the space that should *not* be inhabited, with the urgent search for a habitable home serving as a structuring presence in the narrative. The foreboding presence of the family's uncertain future is reinforced when the couple find out that Mai is pregnant with their third child.

CHRONOTOPES OF MOBILITY IN *METRO MANILA*

Metro Manila achieves the noir look and mood in the spaces of masculinity offered in the narrative: the armoured van, and the security firm's underground parking where the 'debriefing room' is located. The armoured van serves as *Metro Manila*'s prominent chronotope of mobility, given its significance to the configuration of both Oscar and Ong's masculine subjectivities (Figure 6.3). The scenes in which they inhabit the van strengthen their male bonding, starting with the scenes where Ong teaches Oscar to drive. In one scene, Ong drives to a vacant lot outside the city centre, where both practise

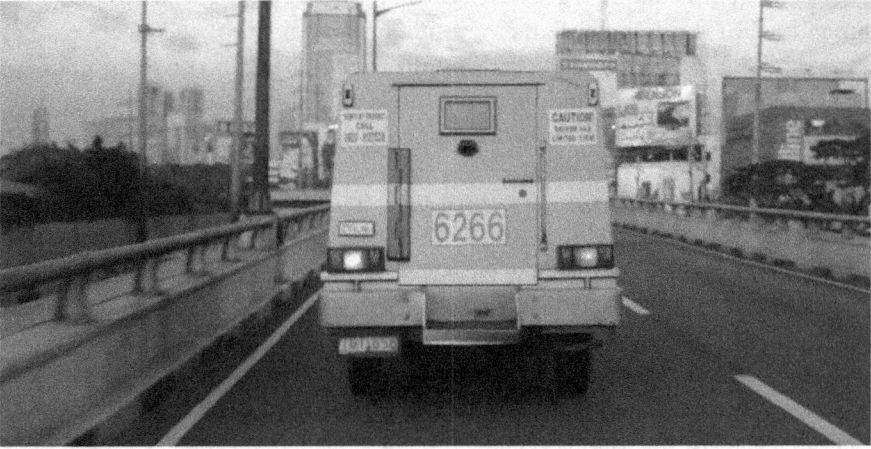

Figure 6.3 *The armoured truck driving through one of the city's main thoroughfares in* Metro Manila.

shooting with the guns they carry with them while on duty; a performance of masculinity and male bonding. More significantly, it is in and through the van chronotope that both men reveal masculine anxieties. Oscar's anxiety is easy enough to identify as his inability to perform his perceived role as provider for his family. Ong, on the other hand, reveals his guilt at his inability to save his former partner who died in the line of duty. While driving, Ong's recollection of the death of his previous partner is revealed in a violent flashback: his partner is gunned down in an ambush by a group of criminals as they were transferring money boxes in a bank.

Like the configuration of masculinity in *Kinatay* modelled after the idealised image of the military or police, Oscar is ex-military. This personal history lands him the job at the security company, when by chance a guard spots his army tattoo while he is queuing for an interview. The interviewer, Ong, and everyone else present in the room, guarantees the job of van driver to Oscar when he proves his military experience, even though he does not know how to drive.

It is clear that Oscar does not measure up to Ong's masculinity, symbolised primarily by Oscar's inability to drive. The narrative development shows an uneven relationship between the two men, configured through spatial association. The other men in the security company pejoratively call Oscar 'Oscar-the-peasant', while Ong stands for the male figure who has mastery over urban space. Like in *Kinatay*, driving in *Metro Manila* is a spatial practice that signifies the potential for social mobility. Ong teaches Oscar how to drive, a seemingly kind act that puts Oscar in Ong's debt. As the narrative moves closer to the heist, it turns out that Ong has been grooming Oscar to become his unwitting partner-in-crime.

There are no exciting car chase scenes in *Metro Manila*, which reflects the limitations of the actual urban environment of heavy traffic. The absence of explosive driving scenes also corresponds to the physical composition of the armoured van, as well as adding to the film's slow pacing. In lieu of space and the means for car chase scenes, the film conveys tension through a score that accompanies the tracking shots of the armoured van, shot either from behind or in front as it drives at a steady pace mostly through the EDSA highway. The scenes where the van departs from a straightforward route signal that something might go wrong. The false alarm of robbery in an early scene foreshadows the twist that will occur in the last quarter of screen time.

In *Metro Manila*, masculine mobility means mastery of the urban space. This aspiration to master the city is captured in a critical scene that dialogues with the chronotope of mobility and the slum chronotope, where both men behold a view of the Manila skyline at night, a view that Ong has access to on his balcony (Figure 6.4). Ong remarks, gesturing at the view: '*Look at that . . .*

Figure 6.4 *Ong and Oscar overlooking the city in* Metro Manila.

Metro Manila. Quite a sight. This is where I come to think.' Ong's self-perception of his mastery of the urban space, in contrast to Oscar's lack of mobility, is reinforced when he chides Oscar for squatting in Tondo: '*You work for an armoured truck company. That slum is a haven for the worst type of criminals.*' Ong's perceived mastery of the urban space extends to the heist he imagines. Heist films invest their protagonists with the capacity to imagine, a display of 'creative activity by encoding the values of imagination and creative effort into criminal activity' (Lee 2014: 9). This theory applies very well to a film like *Metro Manila* where the successful enactment of a carefully thought-out plan creates the myth of 'the law-breaking criminal genius ... displaced from a moral or criminological plane onto an aesthetic one' (Lee 2014: 9).

The film deliberately withholds the heist from view for over an hour of screen time, before it shifts to reveal Ong's master plan. The chronotope of mobility collides with the threshold chronotope of an alley that takes Oscar, and the film narrative, onto the film's pathway to spatial injustice. By this I mean that Ong's deception is exposed when Oscar finds the nerve to get out of the van and follow Ong into the alley where the latter is meeting accomplices. This particular alley operates as a threshold chronotope, where the time of Oscar's ethical crisis takes place. Here is where the heist is explained and Ong's true motives are revealed, and here is where Oscar's virtue is put to the test.[10]

It turns out that the ambush that led to the death of Ong's partner left him with an unopened money box. Ong needs to fake another ambush so that Oscar can gain access to the processing centre that holds the key to the money box. More importantly, Ong plans to frame Oscar for the crime if he refuses to participate. Ong explains where Oscar needs to go, with very specific instructions, in order to retrieve the key in the processing centre. Ong forces Oscar's complicity in a significant line that dialogues with the film's main chronotope of mobility, a command that makes Oscar part of the crime whether he likes if or not: '*Ok. You drive.*'

As with most heist narratives, something in the master plan goes awry. While Oscar is behind the wheel and Ong gets out to stage the fake ambush, Ong is unexpectedly killed by the same thug that shot his ex-partner. The sudden appearance of this assassin from Ong's past is somewhat abrupt; his motivation for killing Ong is never explained and results in what I consider to be one of the film's narrative gaps. Putting that aside, however, Ong's death allows Oscar to emerge as the film's unlikely noir anti-hero. Ong's death was supposed to signal Oscar's literal and symbolic immobility – but instead, this drives Oscar to act on his own terms. Ong's last words demanding that Oscar take the wheel takes on more significance – it is a demand that Oscar 'man up', so speak, that he overcome his masculine anxiety in order to do the job.

Metro Manila's last few minutes compress time and space in the rendering of the heist. The day turns into night through tracking scenes of the armoured van as it moves along the main highway, similar to the tracking shots used earlier in the film when Oscar was just beginning his journey into the big city. When the van returns to the processing centre, Oscar stages his one-man heist. There is something rather crude about the mechanisms of this heist, far from the technologically advanced stunts in Hollywood heist films. The processing centre itself isn't exactly a sophisticated fortress. Oscar, using a torn-up strip of cardboard and tape manages to keep the door to the processing centre unlatched when someone exits. When he enters, the noir elements of suspense and darkness are ramped up through claustrophobic shots and intense scoring. The film tracks Oscar through the dimly lit hallway and stairway leading to the room that holds the literal and metaphorical key to his family's survival. The heist culminates in Oscar's death when he is shot in a bloody scene by security guards.

The last few scenes reveal Oscar's creative efforts in reconfiguring Ong's heist. As explained by Ong in earlier parts of the film, Oscar's death guarantees the transfer of his belongings to his wife, Mai. When Oscar died, he was wearing a locket containing an imprint of the key that will open the money box. During the heist, Oscar grabbed a decoy key number so that the security company will no longer track the money box in his family's possession.

The imprint is hidden behind the image of the Virgin Mary inside the locket, an allusion to the film's interlocked themes of faith and survival. These values are much more embodied in Mai's character than Oscar's. Her character development is quite limited, an area where this film falls short. Mai's role in this narrative, it seems, is to reinforce Oscar's emasculation given his inability to provide for the family. In fact, as part of blackmailing Oscar, Ong's strongest taunt directly challenges his masculinity: '*What kind of man lets his wife whore herself out in a bar?*'

It is in this sense that Mai somewhat functions as a reformulation of the femme fatale in the form of the suffering female, sans deception. When Oscar finds the money box in the apartment and tells Mai about the ruined plan, she demands that Oscar return the box. When he says he might be blamed for his partner's robbery, Mai's reply pushes him over the edge: '*We can't stay here. We have to escape . . . We made a big mistake coming to Manila.*' Mai's defiance in this last statement is even more understandable if we link it to the scene in the bar earlier that night, where the pimp suggested that her young daughter could be offered to special clients. Ultimately, then, it is Mai, not Ong, who sets the narrative's final test of masculinity, which Oscar satisfies through death.

What are we to make of the sub-story that unfurls in *Metro Manila*? As I suggested earlier, this sub-story that takes place in a plane can be considered another chronotope of mobility that dialogues with the van chronotope, with Oscar having more control over the imaginary plane's transit. The story of Alfred Santos is used to bookend the film with Oscar's voice-over, presumably reading his farewell letter to Mai, where he explains his self-sacrifice. Desperate after the family business goes bankrupt, Alfred robs fellow plane passengers mid-flight, inspired by a dream that he could escape with a homemade parachute. Oscar likens his own story of escape to Alfred's story, which both ended in death. Unlike Alfred, however, Oscar asserts that his plan was not based on a dream, but on the reality that there was no other way out.

In contrast to *Kinatay*, there is a small sense of justice to be found in *Metro Manila*'s closure, but it is one paved by the protagonist's death, and one that signals departure from the city. Oscar contrasts Alfred's story with his own decision to take the similar route as one of redemption rather than hopelessness. Moreover, the film's opening lines preface Oscar's death as masculine sacrifice, contrary to the notion of endurance ascribed to a church proverb.[11] Oscar's death might have been inevitable, but the proverb suggests that the film imagines his agency through his capacity to set the terms of his death. By taking over the heist, Oscar successfully hijacks the master plan from Ong, ultimately redeeming his masculinity in death by providing a way out of the city for his family. The film closes on a somewhat hopeful tone. Mai and her children, carrying with them a bag full of money, are travelling by bus – suggesting a possible return to the countryside. In a way, the Ramirez family got the relief they came for in making their way to the big city, but in exchange the city took Oscar's life.

ON THE JOB AS MANILA NOIR

If *Kinatay* and *Metro Manila* feature male noir figures in the process of being corrupted by the city, *On the Job* presents characters who are already in too deep. Established Filipino filmmaker Erik Matti's *On the Job* takes us deep into the labyrinth of the city as crime scene.[12] Among the films in this chapter, *On the Job* lends itself most overtly to the noir narrative of the crime thriller, with its cops versus criminals and whodunit narrative trajectory.

Inspired by true events, as announced by the film's opening scenes and the use of actual news footage, the film tracks the movements of two prison inmates, Mario and Daniel, who are regularly contracted as hitmen by powerful clients. The movements of the prison inmates parallel the storyline of the detectives who are investigating the murder that sets off the narrative. The narrative unravels through the intersections and collisions of the killers and the detectives, which take place in the urban spaces of Metropolitan Manila whose roads, streets, and alleys are rendered confusing and un-mappable by the film.

On the Job grounds itself strongly in the urban spaces of Manila, and is effectively able to navigate the city's built environment in ways that produce suspense and tension through its visual and aural elements.[13] *On the Job* sets itself apart through its thoughtful use of space, particularly in the configuration of the prison space as slum chronotope. The slum chronotope runs through the narrative of *On the Job*, not just through the scenes that occur in slum spaces, but also through the configuration of the prison space itself. I argue that the prison space can be read as a simulation of the overcrowded, self-sufficient, makeshift nature of the slum space.

Prisons and jails in the Philippines are infamous for being chaotic, undermanned, dirty and, most of all, overpopulated and congested. Human rights violations are rampant in the seven national prisons and over 400 jails in the Philippines. There is a huge lack of basic services like food, clean water and toilet facilities.[14] According to data from the Bureau of Jail Management and Penology (2017), the congestion rate for jails in the National Capital Region is a staggering 547 per cent. Jails with an 'ideal capacity' for 4,801 inmates actually contain 31,043. In August 2016, just three months after the Duterte administration launched its war on drugs, Philippine prisons made international headlines when the Agence France-Presse (Celis 2016) published photos of the 'hellish' conditions at Manila's Quezon City Jail, a jail initially made for 800 bodies crammed with almost 4,000 prisoners.

Overcrowding and a lack of guards have resulted in some form of self-regulation among prison inmates. A CNN report (McKirdy 2016) exposes the gang system that exists and keeps a sense of order inside the Quezon City

Men on the Move 123

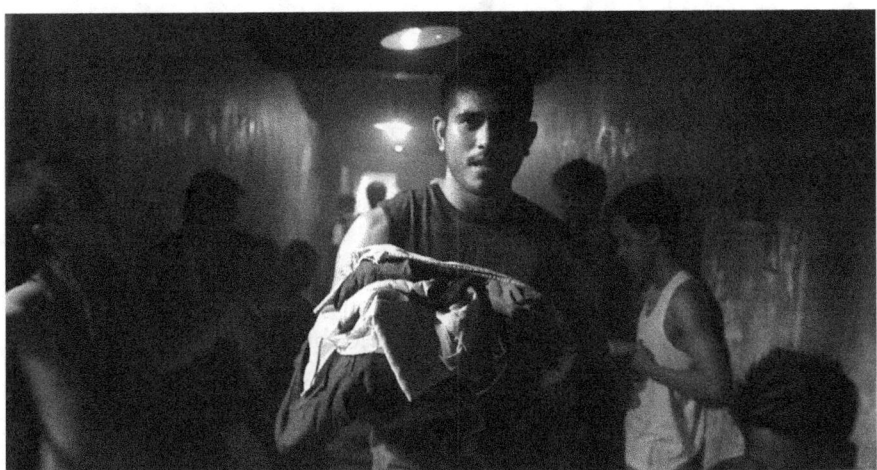

Figure 6.5 *Daniel's walk introduces the prison space that resembles a* looban. *Screen grab from* On the Job.

Jail. These group dynamics exist in prisons and jails across the country. In an earlier study, Filomin Candaliza-Gutierrez (2012) identifies *pangkats* or gangs that operate in the New *Bilibid* Maximum Security Compound, citing ethnolinguistic similarities as a basis for belonging.

The view that prisons are self-contained spaces that produce particular socio-spatial relations makes it possible to liken prison communities to slum communities. The prison space as depicted in *On the Job* resembles and functions in similar ways to slum communities, particularly *loobans*. Like *loobans*, the prison space is literally hidden from view, and yet it is a space teeming with human activity precisely because of its invisibility. *On the Job* certainly attempts to imagine the congestion and squalor in Philippine prisons through constructing the set of the film's *Bagong Yugto* (New Chapter) City Jail.[15]

A memorable three-minute sequence that tracks Daniel introduces the prison space as slum space in *On the Job* (Figure 6.5). In the absence of wide establishing shots of the prison interiors, this scene captures the spatial and social dynamics of the prison space, comparable to the tight tracking shots executed in *loobans* in the previous chapters. We see different areas of the prison space, such as the kitchen, gaming and laundry sites, as the camera tracks Daniel's swaggering walk. If not for the presence of guards and passing views of cell bars, it is possible to forget for a moment that this scene is set inside a prison.

The slum-prison chronotope organises time in the vein of the futuristic-present in relation to the workings of prison time. For the inmates, their time depends on the duration of their sentence or their time outside the prison while on the job. Prison time is not fixed – it can be negotiated. The inmates subject themselves to these ever-present negotiations in order to provide for the future of their families. The ageing Mario is about to be released from prison which signals the end of his hitman days, while the youthful Daniel is eager to take Mario's place as top hitman. The slum-prison chronotope also configures the inmates' relations with other characters: the guards and warden who allow the inmates to go in and out of prison within a negotiated period; and with Thelma, the femme fatale contractor who arranges the hitmen's pick-ups and returns. Mario's visits to his family and Daniel's phone calls to his mother are determined by the time allowed through these negotiations.

What *On the Job* is able to execute through the prison-slum chronotope, is a complex dialogue with other chronotopes that structure the narrative according to the movements of the characters. The inmates find themselves in-between times as they move from inside and outside the prison space, in the process revealing the power structures that allow for such a guns-for-hire system to exist. The film illustrates how the system works in a manner that reveals the contradictions in the seemingly porous movements of the inmates from inside to outside the prison space.

CHRONOTOPES OF MOBILITY AND SPATIAL INJUSTICE IN *ON THE JOB*

Masculine authority is embodied in the police and military figures in *On the Job*, just like in *Kinatay* and *Metro Manila*. General Pacheco is the top man behind the orders to kill. The plan is to groom Francis Coronel, a rookie agent, into the youngest National Bureau of Investigation Chief to serve the political aspirations of the general's entourage – which includes Coronel's father-in-law. Coronel graduated top of his class in the Philippine Military Academy, where his late father was also educated.

If the military men are at the top of the chain, the contract killers are at the bottom. However, the hitmen are actually key players in the corrupt system. The contract killers, hidden from view, are the ones who carry out the dirty work in order to sustain the system of corruption embodied by General Pacheco and the men who support him. What places the prisoner-hitmen at the bottom of the power scheme is that fact that their lives are dispensable.

Like in *Kinatay* and *Metro Manila*, chronotopes of mobility in *On the Job* take the form of the private vehicle, where scenes of transit signal social mobility. The vehicle in *On the Job* is a clear assertion of symbolic power given that the private vehicle that takes Mario and Daniel from the prison to their targets bears a police licence plate.[16] For Coronel, the film's naive detective figure, the private vehicle also functions as chronotope of mobility in that it signals the potential beginnings of his entry into political corruption. At the start of the investigation, Coronel's congressman father-in-law gifts him with a new Range Rover, which he reluctantly accepts upon the prodding of his wife. Later, when Coronel decides to arrest his father-in-law and General Pacheco, he returns the Range Rover as a symbolic gesture of turning away from corruption.

In contrast, the chronotope of mobility ascribed to the hitmen is the domain of the female contractor who the film introduces as the chain-smoking, red-lipped Thelma, the film's femme fatale. In *On the Job*, the femme fatale calls the shots, to some degree. Thelma's role as contractor means she has a say in approving or disapproving special requests from the hired guns, such as asking for payment in advance or getting an extra day outside the prison space. In fact, Thelma is the one who articulates that Daniel is ready to take Mario's place as main contract killer.

The presence of the femme fatale in the vehicle occupied by Mario and Daniel serves to temper their masculinity, which has little effect in the face of a female figure who holds monetary capital. Thelma's tough femme fatale character can be juxtaposed with the alluring character of Nicky, Coronel's wife. Although Nicky is portrayed as a sweet character in the beginning, she turns out to be the real danger to her husband later on, when she questions his loyalty to her and to her father. Nicky's decision to choose her father over her husband can be considered a symbolic collusion (rather than collision) with Thelma, who hands over the envelope with Coronel's picture to Daniel, making him the target of the film's bloodiest scene.

Along with scenes of transit involving private vehicles, *On the Job*'s chase scenes done on foot operate as chronotopes of mobility. These critical chase scenes are ignited by a collision of masculinities, which in this narrative is also a collision of ethics. These chronotopes of mobility are instances that test not just the male figures' capacity to move, whether on foot, or through the act of driving, but also the capacity to make moral choices. The first chase sequence is set off in the maze-like alleys of a *looban* and tracks the characters as they move towards larger streets. The chase leads to a hospital shoot-out, and tracks the male characters as they move to a construction site and Manila's overground train. Meanwhile, the second chase sequence is the final car chase spurred by the bloody shoot-out that results in the death of Coronel.

The chase scenes in *On the Job* are devoid of obvious special effects; instead they rely on the classic interplay of light and darkness, as well as an effective music score to aid the creation of suspense. There are no overtly grand spectacles or death-defying stunts, other than the sheer force and energy generated by the act of running after someone, or running away. The camera cuts from one to the other, ascribing panic not just to the figures fleeing but also to the figures chasing after them. The effect is what I view as the dispersal of audience excitement and sympathy, as well as the dissolution of the moral roles of the chaser versus the chasee. This sort of frenzied camera work that also uses quick cuts and shaky effects encourages the shifting of audience allegiance, with us simultaneously rooting for the chaser to catch up and the chasee to get away. This effect of dispersing audience sympathy is accomplished in the first chase sequence in *On the Job*, in which the film makes use of the slum's *eskinitas* as the space in which the two sets of partners – the cops and the killers – literally collide for the first time.

In the chase sequences done on foot, the male figures themselves function as embodied chronotopes of mobility. This first chase sequence occurs after Paul, an ex-cop, reveals how the killing system works, in a desperate attempt to solicit police protection now that he knows he is next on the kill list. The political motive for the recent spate of hits is revealed: General Pacheco wants to get rid of his contractors to make sure there are no loose ends for his senatorial bid. Coronel and company arrive at the mouth of the *looban* just before a gunshot is heard, spurring the first part of the chase. The first part makes use of the alleys of the *looban* as channels of mobility, which means that the figures who know this terrain better would more likely get away. And so Mario and Daniel, men of the street who don't own private vehicles, manage to get ahead in the chase scenes within the *looban*.

The second part of this chase sequence paints a clearer intersection of *On the Job*'s male noir figures, with the father figures (Acosta and Mario) and the son figures (Coronel and Daniel) taking different routes, at the same time depicting the playing out of two different times and spaces through quick cuts and jerky framings. Acosta chases after Mario through a construction site, while Coronel chases after Daniel in a memorable scene inside a train carriage. What this second part of the chase sequence is able to do, especially the train scene (which is also featured in the film's promotional poster), is to ground this narrative of corruption even more so in Manila's urban context. In this chase scene, the film's urban space activates its potential as 'any-space-whatever' where 'characters practically disappear in order to foreground the spatial narrative' (Martin-Jones 2011: 156).[17]

The running sequences foreground, as the camera chases after the male figures on the move, images that stand particularly for Manila's urban landscape – the streets, the jeepneys and cars in the night-time traffic, the construction site, the overground train. These are Manila-specific images that are not foregrounded in the same manner in any of the other films included in this study, precisely because of the faster pace of running offered in *On the Job*. Mario and Daniel, the ones being chased, make full use of the spaces they find themselves in, attempting to blend into these spaces in order to lose their trackers. In their attempts to disappear into space, we are compelled to pay more attention to the spaces they occupy. This chase sequence proves critical to the film's most naive detective figure, Coronel, who then drives to confront his father-in-law about his possible involvement in the guns-for-hire system. What this chase sequence does, then, is urge Coronel (and the viewers) to cast a wider net of investigation, beyond the killers he was chasing after, in order for him to finally realise that the real culprits behind the system are those right at the top.

From the running sequences, I turn to the film's dramatic car chase sequence which functions as its final chronotope of mobility. This particular car chase literally depicts a collision of masculinities through the collision of vehicles, overcast by a flurry of gunshots. The chase sequence is prompted by the assassination of Coronel at the hands of Daniel, a symbolic turning over of the role of prime hitman from Mario to his protégé. Coronel's assassination by Daniel signifies the collision of masculinities of these younger male figures in the narrative, with Coronel at the losing end. Daniel shoots quickly, and the scene cuts to a wide shot from above showing Acosta bleeding out in the square, emphasising the young man's tragic end. That this scene was staged outside Manila City Hall, a site recognisable to the Filipino viewer, strongly signifies the political motivations behind this death.

Coronel's murder spurs his stand-in mentor figure, Acosta, who has not been shown behind the wheel at any point in the narrative, to get into his beat-up car in order to intercept the general's convoy. Unlike the edgy tone of the running scenes, this car chase sequence is accompanied by a tragic song, which suggests that Acosta's attempt to apprehend Acosta for his crimes is futile. Shouting accusations of murder as his old car catches up with the general's larger vehicle, Acosta swerves to block the latter, gets out and starts shooting in vain at the bulletproof vehicle. The camera cuts from medium to wide shots during the shoot-out, with Acosta quickly being surrounded (Figure 6.6). He takes cover inside his car, which is riddled with bullets. Throughout this entire scene, the congressman and the general never step outside their vehicle. When the rain of bullets ceases, a curious gesture marks the end of this chase: a tight shot of Acosta's raised bloodied middle finger as proof of life and act of defiance, even though he has actually been cornered by the powers-that-be. This final car chase sequence grants Acosta the role of the film's unlikely noir hero, at least within roughly three minutes of screen time.

In contrast to Acosta's act of defiance, his counterpart, Mario, enacts a fatalist end for himself. Mario kills Daniel just as the latter was bidding his affectionate farewell as an act of self-preservation. Then Mario kills his wife's lover in front of his family. The structuring presence of home for Mario is no more, and he returns to the private vehicle to get on with the job of living,

Figure 6.6 The final collision of masculinities in On the Job.

even as he has no one else to live for but himself. Mario's fate is sealed inside the private vehicle, in a final shot where he defiantly looks straight at the camera through the clatter of rain on the car's windshield.

The windshield scene is the final cut in *On the Job*'s international DVD and streaming versions.[18] In the version screened earlier in Philippine cinemas, the film's final scene shows the late Coronel's young partner retrieving the mobile phone that contains a recording of Pacheco's involvement in the guns-for-hire syndicate. The international version's ending might be said to drive home the point of Mario's fatalistic closure; the Philippine version's ending puts emphasis on corruption within the system. These two endings, in my view, do not drastically alter the film's overall capacity to reveal imaginaries of spatial in/justice through the movements of its male subjects, whose collisions gradually reveal that corruption extends far beyond the hitmen's prison spaces. The final car chase sequence demonstrates the culpability of the state and its institutions for enabling a kill-or-be killed system that relies on its underclass in order to survive.

Conclusion

Kinatay, *Metro Manila* and *On the Job* are examples of male-driven narratives that can be approached as Manila film noir grounded on the slum chronotope. Such an approach enables the productive exploration of chronotopes of mobility, or scenes of transit that drive narrative and character configuration. Read through the dialogue of the slum chronotope and film noir, I have argued that it is possible to locate moments in which the male noir figures struggle for spatial justice even as they ultimately fail in the films' narrative closures. It has also been noted that unlike classic noir, the structuring presence of home runs through Manila noir, as the desire for a better future for the family drives the male characters' crimes.

This chapter explored how masculine anxieties are spatially conveyed, as contextualised in Metropolitan Manila's urban spaces where spatial mobility is strongly linked with the desire and potential for social mobility. This reading forecloses the construct that driving is imagined to be a masculine spatial practice, at the same time that this spatial practice is ethically charged, given the theme of crime that underpins the narratives. In these representative films, the struggle for spatial appropriation is signified by who is able to literally and symbolically sit behind the wheel.

The act of driving is never granted to the male lead in *Kinatay* who finds himself an unwilling passenger in the van that ultimately tests his will to survive for the sake of his family. In *Metro Manila*, a sense of moral agency is granted to the male lead who decides to take the wheel in enacting the heist that leads to his death, so that his family can escape the same tragic fate. Meanwhile, *On the Job* configures the slum chronotope as prison chronotope, which further grounds the narrative in Manila's sociopolitical conditions. The film, through literally covering more ground in Manila's urban space, offers a relatively more complex narrative depicted through the intersecting paths of its male figures. Through its chase sequences, the film offers ethically charged collisions of masculinities, leading to tragic ends for all but the male political figures of state corruption. The film's narrative closure undoubtedly indicts the state as responsible for the crime and corruption that permeates the city.

In this chapter, the study moves beyond the immediate slum spaces of Metropolitan Manila, with the slum chronotope remaining as its organising centre. I have argued that the chronotopes of mobility in Manila noir reveal the male figures' tragic struggle for spatial justice, prominently signified by the act of driving that indicates the in/ability to map or master the urban space. Despite the darkness of Manila noir, it is possible to examine the means by which the tragic male characters are configured as the films' moral social agents, while at the same time their masculine anxieties are revealed and challenged.

Notes

1. Brillante Mendoza was the first Filipino to win the Best Director award for a feature film at the 2009 Cannes Film Festival. American critic Roger Ebert (2009) infamously called *Kinatay* the 'worst film' in the history of the Cannes Film

Festival. In contrast, fellow nominee Quentin Tarantino praised exactly what Ebert denounced, citing the film's effects on its viewers as its strongest feature (Lodge 2009).
2. One US-based review expressed generic expectations from this Mendoza film upon its opening: 'The first 15 minutes or so showcase what Mendoza does best: capturing the chaos of life in the teeming slums and streets of Manila' (Weissberg 2009).
3. See Pühringer et al. (2006).
4. Patrick Flores (2012) reads *Kinatay* as a critique of urban modernity via the long take. Meanwhile, critic Patrick Campos (2016: 320) argues that *Kinatay* invokes paralysis in its viewers because of its brutal rendering of murder: 'In such films, there can be no heroes, neither triumphant nor tragic. Violence, not heroes, defines such films.'
5. In her reading of South Korean noir, Susie Jie Young Kim (2010) offers the notion of 'driving views', which refers to images one sees through a car window that are ultimately marked with ambivalence.
6. Reacting to negative reviews of *Kinatay*, Mendoza explains that outrage is part of his intended effect: 'I think I managed to manipulate the audience without their being aware of it. They get trapped in the film. That's why it angered many viewers. They say, "You trapped us. You didn't give us a choice"' (Zafra 2009).
7. In the Philippines, the term 'chop-chop', and the story itself of *Kinatay*, recalls sensationalised murders of 'chop-chop ladies' reported in tabloid news. There were a number of popular massacre films in the 90s based on these reports.
8. Local reception of *Metro Manila* was not that generous. See David (2015a).
9. The film premiered and was warmly received at the Sundance Film Festival. It was also critically acclaimed at the British Independent Film Awards, where it won Best British Independent Film, Best Director, Best Achievement in Production, and was nominated in the category of Best Film Not in the English Language.
10. To cite one reviewer who phrased it in spatial terms: '*Metro Manila* is so spellbound by its setting that it is a good hour before we discover what kind of film it is going to be. It begins as a swirling drama of survival in the Filipino capital – but then suddenly it slips off down an alleyway, only to emerge a scrupulously engineered, Christopher Nolan-ish crime thriller' (Collin 2013).
11. The line cited in the film goes: '*There's a Filipino proverb. No matter how long the procession it always ends at the church door. I prefer the version we learned in the military. If you're born to hang, you'll never drown.*'
12. Already a well-known filmmaker prior to the digital turn, Matti sets himself apart from Philippine indie auteurs in terms of visual style. Unlike the other films discussed so far, *On the Job* is a film backed by a major studio, Star Cinema Productions, in partnership with Matti's own independent production company. Its budget of PHP45 million certainly sets it apart from the modest budgets of earlier Philippine indie films (*Ang Pagdadalaga* was made with a budget of roughly 1 million). The film, which premiered in the Director's Fortnight at the 2013

Cannes Film Festival, generally received warm reviews in both the local and international scene. In the absence of precedence from Philippine cinema, some foreign reviews (Tobias 2013; Toro 2013) could not avoid comparing *On the Job* to regional counterparts, particularly to the Hong Kong noir, *Infernal Affairs* (Lau 2004). Matti recounts how foreign funders were hesitant to finance this film which funders thought was like a Hong Kong movie (Boo 2013).

13. A review published in a national broadsheet articulates local reception of *On the Job*: 'It's so good, it doesn't seem like it's a Filipino film' (Cu-Unjieng 2013). Leading Filipino critic Joel David (2015b) states that the film is indeed 'a qualitative leveling up' in Philippine cinema given its successful rendering of the urban space in order to represent the 'proliferation of dramatis personae representing various social strata and performing diverse conflicting functions'.
14. See reports by the Commission on Human Rights – Philippines (2015) and the US State Department (2013).
15. Matti (2013) notes that their research for *On the Job* revealed that Philippine jails are like 'little cities'.
16. In the Philippines, displays of authority through commemorative plates and stickers on vehicles are not unusual. The intention is to gain special treatment from traffic enforcers. This shameless display of authority through vehicle accessories such as police sirens and government plates is such a well-known practice that then President Benigno Aguino III (2010–16) used the siren (*wang-wang*), often used in convoys for officials, as a metaphor for corruption in his first State of the Nation Address.
17. Martin-Jones (2011: 156), citing Michael J. Shapiro's (2008) *Cinematic Geopolitics*, explains that a shift from a 'focus on the aesthetic rather than the psychological' can yield productive geopolitical film readings.
18. There are a number of deleted scenes in the international DVD version of the film compared to the Philippine release, which include sex scenes and some scenes related to Acosta's family life.

CHAPTER 7

Migrants in Transit*: The Slum Chronotope and Chronotopes of In/Visibility in the Overseas Filipino Worker Genre*

> The OFW may be the most intriguing spectacle of this new millennium. (San Juan Jr 2009: 122)

> The OFW film, at best, is an ironic genre; at worst, a genre – perceived from another time and place – that never should have existed, but does. (Campos 2016: 531)

In this chapter, I push for expanding the scope of the slum chronotope in order to place it in dialogue with the 'chronotopes of in/visibility' enabled by a genre that is arguably distinct in Philippine cinema. Here I explore how the slum chronotope in Philippine urban cinema expands its coordinates to create a dialogue with the configurations of spatial in/justice in the Overseas Filipino Worker (OFW) genre through a reading of Hannah Espia's *Transit* (2013).[1] If in the previous chapters, the men, women and children of Philippine urban film narratives navigate the urban spaces of Metropolitan Manila, the migrant characters in the ensemble narrative of *Transit* navigate the spaces of the foreign city of Tel Aviv.

I propose that the slum chronotope can productively be placed into dialogue with the OFW genre's preoccupations with depicting the migrant figure's struggle over space in foreign urban landscapes. While *Transit* does not take place in the spaces of Manila, it is possible to approach *Transit* as a product of Philippine urban cinema in its capacity to take into account the spatio-temporal configurations of Filipino migrant subjectivities and spatial practices in the foreign urban spaces of Tel Aviv. *Transit* tracks the fragmented narratives of the members of a Filipino migrant family in Israel who navigate the foreign spaces through strategies of visibility and invisibility to escape the perils of deportation.

The slum chronotope's productive dialogue with the OFW genre underscores the global scope of the urbanisation of poverty – aligning the OFW class with the global underclass who stake their claims for spatial justice in global spaces of development where migrant labour is considered both a necessity and a threat. The production of *Transit* on the heels of the films I have so far approached as Philippine urban cinema might be considered the logical expansion of the coordinates of the slum chronotope, as the figure of the OFW in the global context is comparable to the urban refugee in the local context – both figures of the neoliberal world who are compelled to create spaces of dwelling in spaces of injustice for the sake of survival. Like all the characters in the urban films discussed so far in this study, the migrant figures in this chapter are moral social agents who grapple with issues of social justice through the production of space.

THE SLUM CHRONOTOPE AND THE OFW DIASPORA

In proposing the productive dialogue between the slum chronotope and what I call chronotopes of in/visibility, I draw attention to the global scope of the phenomenon of slumification and the OFW diaspora. This is not to say that the slum inhabitant and the OFW figure share homogenous struggles and experiences. However, it is not difficult to cite elements of solidarity between the two figures, as both are subjects and subjected to spaces of in/justice brought about by urbanisation in the age of neoliberal global capitalism. As eminent Filipino-American academic Epifanio San Juan Jr (2009: 121) puts it in his essay on the OFW diaspora: 'Homelessness and uprooting characterize the fate of millions today – political refugees, displaced persons, émigrés and exiles, stateless nationalities, homeless and vagrant humans everywhere. Solidarity acquires a new temper.' If slumification across the globe saw the emergence of the new urban poor, so too can the OFW figure located in urban centres everywhere find solidarity with figures of the global underclass.[2]

Apart from solidarities in terms of class formation, the dialogue between the slum chronotope and chronotopes of in/visibility in the OFW narrative can be established along spaces of occupation. Like the subjects grounded on the slum chronotope, the migrant figure finds himself or herself performing place-making strategies in spaces of informality. In other words, both figures might be said to inhabit spaces of injustice. According to a report on environmental changes and migration: 'Migrants often settle in slums where they establish a social network necessary to find employment, earn wages, and send remittances home to support family members' (Warner 2010: 2). In many cases, the choice of spatial location, for both the slum inhabitant and the OFW, are global urban centres that promise economic and social returns despite the physical and emotional risks taken to get there and stay there.

In the Philippine urban context, Neferti Tadiar (2004) argues that rural migrants in Manila, or the 'urban excess', can be considered urban refugees. Their movement to the cities are prompted not just by economic need but the need to flee the dangers of military counter-insurgency operations against revolutionary groups in the countryside (Tadiar 2004). The same economic and social motivations can be attributed to the migration of Filipino workers to urban centres in economically advanced countries. In a study on the citizenship status of Filipino domestic workers abroad, Rhacel Salazar Parreñas (2001) introduces her essay by citing popular cities of OFW destination: 'Located in more than 130 countries, migrant Filipina domestic workers have settled in the cities of Athens, Bahrain, Rome, Madrid, Paris, Toronto, New York, Los Angeles, Hong Kong, and Singapore.'[3]

Like the rise of slumification, the emergence of the OFW diaspora was driven by the demands of neoliberal global capitalism. Although the Philippine government denies the existence of an official labour export policy, it is undeniable that existing policies and institutions absolutely encourage labour migration. In fact, Robyn Rodriguez (2010) characterises the Philippines as a 'labor brokerage state' because of its central role in facilitating the global mobility of its migrant workers. Next to Mexico, the Philippines is the world's largest source of labour globally (San Juan Jr 2009), with an export labour policy that is often referred to as 'a successful overseas employment program' (Abella 1993: 250). It is estimated that there are 10 million OFWs across the globe, roughly 10 per cent of the national population (Philippine Statistics Authority 2013). Migrante International (2015), a progressive organisation that advances Filipino migrant rights, estimates that there are 12–15 million OFWs, if undocumented workers are included.[4]

Maruja M. B. Asis (2008: 80–1) has identified four distinguishing characteristics of Filipino labour migration. First, the migrants are 'more widely distributed' globally; second, they have a 'wider range' of skills, but have 'secured a niche in nursing, seafaring, and domestic work'; third, Filipino workers are said to be relatively more educated than other Asian counterparts. The fourth distinguishing characteristic of OFWs is the centrality of female migrants, considering the 'feminine' nature of the jobs available to them.[5]

Although the Philippines has had a long history of labour migration which can be traced back to the Spanish and American colonial period (Aguilar Jr 2003), most researchers agree that the present OFW phenomenon traces its roots to the dictatorial regime of Ferdinand Marcos. Having declared Martial Law two years prior, Marcos issued the 1974 Labour Code, which essentially aimed to 'promote overseas contract work and reap the economic benefits to be gained from the outflow, especially in terms of foreign exchange and employment' (Gonzalez 1998: 163). This was Marcos's response to growing international debt and unemployment in the country. Through this issuance, agencies providing the mechanisms for overseas contractual work were established. The labour export policy was initially designed as a temporary measure for national unemployment; however, it has now turned out to be the 'cornerstone' of the Philippine economy (Rodriguez 2010: xvii). Following the Marcos ouster in 1986, the succeeding administration of Corazon Aquino continued encouraging labour migration, but attempted to differentiate itself from the previous regime by legislating more protection for OFWs (Rodriguez 2010). Most significant, however, was how the administration aggressively linked the OFW phenomenon to nationalist discourse (Rodriguez 2010). In an infamous speech delivered in Hong Kong, Aquino dubbed Filipino migrant workers *bagong bayani* or the 'new heroes'. As Rodriguez (2010: 84) explains: 'Aquino portrayed international migration as a voluntary act of self-sacrificing individuals living in a democratic society rather than a kind of forced conscription under a dictatorial regime ... a sacrifice that requires some degree of suffering but ultimately advances the greater national good.'

From the above historical overview, what I wish to emphasise is how the unprecedented development of the OFW phenomenon is inarguably indicative of the significance of the Philippines in global capitalism, inextricably linking Philippine development with neoliberal global development. As Rodriguez (2010) has argued in characterising as well as criticising the Philippine state's neoliberal strategy of labour brokerage, the discourse of migrant labour as nationalist sacrifice is an example of the kind of 'flexible' workers that global capitalism demands. And as one of the world's largest sources of migrant labour export, it is clear that the Philippines is, as Tadiar (2004: 5) has argued, 'a constitutive part of the world-system'.

To return to the dialogue I am establishing between the slum chronotope and the OFW genre, I once again reference San Juan Jr (2009), who establishes a strong link between the urban spaces of Manila and the global urban centres OFWs struggle to occupy. San Juan Jr (2009: 122) suggests that Manila has become the 'conduit' through which OFWs wait to be deployed into the neoliberal global economy. The OFW's position as a kind of mobile subject of the global underclass is represented in the OFW film genre, moving to and from local and global urban spaces.

CHRONOTOPES OF IN/VISIBILITY IN THE OFW GENRE

I propose to locate chronotopic configurations of in/visibility in the OFW genre, instances within the narrative structure that surface the contradictory positions that OFWs occupy in the global landscape. Chronotopes of in/visibility are key scenes where the OFW figures enact or articulate imaginaries of spatial in/justice in a space where their very survival depends on how they are able to slip from visibility to invisibility. I locate these moments in *Transit*'s emotionally charged scenes, where the characters are compelled to come to grips with their subjective struggles in the foreign spaces of injustice.

My conceptualisation of chronotopes of in/visibility is influenced by the view of the OFW figure as 'partial citizen' whose political, civil and social position in the host country is incomplete, even as his/her labour proves indispensable (Parreñas 2001: 1130). I also draw from the use of invisibility as a common idiom used to characterise the marginalised conditions of migrants in host countries. Despite and because of this position as partial citizens whose rights are always in question, migrants find the means to negotiate and lay claim to the right to belong in the host country. In other words, they find a way to become visible while remaining invisible.

With the mode of melodrama present in the OFW genre, chronotopes of in/visibility are also invested with affective capacities, which are often linked to the nationalist discourse of suffering. As Rolando Tolentino (2009a) and Patrick Campos (2016) have argued, Rory Quintos's *Anak* (2000) is the best example of how melodrama works effectively to romanticise and legitimise the state's nationalist discourse that helps sustain the country's labour export policy. In my discussion of *Transit*, I examine how the melodramatic mode is reconfigured in a way that disassociates sacrifice/suffering from the nationalist drive of previous OFW films. I further want to suggest that the narrative's melodramatic excesses are displaced onto the film's recurring use of wide establishing shots of Tel Aviv which are contrasted with the way migrant spaces are portrayed.

The spatio-temporal configrations of the OFW genre that enable chronotopes of in/visibility depend on where the film is set, and what strand of OFW narrative it belongs to (biographical/fictional/diasporic). Like the melodramatic mode's 'return to innocence' (raised in Chapter 5), I propose that the OFW genre is governed by the 'structuring presence of return', be it to the homeland or to the host country, or back and forth. *Anak*, for example, narrates the return of the OFW figure to the homeland, but the female lead's narrative is often interrupted by flashbacks of her suffering as a domestic helper in Hong Kong. The narrative then moves back and forth in terms of time and space, ultimately ending in the OFW's decision to return to the host country when her savings run out. The character's movements shift from visibility in the homeland to invisibility in flashbacks: visibility when she reconnects with her family, and invisibility when she returns to Hong Kong. Contrary to the film's exposition, the OFW figure returns not to the homeland but to the host country, with the film's ending suggesting complicity with the state's policy of labour brokerage.

The flipside of OFW films like *Anak* are films set in the host country where time and space are also fleeting and threatened by the time of return to the homeland. *Transit* is an example of this kind of OFW film, mostly set in Tel Aviv. The migrant figures are often confronted by the threat of abuse, deportation and even death. Because time and space can run out any moment, the affects of suffering and sacrifice provided by the melodramatic mode can be coupled with the affect of fear. The irony is that the migrant figure strives to remain in the precarious foreign space, for fear of returning home without economic gain. The time of return that is feared, in this sense, is the time of *premature* return.

TRANSIT

Transit's tale of OFW struggle in Israel is told through the intersecting vignettes of its five characters, set roughly during the period that Israel issued a new law which sought to deport migrant workers' children below the age of five (roughly 2009–10). There's middle-aged Irma, the domestic helper whose work visa has run out, and her teenage daughter, Yael, who is half-Israeli and does not understand Tagalog. The other pair in the cast of characters is father and son, Moises and Joshua. Moises is Irma's younger brother who works as a caregiver, while the four-year-old Joshua is his Hebrew-speaking son from his estranged Filipina partner. Finally, there's Tina, a newly arrived domestic worker who Irma helps settle into Tel Aviv.

By using a non-modular narrative format, the film already attempts to distance itself from the typical OFW film narrative, inviting a complex reading of the different ways by which the five characters negotiate their precarious emplacement as members of the OFW diaspora. Each vignette adds more depth to the characters' individual conflicts as they contend with the implications of the new deportation law. The film is bookended with scenes at the airport, with the vignettes gradually coming together to reveal how Joshua is discovered by immigration police. The vignettes are told from the perspective of the oldest character to the youngest, with the story of the newcomer Tina's episode serving as the film's halfway mark.

Apart from the non-modular narrative structure, *Transit*'s choice of filming in Israel is new in the OFW genre.[6] A brief account of OFWs in Israel helps locate this chapter's analysis of *Transit*.

There are roughly 29,000 OFWs in Israel.[7] Despite the relatively low population compared to top OFW destinations (2.4 million in the top OFW destination of Saudi Arabia), Filipino caregivers have become a recognisable migrant group since Israel started to import more workers in the 90s, next to Romanians who work in construction and Thais in agriculture (Bartram 1998). The Hebrew word for 'caregiving' (*metapelet*) has come to stand for Filipina in Israel (Margalit 2017), just as Filipina is defined in the Greek dictionary as 'domestic servant' (Aguilar Jr 2003; Tolentino 2009a).[8]

It was in 1993 when *ovdim zarim* or non-Jewish 'foreign workers' started arriving in Israel following a recruitment campaign in response to the shortage of workers (Bartram 1998; Jackson 2011; Liebelt 2011). The need for non-Jewish foreign workers in Israel emerged shortly after the removal of Palestinian workers from the Israeli labour market, following the 1987 Palestinian Intifada (Bartram 1998; Jackson 2011; Liebelt 2011). Some of the policies that the Israeli government have formulated for foreign migrants were derived from restrictions made on Palestinian workers, such as carrying work permits that bear the name of the worker's Israeli employer. Liebelt (2011) explains that the Israeli Ministry of Health specifically targeted the recruitment of Filipino workers in 1995, with the desire to shift nursing care work from public care institutions to private homes in order to cut costs. This recruitment drive was actually named the 'Filipino Plan' which 'points to the policy-makers' ethnic preference for carers (2011: 28). The Filipino carers community in Israel gradually grew. What the Israel government did not anticipate was that despite the temporary nature of the international labour recruitment policy, many foreign workers would overstay their visa and would seek to reside permanently in the country, albeit illegally.

The visible core of international labour migration in Israel is undoubtedly Tel Aviv, with a quarter of the city's overall population now made up of roughly 60–80,000 migrant workers (Willen 2003). The neighbourhoods in the southern areas of Tel Aviv, particularly Neveh Sha'anan where the Central Bus Station is located, are now known as the parts of the city where Filipino migrant workers gather when they are able to take time off from their employers (Liebelt 2011; Willen 2003).

The migrant spaces of Tel Aviv are indicative of the larger social divide within the city, particularly between the affluent spaces in the 'White City' (areas north of the city) and the impoverished spaces of the 'Black City' (south of the city) (Rotbard 2015). The White City covers neighbourhoods north of Tel Aviv where 4,000 buildings are modelled after the modernist Bauhaus architectural style (Rotbard 2015). The 'Black City', which covers the southern parts of Tel Aviv and the once Palestinian-inhabited area of Jaffa, now stands in direct contrast to the White City. It is 'an out-migration of middle-class residents, a public image of crime and insecurity, infra-structural neglect and a generally low standard of living' (Liebelt 2011: 131). Within the Black City spaces of Tel Aviv, OFWs produce their own Philippine spaces: in their shared rented rooms in abandoned old tenements, in the Central Bus Station (CBS) that Filipinos called *takana* (the shortened and 'tagalised' version of the Hebrew word for the station), and more significantly, a passage in the shabby CBS building called 'Manila Avenue' (Liebelt 2011: 129). CBS is 'the most important space for sociality of Filipinos in Israel' (Liebelt 2011: 149), a space referenced in *Transit*.⁹

The spaces of migrant workers in the Black City became targets of the state's deportation campaign (Jackson 2011; Willen 2003). The state ramped up its anti-immigration policies in 2002 under then Prime Minister Ariel Sharon through the creation of the Immigration Police and other agencies dedicated to deportations (Willen 2003). The deportation campaign enforced police surveillance, racial profiling, and set up an information hotline where illegal migrants can be reported (Willen 2007). In 2009, Israel's deportation measures targeted the estimated 1,200 children below the age of five of undocumented foreign migrants, and this serves as the backdrop for *Transit*'s narrative (Guarnieri 2010).

Israel's hostile attitude towards foreign workers has created a 'topography of fear' and a sense of fatalism that one can be deported at any time (Liebelt 2011: 144). More significantly, according to Sarah Willen's (2003: 23) ethnographic research among illegal migrants in Israel: 'Changing configurations of illegality in Israel have reshaped not only migrants' experiences of embodiment and time, but also their experiences of space.' Migrants have had to learn to behave in certain ways in order to avoid suspicion, with illegality manifested in the ways migrants 'use, move around in, and present – or hide – their bodies' (Willen 2007: 19). It is within the precarious conditions outlined above that the migrant narrative of *Transit* takes place.

CHRONOTOPES OF IN/VISIBILITY AND SPATIAL IN/JUSTICE IN *TRANSIT*

While composed of vignettes, the narrative structure of *Transit* might be viewed as progressing from the past to the future of a migrant family, as it begins from the perspective of the oldest character and ends with youngest. In terms of screen time, Joshua's final story occupies the longest, making him the privileged character in this narrative told through the mode of melodrama. His potential deportation is the overall narrative's core conflict, the point where all the other narratives converge. It is Joshua, after all, who is in the most danger of deportation by virtue of his age.

What is immediately noticeable in the first viewing of *Transit* is the regular use of wide establishing shots of the city's skyline as transition markers, which contrasts with the more prevalent use of tight framing throughout the film, especially in scenes shot inside the migrant family's apartment. The wide shots of the sky, rooftops, roads and coastline, all serve to signify the available spaces in the city. These are not necessarily spaces of affluence, but spaces that convey a range of positive values like beauty, peace, joy and justice – that this migrant family do not regularly have access to because of their difficult emplacement between visibility and invisibility.

In the following discussion I analyse chronotopes of in/visibilty as configured by the characters that can usefully be contrasted in terms of how they navigate through the difficulties of partial citizenship. I contrast the character configurations of Irma and Moises, the parental figures of the narrative, followed by a discussion of the young female characters, Tina and Yael. I then examine Joshua's character who serves as the film's most radical figure of spatial appropriation, even though this attempt ultimately fails. Finally, in the last section, I will examine the montage of spaces that the film uses in its concluding scenes, up to the rolling of credits where the father and son are waiting for their luggage at Manila airport.

Irma and Moises' Chronotopes of In/Visibility

Irma and Moises can be juxtaposed in terms of how they choose to navigate the foreign spaces of Tel Aviv given the similarities and differences of their subject positions. They both made the conscious decision to remain in Tel Aviv, with some degree of assimilation signified by their ability to speak Hebrew. Both have chosen to continue raising their children in Israel despite the new law aimed at deporting children below the age of five. While both are employed in care work, the most striking difference between the two is that Irma's visa has run out, while Moises is a documented caregiver. In the following discussion, what I want to show is how both characters stand for migrant parents who stake their claims in the foreign space in order to pursue a better life for their children.

Irma, the mother figure, seeks a stronger bond with her daughter who identifies as Israeli. Despite the restrictions she faces as an undocumented worker, she expresses an urge to connect with other migrants, especially in her efforts to help the newly arrived Filipina migrant, Tina. On the other hand, Moises, who can be considered a feminised figure given his job as caregiver, is portrayed to be the more reserved character, whose main concern is to keep his child safe by hiding him from the authorities. Despite their conflicting means of striving towards spatial justice in the foreign space, they do so out of the desire to keep their family together. Let me explain my assertions further through locating each character's chronotopes of in/visibility that reveal the different means by which these migrant characters stake their claims over the foreign space.

IRMA AS MIGRANT MOTHER

Transit opens with a wide shot of Joshua's small figure inside an airport, his back turned, looking out towards the planes on the tarmac (the same scene the film returns to at the end). It then cuts to a close-up of Irma, whose character sets off the film's non-modular narrative. Irma's roughly ten-minute vignette begins and ends with her failing to reach her teenage daughter – who has gone out against Irma's explicit warning to stay indoors – by mobile phone. This scene points to Irma's main conflict: miscommunication between her and her daughter who does not speak nor understand Tagalog. This language barrier is just the surface of Irma and her daughter's cultural and social differences, articulated fully in Irma's emotional outburst when her daughter returns home.

Irma stands for the illegal migrant who has opted to overstay her visa and raise her daughter in a country not her own. Informed by this initial characterisation, there are two key scenes that function as Irma's chronotopes of in/visibilty. The first is a sequence leading to a brush with an immigration officer, and the second is a powerful confrontation scene with her daughter.

On the first chronotope of in/visibility: Irma moves cautiously on the streets of Tel Aviv as she makes her way to her employer's house. Unable to leave Joshua with a Filipino neighbour who on that day is already hiding a number of Filipino children in her apartment, Irma opts to take Joshua with her to work. In this walking sequence, Irma's sense of fear can be seen in her gestures. Wearing sunglasses, she looks around and carefully chooses which street to walk through. She urges Joshua to walk faster. When stopped by a policeman and asked for her visa, Irma pretends that she left it at home. Luckily, her employer comes out to vouch for her and Joshua. Inside, as Irma starts cleaning as though nothing happened, her well-meaning employer berates her, reminding Irma to think of the safety of Joshua and her daughter.

This scene brings to light the risks that Irma knowingly takes on a daily basis, as well as the sense of fear she carries with her as she makes her way through the visibly affluent spaces of the city. Irma's good relationship with her employer is what saves her in that moment of crisis, but at the same time it reveals the servitude on which their relationship is predicated. Irma's employer says to the officer: '*They are with me. I'm Devorah Katz. I'm sorry but they are with me.*' By stating her name, Irma's employer asserts the validity of her full citizenship, on which her migrant employee's partial citizenship is based.

And yet in the space of the dwelling that she shares with her family, Irma slips back into comfortable visibility. Despite the cramped and shabby interior of her apartment, here, Irma is fully in charge. She becomes just one of the many residents of Tel Aviv, as signified by a wide shot of the row of buildings where Irma's apartment belongs, her dwarfed image shown draping the day's laundry on the balcony. Irma also welcomes Tina, the newcomer, with open arms when she arrives at the apartment and is offered a small room to stay in. In the kitchen, Irma cooks *adobo*, a Filipino dish, commenting in jest that her daughter doesn't know how to cook the dish: '*Every Filipina knows how to cook adobo.*'

I locate the second chronotope of in/visibility in this vignette's melodramatic scene, where the dialogue's use of the idiom of in/visibility reveals the depth of Irma's precarious emplacement in the foreign space that she fears she cannot share with her daughter, Yael. Upon her daughter's return, Irma explodes with the following lines, symbolically delivered in Tagalog:

> **Irma** (in Tagalog): *Can't you see me? Here I am. Your mother! Don't you see me? Don't you know what I'm going through?*

The full force of this emotional outburst, however, is not conveyed fully to her daughter who can only sense Irma's anger, and fails to grasp the words.

> **Yael** (sobbing, speaks in Hebrew): *What are you saying? I don't understand you.*

> **Irma** (in Tagalog): *You don't understand? Why don't you understand? You are Filipino, you should know how to speak Filipino. You are Filipino! You are not Israeli!*

When Yael protests, Irma slaps her and reiterates: '*Your mother is Filipino. You can't change that.*' The scene then abruptly cuts to and ends with the opening scene where Irma fails to reach Yael on her mobile.

This chronotope of in/visibility wields the melodramatic mode in a way that reveals Irma's wager in staying in the foreign space where she is not only a partial citizen, but an invisible one given her undocumented status. Through dialogue, the film compresses time and space for this migrant mother, all the years of struggle and hiding in the foreign space where she raised her daughter whose Israeli father has long disappeared (Irma's explanation: '*Let's not talk about that. That's a long time ago*'). This affective scene surfaces Irma's fear as a migrant mother – that as she struggles to keep herself invisible as an illegal migrant, she is also becoming invisible to her daughter who is more at home in the foreign space that rejects Irma's presence.

MOISES AS MIGRANT FATHER

The relative mobility of Moises as a documented worker compared to Irma's illegal status is immediately conveyed through his entry in the narrative. Moises is on board a moving bus, making his way through idyllic coastal scenes from Herzliya (where his employer resides) back to Tel Aviv. Covering twice the screen time of Irma's vignette, Moises' episode is overlaid by his voice-over, which tells the legend of 'The Sun and the Moon' that he uses to explain the absence of Joshua's mother from their lives.

Even as a documented migrant worker, Moises expresses fear over deportation not so much for himself but for Joshua, who is the target of the new deportation law. In contrast to his older sister, Moises favours a more conservative approach against anti-immigration policies. He dissuades his sister from signing a petition against the deportation law, raising suspicion and resignation. When Irma asks if Tina, who by this time is in danger of being deported, can hide with them, Moises vehemently rejects the request saying it will just cause them more trouble: '*What's with you? Do you want Yael to get in trouble? You want to risk everything because Tina wants to break the law?*' In short, Moises thinks that if they try to keep within the law as best they can by hiding from it, there is a chance they might actually escape it.

The very inclusion of Moises in this migrant narrative as a caregiver is a valuable expansion of the discourse of labour migration that has so far focused on female workers. While not entirely subscribing to post-feminist claims that question the discourse of the feminisation of labour, there is definite value in casting a wider net in migrant studies to include the particular struggles that male migrants contend with. Interestingly, Moises in *Transit* is engaged in care work, broadly considered feminine work, unlike seafaring or construction, which are popular professions for male migrant workers in the Middle East. The character of Moises, and the subjective conflicts he contends with in *Transit*, shore up the possible reconfigurations – although not necessarily progressive values — of traditional gender roles brought about by the phenomenon of global migration. The instances when Moises stands his ground against his older sister's wishes might be considered masculine assertions in a space where he feels emasculated.

This gendered dimension of emasculation that underpins Moises' struggle over space is reinforced in the scenes I locate as chronotopes of in/visibility in his vignette. There are two affective scenes that I explore further: first, the scene where he seeks out his estranged wife, and second, the scene of his emotional outburst at the detention centre where he resists Joshua's deportation.

The emotional scenes that function as chronotopes of in/visibility are preceded by tender moments between father and son, such as a scene of Joshua playing by the port while his father watches, and the two playing in the garden of Moises' employer. Moises' relationship with his employer, Eliav, is also portrayed as an affectionate one, with Eliav expressing genuine concern for Joshua, although it is one that is still uncomfortably underpinned by money. The conversation that ensues when Moises is pushing Eliav on his wheelchair through an idyllic neighbourhood reveals this employer-employee relationship framed through the economy of care. Eliav finds out that it is Joshua's birthday and insists on giving the boy some money. Eliav challenges Moises' refusal: '*Don't argue with me. I have a lot of money you know.*'

The first chronotope of in/visibility is framed through Moises' voice-over, recounting the legend of 'The Sun and Moon' to Joshua as a bedtime story. The story explains that the Moon had to hide his child from the Sun to keep it from burning. In the encounter that ensues, Moises suggests that the Sun in the legend is Joshua's mother, who left to marry an Israeli man.

The encounter between Moises and Susan (the estranged wife) in a dream-like scene by the coastline is possibly the film's most visually striking moment. The scene is framed in a wide shot that includes sea and sky, foregrounded by the coast, as Moises' small figure approaches a woman standing on the beach. There is nobody else there. The scene then cuts to a medium close up of the two figures in a sparse, yet emotionally charged, conversation. Moises implores Susan and her Israeli husband to adopt Joshua until he turns five and is eligible for residency. Susan refuses, followed by an exchange where Susan chastises Moises for putting their child at risk. The conversation reinforces the dialogue between the imaginary of the migrant worker with the urban imaginary of Manila, just as it emphasises that the choice to move and remain overseas is a valid one:

> **Susan:** *Why don't you just go home to Manila? Get a job there!*
> **Moises:** *We have a good life here. And what job will I get there? It's better to hide here than to starve there.*

This dream-like scene is abruptly interrupted by the scene of the second chronotope of in/visibility, where Moises is interrogated by an officer about Joshua. Moises tries to reason with the officer by saying that his son is almost five and speaks Hebrew. Moises starts sobbing. The officer abruptly asks about his wife, and when Moises responds that he does not have one, the officer suspects that he might be hiding her identity as an illegal migrant. This provokes an outburst from Moises who shouts, through tears: '*She's not my wife! She's married to an Israeli. She left us, okay? She's not my wife!*' To this, the officer responds definitively that Joshua has to be deported, and the vignette closes with Moises shouting his protests.

Similar to Irma's vignette, the melodramatic mode is utilised in the above chronotopes of in/visibility to shore up Moises' masculine anxieties as a significant dimension of his subjective formation. His masculinity is reconfigured in the foreign space both by the nature of his profession and by the absence of his wife, recasting the male migrant figure in a different light that serves to expand the discourse of the feminisation of migrant labour.

The scene with the wife, while brief, also points to the reconfiguration of parenting itself in the migrant space.[10] Is Susan a bad mother in suggesting that Moises stop hiding Joshua from the law, or is Moises a bad father for wanting to hide Joshua? The confrontation scene does not offer a definitive answer. Although the film is clearly more sympathetic to Moises, the film does not condemn Susan for wanting to have a better life. In fact, the sun and the moon legend absolves Susan to a degree. The fictional story, just like the dream-like scene, displaces Susan's story to another time and place, far from the struggles of father and son in Israel.

Ultimately, it is the desire to protect Joshua through the strategy of hiding that matters most when Moises is faced with the real threat of Joshua's deportation. His earlier conservative stance of trying to keep out of sight from the law through the strategy of hiding erupts into outrage when he is told that Joshua has to go, his words finally articulating the injustice of the situation: '*No, you cannot do this, you cannot do this*', he protests, as the screen cuts to black.

TINA'S AND YAEL'S CHRONOTOPES OF IN/VISIBILITY

The young female characters in *Transit* can be contrasted in terms of their subjective struggles towards a notion of belonging in Israel. Tina stands for the female foreign migrant who has to learn how to orient herself in the foreign space she has just set foot in, while Yael struggles to assert her Israeli identity against her own self-doubts, as well as against her mother who takes her subjective formation as Israeli citizen as an affront to her Filipino heritage. While these two young female characters take different paths towards their notions of belonging, they are remarkably similar in terms of the aspirational desire to lay claim to a sense of full citizenship in the foreign space. Unlike the film's parental figures, Tina and Yael are more defiant in articulating their desire to become visible; their vignettes lay bare the forms of social injustice they face in their own subjective formations in the foreign space.

TINA AS NEW MIGRANT FIGURE

While her vignette runs just over ten minutes and is identified in some reviews as a weakness in the narrative, Tina's figure is significant in unravelling the gradual configuration of the new migrant into the foreign time-space. Through Tina, the film shows how the new migrant is compelled to inscribe strategies of in/visibility, contrary to one's good intentions. In a gathering among other Filipino migrants, Tina raises the scarce presence of Filipino children playing outdoors. The migrants explain that this is simply the way of life here, if you want to keep the children from being deported. In this scene,

Tina is cautioned by the older migrants to be careful, as there are cases of migrants themselves snitching on other migrants.

Tina's vignette begins and ends with a medium close up of her walking mindlessly through the city with a dazed expression. As the vignette develops, we find out that Tina is pregnant, which, according to Israeli law, means she will have to be deported. Grounded on this subjective conflict, two instances in Tina's short vignette can be located as chronotopes of in/visibility. The first takes place in an emotional scene with Irma in the small room she inhabits, which transforms from a welcoming space to a foreboding one. The second instance occurs when she articulates her desire to stay in Israel by hiding, which Moises staunchly refuses.

The tiny room Tina is offered in Irma's apartment is significant in configuring her desire to belong in the foreign city. From the beginning of her vignette, her aspiration to belong is rendered visually and spatially. She sets foot in the dark hallway leading up to Irma's apartment, and the scene brightens as they ascend the staircase, with Tina's entry taking on a bright and hopeful mood. In a scene overlooking views of the city from the balcony of the apartment, Tina receives specific directions from Irma to her employer's house, suggesting that learning to map the foreign city space is key to assimilation.

This hopeful mood is cut short with the scene of Tina walking in a daze as she makes her way back to the apartment. She ascends the staircase in a mood completely opposite to the brightness of the scene when she first arrives. In this scene, which functions as her first chronotope of in/visibility, she is weeping on the bed of her tiny room while Irma listens in silence, the vignette giving Tina time and space to articulate the injustice of her situation which is ascribed a gendered facet: '*I wish I could just lie here. But that's not how it is. Because women can't just lie down.*' She continues with a line that signals her desire to stay, not just in the room, but in the foreign space: '*The guy who got me pregnant, why doesn't he have to go?*' She further articulates the fear of premature return when she says: '*I haven't earned enough yet.*' The scene cuts to the next morning, with Tina defiantly standing her ground in her tiny room when she flings open the window that overlooks the city.

The second scene that functions as chronotope of in/visibility once again features a defiant Tina who counters Moises' refusal of her desire to stay in Israel: '*What about my child? What about me?*' What this scene does is strip Moises of his moral ascendancy, as his desire to hide Joshua from authorities is not so different from Tina's desire to remain in Israel as an undocumented worker. The highway corner on which this scene is set contributes to the levelling off of Moises and Tina, who are both just trying to find available spaces in the vastness of the foreign city.

Tina's vignette reinforces the film's overall use of the melodramatic mode to surface subjective wagers for spatial justice. Her emotional outbursts grant her time and space to lay claims to spatial justice in her desire to remain in the foreign space, albeit through hiding. The chronotopes of in/visibility succeed in interrogating the ironic grounds of immigration laws, where 'These workers provide care for the citizenry of various receiving nations at the cost of the denial of their own reproduction . . . and membership in the nation-state that they are reproducing' (Parreñas 2001: 1130).

YAEL AS FEMALE MIGRANT FIGURE

Among all the characters in *Transit*, it is Yael who naively believes she can lay claim to full citizenship, not fully understanding the precarity of her situation as the daughter of an undocumented female migrant. It is useful to contrast her social and cultural embeddedness in Tel Aviv with Tina who is just beginning to emplace herself within the city. That Yael does not speak nor understand any Tagalog is indicative of her distance from her mother's culture, and she also does not express any strong desire to do so. In a scene where she is among other children of Filipino migrants who express thoughts of going to the Philippines given the new immigration laws, Yael retorts in Hebrew: '*That's silly. We passed the residency criteria. I don't think the Philippines is our home.*' And yet, in other instances, she reveals a degree of understanding of her precarious position. An example is the scene where her Israeli boyfriend, Omri, suggests that they do something to oppose the new deportation law. Yael replies: '*We're not Israeli like you . . . so all we can do is obey the rules or hide.*' As opposed to her Israeli boyfriend, Yael does not consider herself Israeli, but against her mother, she tends to assert her Israeli identity.

The film's fourth vignette opens and closes with a view of Yael from above as she looks up at the sky with a pensive facial expression, conveying her mood as she attempts to understand her situation in Tel Aviv. This rather peaceful scene on the rooftop of the tenement building contrasts with the emotional scene between mother and daughter, staged on that same rooftop the night before.

There are two scenes that function as chronotopes of in/visibility in Yael's vignette. The first is a scene inside the house, where Irma orders Yael to stay indoors. Having come home to see her daughter in a tender moment with her boyfriend, Omri, just outside their apartment, Irma berates her daughter for her public display of affection, but her words belie deeper reasons for her anger that is laced with fear. Irma perceives the Israeli boyfriend's presence as a threat to her daughter's security. The exchange between mother and daughter is the film's most dramatic scene:

Irma: *You know what's unfair? This new law is unfair. The government is. Life is unfair. What if they deport you?*
Yael: *They won't! I'm qualified to stay.*
Irma: *You're not sure of that! You are Filipino!*
Yael: *No! You are Filipino! I am Israeli.*

This last line from Yael leaves her mother stunned and silenced, at the same time that it reveals the chasm between mother and daughter triggered and exacerbated by the new deportation law. This emotional exchange reveals that Yael considers herself to be deserving of remaining in Israel, to become visible, and she believes that her mother is denying her right to citizenship.

Yael stages a defiant attempt to distance herself literally and symbolically from her mother in her foray outside the city of Tel Aviv, risking a trip to Jerusalem's Western Wall with Joshua, upon the invitation of Omri. Skyline views similar to those used in Tina's vignette as she was looking outside her window beckon Yael, as she looks out over the balcony from her bed on the day she is forbidden to go out. What follows is a romantic montage set at the Western Wall. Yael affectionately watches Omri and Josua from behind a fence overlooking the male section of the wall. These are images of Israeli-Jewish identity that Yael does not have access to. Yael gazes at the scenes with a strong sense of longing and even joy, and yet she cannot fully participate in the prayers. Ironically, it is Omri's voice, not Yael's, that accompanies the beautiful images in this montage.

This emotional scene moves to the rooftop that functions as the second chronotope of in/visibility in Yael's vignette, where mother and daughter attempt to bridge their distance. Both are weeping, with the camera showing reverse shots of facial close-ups. The idiom of spatial distance is used in their exchange, as Irma apologises for slapping her daughter. When Yael insists that she wants to be left alone, Irma replies with these dramatic lines: '*Leave you alone? I've been doing everything so they couldn't take you away from me. Because for me, nothing can separate us. You may choose to run away. But you will always, always be with me.*'

With this, mother and daughter embrace, with the backdrop of the city adding poignancy to the scene (Figure 7.1). This tearful exchange is, undoubtedly, wrought with melodrama, but is in keeping with the film's overall deployment of affect as a means of surfacing spatial in/justice according to each character's subjective concerns. In this particular scene, Yael's distance from her mother grows smaller. Irma's efforts to keep her daughter close become visible to Yael. More importantly, although Irma's lines invoke the affect of personal sacrifice for her daughter, they are completely devoid of the nationalist discourse of sacrifice typical of mother figures in the OFW genre.

This vignette's final scene suggests that there is room for Yael to grow

Figure 7.1 Bridging the distance between migrant mother and daughter in Transit.

up in this foreign space. Joshua exclaims that Yael has grown taller when he measures her height on a concrete wall which bears marks of both of them growing up over the years. The height markers on the wall further illustrate these migrant children's attempts to make themselves visible in the foreign space.

Both Tina and Yael, despite knowing the risks, articulate and enact their desires to carve spaces and times for themselves in Israel, a country that rejects their presence. Both young women are depicted to be in the process of discovering themselves and their emplacement in spaces of injustice. While their individual vignettes expose the legal difficulties surrounding their struggle for space, the narrative unfolding does not portray their desires as unfounded, as they struggle to make sense of the randomness of the law that determines who stays and who goes.

Joshua's Chronotopes of In/Visibility

Finally, we arrive at Joshua's vignette, which takes up the last half hour of the film's screen time. Comparable to the child seer (discussed in Chapter 4), Joshua's character functions to provide an enhanced vision of the overall narrative, as he bears witness to how the deportation law that puts him at risk affects his family members in different ways.

Learning how to become invisible in the foreign space runs strongly through Joshua's vignette as a normalised practice. He follows his father and aunt's instructions to stay indoors, and does not make a fuss over being transferred from Tel Aviv to Hezriyah. This does not mean, however, that Joshua is portrayed without a sense of agency. Joshua is shown to be aware of his older cousin's sadness at remaining indoors, even suggesting he can take care of himself if Yael wants to go outside. He moreover develops his own practices for becoming invisible. In the scene where Irma takes Joshua to her employer's house, she gives him a scarf to wear, telling him it will make him invisible. Joshua takes Irma seriously, and wears the scarf in instances when he wants to become invisible, not only when he is out on the streets. He puts it on inside the family's apartment, for instance, when he is caught in the middle of the emotional confrontation between his aunt and cousin. Joshua is, moreover, shown to be aware that it is his age that puts him at risk, given the new law. This is why he is keen to learn about how boys 'grow up', for example when he asks about whether he will have a Bar Mitzvah, or when he asks about the practice of male circumcision as a rite of passage in the Philippines.

Joshua's interactions with Israeli characters are disassociated from the state policy of deportation. His father's and aunt's employers are affectionate towards the boy. Joshua's encounters with them suggest his embeddedness in Israeli-Jewish culture. For instance, Irma's employer serves him a piece of Israeli halfa cake. Eliav teaches Joshua how to read from the Torah. It is also impossible to forget Joshua's scenes with Omri at the Western Wall, where Omri teaches Joshua how to pray.

In the vein of melodrama, *Transit* attempts to save Joshua in the nick of time for dramatic excess to come to fore. However, the narrative ends not with Joshua escaping the law, but with his discovery and deportation. This is the film's narrative closure, despite his innocence, kindness and performance of worth as a potential full citizen. And it is precisely this narrative closure that sets *Transit* apart as an OFW film, revealed in the succeeding chronotopes of in/visibility.

Two scenes function as chronotopes of in/visibility in Joshua's vignette, which both reveal the arbitrariness, cruelty and injustice of the deportation law through Joshua's affective acts of spatial appropriation. These scenes occur towards the end of the vignette, also serving as the film's culminating scenes as a whole. The first chronotope of in/visibility can be located in the scene that opens Joshua's vignette, where he is running down a street with his invisibility scarf on; the second is when he sings lines from the Torah in the deportation centre.

The first scene is arguably the film's most climactic moment, although its rendering is restrained. Joshua is left alone with Eliav, his father's employer, who falls off his wheelchair. In a panic, Joshua grabs his invisibility scarf and runs into the streets to find help, but when he turns a corner, a policeman spots him. Joshua freezes as the policeman approaches, his hands on his head wrapped in the scarf as he says in between sobs: *'I'm invisible! I'm invisible!'* When the policeman approaches, Joshua makes a conscious choice to become visible by removing his scarf. He grabs the policeman by the hand and leads him back to Eliav's house.

From this street scene, the film cuts to the second chronotope of in/visibility, where Joshua is seated opposite an officer at the detention centre. Moises arrives and pleads emphatically against Joshua's deportation. When Moises starts protesting loudly, Joshua interrupts his father's outburst and starts singing lines from the Torah to everyone's surprise. This is Joshua's assertion of visibility as an Israeli citizen; what can be deemed a literal and symbolic performance of worth for everyone in the detention centre to see. It is a powerful, even endearing scene – but it does not work to keep Joshua from being deported.

The last few minutes of the film are devoted to Joshua and his father preparing to leave Israel; the interim moments before Joshua's departure. '*Let's go out*', Moises says, a statement that articulates visibility, followed by Moises saying that Joshua doesn't need to put on his scarf any more. They go to the beach, where Joshua fills up a small bottle with sand, his father commenting: '*Put a bit of Tel Aviv inside. So you can bring Israel with you.*' This scene on the beach directly dialogues with the scene discussed earlier when Joshua's mother tells Moises to give up his bid to stay in Israel. While this scene does indeed convey a sense of resignation, with father and son preparing to leave Israel, it is not portrayed with a sense of tragedy, but of hope.

Transit's Imaginaries of Spatial Justice

The film's culminating scenes are powerful imaginaries of spatial justice, which is done through a layering of multiple times and spaces that serve to connect this story to the larger story of global migration. The film does this in two ways in its final sequences: through storytelling and spatial montage.

First, the assertion of the imaginary of a better future is rendered through the fictional story worlds that the migrant parents tell their children. Throughout the narrative, Irma and Moises have been telling the legend of 'The Thin Man' to Joshua, a character who sets off on different adventures. The film returns to the opening scene at the airport with Joshua looking out at the tarmac, where he is joined by his father. When the boy tells his father he is scared of losing his memories of Israel, Moises replies by invoking the story of the Thin Man: The Thin Man finds a beautiful piece of pearl in the belly of an octopus he slays with his sword. A parallel moment takes place between Irma and Yael who are standing in the kitchen of the Tel Aviv apartment. When Yael asks her mother about the ending of The Thin Man, Irma provides a different answer from Moises, saying that the story ends with the Thin Man setting off on another journey to look for a rainbow.

The above exchange shows a close-up of the hopeful facial expressions of mother and daughter, before it cuts to the film's spatial montage that

Figure 7.2 An image from Transit's montage of empty spaces set in Tel Aviv.

functions as another layer to the multiple time-spaces that the film offers as imaginaries of spatial justice. A montage of static images is captioned with words that explain Israel's deportation policy, which targets migrant children (Figure 7.2). These static images are all recognisable spaces used within the narrative: a view of the window in Tina's tiny room, the bedroom facing the balcony that the children play in, the rooftop wall where Yael and Joshua have marked their height over the years; a shot of the door of the tenement building; and finally, a wide shot of the Tel Aviv skyline that is captioned with this powerful line: '*Some of the children are still in hiding.*' The credits roll as father and son arrive at Manila airport to join other newly arrived passengers.

The emptying of the film's recognisable spaces, devoid of the fictional characters, allows the film to locate these migrant spaces in the actual situation of foreign workers in Israel, paying close attention to the anti-immigration law that has compelled migrant children to go into hiding. These migrant spaces offered in the captioned spatial montage are invested with affective potentials, evoking a sense of hope as well as quiet rage at the arbitrariness of the deportation law that makes children even more vulnerable.

The film's narrative closure locates itself and its characters within the larger global context of the OFW phenomenon through the final scene of the father and son's return to Manila airport. By ending at this airport, the film invokes the narrative exposition in the Tel Aviv airport. This dialogue between airports situates this particular OFW film in a global non-place belonging to the global underclass, or what Mark Auge (2009: 34) has described as 'the great commercial centres, or the extended transit camps where the planet's refugees are parked'.

The film's final sequence still conveys the affects of sacrifice and suffering ascribed to the melodramatic mode of the OFW film, but significantly, *Transit* is able to delink these affects from nationalist rhetoric. None of the characters articulate a romanticised desire to return to the homeland, even as they certainly strive to retain their sense of Filipino identity in the foreign space. Nothing in the film suggests nationalist rhetoric. Instead, the film links its affective moments to the spatial practice of survival through the thoughtful rendering of emotional moments in the film's chronotopes of in/visibility.

CONCLUSION

Transit can be approached as a new type of Philippine urban cinema, as it locates itself beyond the urban spaces of Manila into the foreign urban spaces of Tel Aviv. What I have sought to prove in this chapter is how the slum chronotope can productively be expanded into dialogue with the chronotopes of in/visibility offered in the OFW genre, which is unique to Philippine cinema. The migrant figure's struggle for spatial justice in the global urban space is productively juxtaposed with the slum figure's struggle for spatial justice in the local urban space.

Contextualised in the spatial configurations of social segregation in the urban space of Tel Aviv, this chapter's reading of the subjective formation of the characters in *Transit* reveals subjective strategies and negotiations of visibility and invisibility. I have argued that the chronotope of in/visibility can be located in the intersecting vignettes that comprise this OFW film, as the migrant figures contend with deportation as a fact of life in a space that views them as partial citizens. The non-modular narrative of the film shows the different ways this foreign space of injustice configures subjective formation and the struggle for spatial justice.

I have shown the contrasting ways the parental figures in the film, Irma and Moises, strive to protect their children, emanating from their different positions as undocumented versus legal worker. Irma's character reveals a mother's struggle to remain close to her child who has been brought up in the foreign space, without any knowledge of her mother's country of origin. Moises reveals a father's masculine anxieties triggered by his perceived emasculation, as a single father engaged in what is generally considered feminised labour in a foreign space.

The young female characters, Tina and Yael, can be contrasted in terms of their means of assimilating in the foreign space. Tina articulates a sense of defiance against the injustice of immigration laws particularly against female migrants. Yael struggles with the threat of rejection from the country she considers her home, just as she strives to close the distance between her and her Filipino mother. The youngest character of the film, Joshua, can be viewed as the most significant migrant figure in the film, who has had to learn spatial practices of invisibility in order to avoid deportation. Despite being born and raised in Tel Aviv, Joshua is the most vulnerable figure in *Transit*. His narrative exposes the injustice of the immigration given its arbitrariness. No matter how much Joshua tries to prove his worth as a full citizen, he is still not spared from deportation.

Finally, I have argued that *Transit* is a valuable example of a new OFW film that manages to depict the migrant struggle affectively through the reformulation of the melodramatic mode in terms of the politics of survival, rather than through the state's rhetoric of national sacrifice. *Transit* ultimately offers a powerful imaginary of spatial justice through its thoughtful selection and use of spaces and intersecting migrant narratives.

Notes

1. The first feature film of Hannah Espia, *Transit* received the Best Film award at the Cinemalaya Film Festival, competed in the Busan International Film Festival, and was the country's entry for the Academy Awards in the category of Best Foreign Language Film.
2. Barbara Schimmter Heisler (1991) suggests a perspective of the underclass in the American urban context, which I borrow here to approach this new global underclass where the slum dweller and the OFW might be linked.
3. The number of countries of destination for OFWs has since increased to 170.
4. In 2015, it was estimated that one out of ten Filipino households has a member working overseas (Mangahas 2015).
5. The OFW phenomenon is emblematic of the 'global feminization of labour' (Standing 1999). Tadiar (2004: 114) emphasises how Philippine migrant labour has indeed acquired 'a female profile, specifically the profile of the domestic helper'. The Filipina OFW is indicative of the workings of the international division of labour in the globalisation of care (Hochschild 2000; Yeates 2009). Parreñas (2000: 561) calls the emergence of female OFWs in care work as the 'international transfer of caretaking'.
6. Saudi Arabia remains the most popular country of destination for labourers and engineers because of the high demand and the high rates of pay, while the United States arguably remains the promised land in the imagination of many Filipinos given its enduring colonial influence (Abacan 2015; Gavilan 2015; Philippine Overseas Employment Administration 2015).
7. Data according to the Philippine Embassy in Israel (2019).
8. In Hong Kong, Filipina has come to mean maid, while in Canada, Taiwan and Italy, it has come to be synonymous with nanny (Tolentino 2009a).
9. Most of the interviewees in Liebelt's (2011) research expressed that Manila Avenue 'feels' like being in Manila. Manila Avenue is not regarded as a beautiful space even by the Filipinos who spend most of their weekends there. OFWs often compare CBS to poor provincial *barrios* (towns) in the Philippines. One

interviewee who previously worked in Japan expressed disappointment when she first arrived at the bus station: 'when I came from the airport and came here, I thought: it's not so beautiful. I thought Israel was a very developed country' (Liebelt 2011: 152).

10. Migration research has indeed pointed to the emergence of the 'transnational family' and the changing nature of childhood and parenting brought about by the OFW phenomenon (Arguillas and Williams 2010; Parreñas 2005).

CHAPTER 8

Sounds of Youth: The Production of Noise and Chronotopes of Performance in Respeto

> *noise is violence*: it disturbs. To make noise is to interrupt a transmission, to disconnect, to kill. It is a simulacrum of murder. (Attali 1985: 26)

In this final chapter I push for the value of studying Philippine urban cinema through the lens of spatial justice at a time when state assault on the urban poor has become even more ruthless and visible. As my final case study I analyse Alberto 'Treb' Monteras II's *Respeto* (2017), an explosive urban film that wields the slum chronotope in ways that enable the production of spatial justice foregrounding the state's war against the urban poor. A film which, according to Monteras, was initially grounded on the theme of the fascist Marcos military regime (Jaucian 2017), *Respeto* developed into a narrative that projects itself into the present by placing itself firmly in dialogue with Rodrigo Duterte's space and time of extrajudicial killings that has seen thousands dead in Manila's slums.

Respeto is centred on Hendrix, a seventeen-year-old aspiring rapper residing in the slums of Pandacan, who crosses paths with the elderly Doc, a Martial Law activist and poet. *Respeto*'s plot follows how Doc becomes an unlikely mentor to Hendrix and his friends, a classic coming-of-age story about intergenerational conflict. The young characters are caught breaking into Doc's bookshop to steal money, but instead of pressing charges, Doc lets the teenagers rebuild the shop as penance. As Doc and Hendrix grow close, the narrative also depicts the poet's strained relationship with his grown-up son, Fuentes, a dirty cop involved in drug dealing. Fuentes and Hendrix collide in the film's tragic closing scene that shows Hendrix violently beating his mentor's son to death as Doc and his friend, Betchai, watch in horror.

Respeto was the breakthrough film that took major awards in the 2017 Cinemalaya awards, including Best Feature-length Film, Best Cinematography and Best Sound Design.[1] Reviews lauded its use of rhymes and music, showcasing *balagtasan* and the vibrant culture of 'Fliptop' battles throughout its narrative.[2] More significantly, it brazenly referenced Rodrigo Duterte's bloody regime of *tokhang* or extrajudicial killings.[3]

Building upon this book's earlier chapters, this final chapter explores how the slum chronotope in *Respeto* firmly locates itself in the developing history of Philippine urban cinema alongside the state's heightened assault on the urban poor in Duterte's era of *tokhang* or extrajudicial killings. The chapter looks at how the slum chronotope in *Respeto* dialogues with the teen film genre and the melodramatic mode, where the struggle for spatial justice is imagined through the interplay of sound and space. Located in the slums and streets of Manila's Pandacan district, the film's liminal youth figures struggle for spatial justice through the production of noise, seen in instances which can be viewed as resounding chronotopes of performance.

This final chapter pushes for the value of studying Philippine urban cinema through the lens of spatial justice, especially in the context of the violent Duterte regime – the film world's space and time that constitute *Respeto*'s slum chronotope. As the title of the film explicitly suggests, what the lead characters share is their desire for respect – from others and from themselves. The film's narrative and character configuration constitute a strong case study for the potential of urban cinema to portray the city's underclass as active social agents struggling for dignity through the noise they create and the social relations they foster in the midst of urban violence.

The slum chronotope in *Respeto* dialogues with the teen film genre which configures liminal characters and chronotopes of performance enabled during the time of youth. The characters primarily move through limited spaces in the film's imagined Pandacan neighbourhood – the rap battle venue, a cemetery, Doc's bookshop – spaces that the youth characters appropriate through the production of noise, or instances which I call 'chronotopes of performance'. These chronotopes of performance enable the configuration of the larger narrative of *Respeto* that leads its spectators to the explosive final sequence, where sound is spatialised to suggest the tragedy of our times, through and beyond the slum imaginary of *Respeto*.

THE SLUM CHRONOTOPE AND THE TEEN FILM GENRE IN *RESPETO*

Respeto is certainly comparable to the coming-of-age films discussed earlier (Chapter 4), especially *Tribu*, which also used rap throughout its narrative. However, if the focal point of *Ang Pagdadalaga* and *Tribu* is the figure of the child, *Respeto*'s central character is the figure of the adolescent, bearing traces of the teen film genre. In the earlier chapter, I opted to read the dialogue between the slum chronotope and the figures of children in the spaces that configure the time of childhood. Here, the slum chronotope configures spaces of justice and injustice during the liminal time of youth.

While it is possible to argue that *Ang Pagdadalaga* and *Tribu* might also be approached as teen films, their central characters are configured with more childlike attributes (that *Respeto*'s youth figures do not possess) given the presence of adult characters in the narrative that the children look to for guidance and affection. This is especially evident in Maxi's relationship with his father and older brothers in *Ang Pagdadalaga*; adult figures who he certainly looks up to despite their conflict over Maxi's object of affection. Ebet in *Tribu*, meanwhile, despite spending time with and running errands for one of the Tondo gangs, was still very much a child who sought attention from his mother. In *Respeto*, Hendrix and his friends are youth figures who exercise a higher level of self-sufficiency – they fend for themselves against their peers and other figures of authority, even as Hendrix is dependent on income from his older sister and her drug-dealing partner.

In American cinema, the films comparable to *Respeto* are the 'hood' films of the 90s (see Chapter 4's discussion of *Tribu*). These films featured young African American men in urban ghettos, making visible the experience of the city space for these marginalised communities (Massood 2003). Similarly, *Respeto* can be considered a recent example of a global youth film that tackles themes beyond Hollywood imaginaries of youth, such as diasporic identity formation, religion and race (Berghahn 2010; Shary and Seibel 2007).

The occupation of the time of youth has a performative aspect, depending on ascribed roles (for instance within the family unit) or legal parameters (Chambers et al. 2005). As Ervin Goffman (1959: 24) has argued, using the language of theatre for the study of the self, one's 'personal front' is made up of various expressions: 'insignia of office or rank; clothing; sex, age, and racial characteristics, size and looks; posture, speech patterns; facial expressions, bodily gestures and the like'. This notion of performativity as it relates to youth identity is useful to the analysis of *Respeto* on a literal and symbolic level, as Hendrix performs his youth through the performative act of rap.

As discussed in the earlier chapter on coming-of-age, the genre often narrates a rite of passage that marks the young person's transition into another stage of life which is facilitated by the rite of passage. If the films in the chapter that focused on children passed through threshold chronotopes that suggest movement into an unknown future (be it escape for Maxi or entrapment for Ebet), *Respeto*'s rite of passage is much more contained within the liminal time-space of youth. Catherine Driscoll (2019) suggests that there are two types of rites of passage in teen films which are not mutually exclusive, and do not necessarily move on to fully fledged adulthood. One is the passage into maturity through an obvious ceremonial rite of passage (e.g. a graduation) while the other could be called 'an experience of limits' (Driscoll 2019: 66). *Respeto* combines these two types. Hendrix's attempts to win in a rap battle is the formal ceremonial rite of passage in the film, while the film goes on to explore his experience of limits when he is unable to defend Candy, the woman he loves, from being sexually assaulted.

Respeto can be placed in the intersections between Philippine urban cinema and the youth film genre, with its focus on liminal youth characters residing in Pandacan slums. What sets *Respeto* apart from other youth-oriented Philippine films in the last two decades is not just its obvious confrontation with the country's fascist periods of military rule and the current war on drugs, but also its novel use of the politics of sound in its configuration of space. Also running through the film is the modality of melodrama that it harnesses in its chronotopes of performance, and even more productively in the film's tragic closing scene.

Pandacan

A brief background to the film's choice of setting is useful to set the scene for analysis. The district of Pandacan features prominently in *Respeto*, in the same way that Tondo signifies a particular slum space in *Tribu* (Chapter 4). In interviews, Monteras reveals that Pandacan's built environment is ideal for the film: '*May ilog, riles* (There's a river, train tracks), squatters, and in some areas, you can see the high rise buildings of Makati' (Agbayani 2017). Producer Coreen 'Monster' Jimenez also adds that Pandacan is more accessible compared to the district of Navotas, which was where Monteras initially envisioned the film to be set (David 2017b).

Pandacan does not automatically signify slums in the same way that Tondo does. The first thing that likely comes to mind with the mention of Pandacan is its function as an industrial site where three big gas depots (Caltex, Petron and Shell) were based from the 1900s up until they were finally dismantled in 2015. The district also calls to mind the Pandacan or Beata station which is one of the stops of the Philippine National Railway lines. Its physical landmarks include the *Estero de Pandacan* which has been the object of river rehabilitation efforts over the years, as well as the Pandacan bridge, a known landmark in the area south of the river.

By choosing Pandacan as venue, *Respeto* can be read to surface the district's significance in Manila's urban history as one of the sites outside Intramuros which was populated after World War II. In a 1960 government special committee report on squatting and slum dwelling in Manila, Pandacan was identified as one of the areas south of the Pasig River with a high concentration of slum dwellers and squatter communities, a result of the damage wrought by World War II (Special Committee Report 1968: 95). Like its surrounding districts, Pandacan was also described in the report as an industrial district which attracted skilled and unskilled workers due to its location near the ports. Historically, Pandacan was once identified as a 'town' that was part of the Tondo province in the eighteenth century (Santiago Jr 2006: 76–7).

Another way that the film converses with the history of Pandacan is through the music and poetry performances that overtly lace the narrative. According to historian Fernando A. Santiago Jr (2006), in the nineteenth century, Pandacan was known as the 'Little Italy' of the Philippines, frequented by various artists, including poets, singers and musicians. Some also called Pandacan 'Little Milan' with the establishment of an opera house in 1887 (Santiago Jr 2006). The famous Filipino poet, Francisco 'Balagtas' Baltazar resided in Pandacan, where he produced the romantic epic *Florante at Laura*.[4] Pandacan's *Plaza Balagtas*, a site which featured in some scenes of *Respeto*, is a physical marker of the poetry's place in Pandacan history.

Santiago further argues that Pandacan was not just a space for poets and artists. Pandacan served as a 'cradle of agitators' when the Philippine Revolution against Spain was gaining ground in 1898 (Santiago Jr 2007: 83). Santiago cites the Filipino friar, Jacinto Zamora, as hailing from Pandacan (one the three friars falsely accused of rebellion and sentenced to death during Spanish rule), along with other Pandacan natives who actively took part in the revolution.

In the Duterte era, Pandacan has been referenced in news reports as one of the hotspots for extrajudicial killings. In 'They are Slaughtering Us Like Animals' (Berehulak 2016), one of the most heavily circulated photo-essays about the killings published by *The New York Times*, Pandacan is described as a 'shantytown' where a drug raid took place. The accompanying photo features children sitting around a lit candle in an *eskinita* paved with blood where a man was gunned down by the police.

Respeto does not refrain from configuring Pandacan as a space that invokes Duterte's era of the war on drugs, the main figure Hendrix himself making money off delivering drugs for his sister's drug-dealer boyfriend. In interviews, Monteras recounts that a buy-bust operation actually took place on their first day of filming in the area (Agbayani 2017; Selzer 2019). Within the film world, rappers incorporate lines about *tokhangan* or extrajudicial killings in their rhymes. There is also a scene that shows residents gaping at a dead body floating along an *estero* in Hendrix's immediate neighbourhood, with a resident casually asking Hendrix for drugs as he walks by the scene.

Respeto thus enables a dialogue between Pandacan's past and present, its narrative invoking the district's history of poetry, performance and rebellion alongside the country's history of state violence, from the Marcos dictatorial period up to the tyrannical Duterte regime.

THE POLITICS OF SOUND IN *RESPETO*

First, I want to bring attention to the film's overall use of sound as noise, not just through the rap and poetry performances throughout the narrative, but through its creative use of noise to signify spatial justice. Of course, what we consider as noise in the urban space depends on what is *not* noise. In common usage, noise is a pejorative term, attributed to sound that is not pleasing to hear. In the urban space, unacceptable sound is considered noise pollution, like the grime and dirt of the city. What we consider 'noise' depends on sound's contextual use. Noise, like space, is 'essentially a relational concept' (Novak 2015: 126).

Even more significant to our understanding of noise in *Respeto* is the notion of the ethics of noise. Pickering and Rice (2017: 8) assert: 'Noise, far more than just "sound out of place," is indicative of an entire moral system.' The kind of noise produced by the urban poor in slums is identified as part of what makes these spaces uninhabitable, just like dirt and the stench produced by its inhabitants. Tripta Chandola (2012), writing about slums in Delhi, talks about noise perceptions between middle-class and slum residents as dependent on their moral perceptions of each other. Middle-class residents spoke of the slum dweller's moral bankruptcy in relation to sounds they produce, including types of music and even boisterous ways of speaking; meanwhile, slum-dweller accounts of affluent areas judge the 'silence' of these spaces as lacking in life and vibrancy, leading to judgements about isolated lives and lack of social relations. Chandola (2012: 12) explains: 'noise is a matter of social and cultural specificity and subjectivity'. This moral underpinning of what constitutes 'noise' in Manila's urban space is something that Neferti Tadiar (2009: 145) has also written about, identifying noise as part of what makes up the urban excess of Manila: 'Such are the flotsam and jetsam produced by the crisis that is the Philippines, collecting in the dump that is Manila. And to the extent that they embody the social contradictions of global modern life, they are noise.'

Respeto engages with urban space, not just through its arrangement of space, but through its thoughtful use of sound as noise throughout its narrative. Noise in the film is embraced in all its potential to unsettle and disturb our sense of hearing. *Respeto* opens by filling the screen with noise of the Fliptop rap battle crowd, before introducing the image of where the cheers, jeers and applause were coming from. This opening immediately suggests the significance of the film's aural elements to the film's narrative development. While this opening scene successfully draws us into the film, the scene that more effectively frames the powerful use of noise in *Respeto*, which consequently configures how we can come to understand the film's chronotopes of performance, is the boisterous confrontation between the slum residents and the police which occurs barely ten minutes into the film. The scene itself is set up aurally, with sound from a radio news broadcast used to signal the attempted demolition of Hendrix's slum community. There is an element of wonder for unsuspecting spectators when Nando, Hendrix's sister's drug-dealing boyfriend, urgently shouts at Hendrix to take a shit: 'Go take a shit!' (*'Tumae ka na!'*). Nando joins his neighbours in the street armed with bags of excrement (*tae* bombs) and shouts, rallying his neighbours: '*Ingay!*' – the Tagalog word that literally translates to the word 'noise' in English. The thunderous noise of residents shouting expletives and the word '*Tae!*' (shit) while throwing excrement at the police barricade fill the screen, enhancing the shock factor of the scene.

Just as noise is understood as sound that is out of place, so too is dirt 'matter out of place' (Douglas 2003: 44) – or in this case, shit.[5] *Respeto*'s shit scene literally equates noise and shit, as the film's Pandacan residents shout the word *tae* in order to amplify noise. From the colonial period until the current era of neoliberalism, hygiene and sanitation are used to differentiate social classes, with colonisers and the upper class pointing to practices like open defecation as signs of inferiority. An opinion piece in a national broadsheet echoes this thinking, saying that the poor *dugyot* (dirty) who have no access to basic sanitation services are innately dirty:

> In Manila, there are dugyot, who do not care about their communities and will just throw rubbish anywhere or urinate and defecate freely. Then there are those pasaway (hard-headed) who would do their thing (wash plates, pots, clothes on the street and throw garbage into esteros and creeks) on the streets, alleys and corners, invoking their poverty as a justification for it. (Tiquia 2019)

As mentioned in my analysis of *Tribu* and rap music, noise is not a neutral sound and is fact a powerful 'articulation of space' and power (Attali 1985: 6).[6] The above scene in *Respeto* effectively reinforces this point, and takes it a step further by subverting the negative value ascribed to 'noise' that is often used to describe sounds produced by the underclass. The scene's articulation of noise calls to mind the infamous use of excrement in another slum film, the unforgettable scene in *Slumdog Millionaire* (Boyle 2008) where the child protagonist dives into a pool of shit. This scene is a direct reference to the poor sanitation in slums, as well as the very mythology of slum dwellers themselves as dirty. *Respeto*, in its own shit scene, cleverly upends this false perception given how it uses shit as a weapon against pejorative representations of slum inhabitants. In this scene, the residents wield noise (and shit) to protect their right to place, or their right to the city.

On a symbolic level, *Respeto* used the productive power of noise to connect Doc to Hendrix and his friends, seen in their very first encounter. As Doc chases after his son leaving the house, he hears the noise of laughter from the teenagers sitting outside his bookshop, prompting the first exchange of words between Doc and Hendrix. When Doc yells at the kids for being 'too noisy', Hendrix counters by breaking into rap: '*Noisy? Noisy? Did you say noisy? Uh, oh, somebody woke up Grumpy!*'[7]

CHRONOTOPES OF PERFORMANCE

We turn to the chronotopes of performance enabled by the slum chronotope's configuration in *Respeto*, which bears more meaning when placed in dialogue with Pandacan's history of poetry and rebellion. These chronotopes of performance can be located in the various instances in which the characters take up space by filling it with noise, their means of producing spatial justice in their immediate community. I use the term performance here to convey what I have raised as the performative nature of youth. As Karen Malone (2002) explains, speaking of streets as public spaces that lend themselves to youth performances, young people use public space to perform the construction of social identities. She continues:

> Visible expressions of youth culture could be seen as the means of winning space from the dominant culture . . . they are also an attempt to express and resolve symbolically the contradictions that they experience between cultural and ideological forces: between dominant ideologies, parent ideologies and the ideologies that arise from their own experiences of daily life. (Malone 2002: 163)

The chronotopes of performance in *Respeto* use noise to articulate claims to space, while in dialogue with the youth film genre's configuration of the time-space of liminality. These scenes are transitional and intense moments of performance for the film's young characters. *Respeto* carefully uses sound to produce aural landscapes throughout the film, using acoustic properties as cues to add depth of space and time, which we can understand by looking more clearly at the film's chronotopes of performance.

In Philippine local slang, Hendrix and his friends are archetypes of the *istambay* figure (derived from 'stand by') a term usually attributed to male youths who are seen idling in public spaces of urban slums. The *istambay* is generally defined as a 'person who does not have work and who usually hangs out on street corners' (Batan 2010: 82). Sociologist Clarence Batan argues that the negative perception of the *istambay* assumes that these idle youths choose to be idle, neglecting the real structures of poverty that prevent them from formal education and employment. There is a sense of stillness conveyed by the term. *Istambay* implies standing still, transfixed in the time and space of idle youth. The *istambay* is a particulary urban figure considered deviant by the state, comparable, for instance, to 'chavs' in British urban slang, which popular British pundit Owen Jones (2011) has argued to be a caricature of all the negative associations of the working class, including laziness.[8]

In June 2018, the '*istambay*' was targeted through the anti-loitering campaign of the Duterte regime, when the president gave a verbal order to arrest those seen loitering in public spaces. Five days after this unofficial directive, the Philippine National Police announced they had made 3,000 arrests, which included over 900 minors, for violating local curfew laws (Talabong 2018). Many of these arrests occurred in urban slums. This happened despite the fact that loitering and vagrancy were decriminalised in the Philippines in 2012. The directive was criticised widely by human rights organisations who decried the criminalisation of the urban poor. As journalist Luis Teodoro points out:

> Why *istambay* are in the streets or at the corner store rather than at home sociologists have attributed to the poverty that afflicts them, among the consequences of which is poor, even primitive housing in which space and ventilation are at such a premium the streets, no matter how mean and dangerous they often are, at least offer enough room to breathe and move around in. The brutal heat of the Philippines' tropical climate also explains why many of them go shirtless in the streets and in their homes. (Teodoro 2018)

Respeto adds to the local works of popular culture that attempt to overturn the pejorative perception of the *istambay* by privileging their stories. Like *Tribu*'s privileging of Tondo, *Respeto* adds to Philippine urban films that make visible and audible otherwise invisible experiences and geographies of youth in Manila's urban space. *Respeto* gives voice to the *istambay* figures of urban Manila who assert their right to the city through their very presence in the streets and other public spaces they occupy.

The rap battle is a clear metaphor for Hendrix's ceremonial rite of passage in which he fights for his voice to be heard among other competing voices. But while Versus – the Fliptop rap battle venue – signifies the space of respect and prestige that Hendrix desperately wants to break into, his more significant chronotopes of performance are located outside of this official rap space. In fact, his words flow more easily when he's out and about with his friends, as illustrated in an early scene where he joins another group of rappers on the street just outside his neighbourhood, the blurred images of the larger city space serving as their background.

Hendrix's rap outbursts on the streets and in official rap battles bear more meaning when amplified by his voice-offs and voice-overs, film sound techniques used in three significant instances throughout the film, which I consider the film's chronotopes of performance. These three scenes that feature Hendrix's 'voice' illustrate Hendrix's liminal configuration visually and aurally, and at the same time they function to connect the film's fictional world to the 'real' world where the violence of the state war against the urban poor exists beyond the screen. These sound techniques are quieter, gentler, controlled and seemingly more carefully constructed than the spontaneous outbursts in Hendrix's rap scenes, but through them the film gives him a sense of control and comprehension about what is going on around him. I think Hendrix's voice can still be framed as having the power of noise as opposed to mere dialogue given its ability to disrupt the film's narrative flow, and the very fact that it is Hendrix's voice, which is representative of disenfranchised urban youth.

Hendrix's voice-offs/voice-overs are placed strategically throughout *Respeto*, occurring immediately after Hendrix's intense, often violent, collisions with the adults around him, parallel to the official battles he joins at Versus. The first occurs after Hendrix is bullied by his sister's partner, Nando, to get money from Doc; the second after Hendrix and his friends are assaulted by the dirty cop Fuentes. The first and second chronotopes of performance precede significant spectral scenes in the film, where the ghost of Doc's late wife appears, adding to the layering of history that *Respeto* executes throughout the film through its use of sound. The third and last chronotope of performance is slightly different, preceded by an intense exchange of words between Hendrix and Doc. This third chronotope of performance is significant as it is actually the last instance in the film where Hendrix performs via rap/poetry, paving the way for the film's ending which I will discuss in the last section of this chapter.

Hendrix's voice in these particular scenes shifts from voice-off (voices heard outside the frame) and voice-over, which means they function both to expand the film's diegetic space at the same time that we are made privy to Hendrix's inner monologue. Following Mary Anne Doane's (1980: 40) thoughts on film sound and space, the voice-off 'deepens the diegesis, gives it an extent which exceeds that of the image, and thus supports the claim that there is a space in the fictional world which the camera does not register'. The voice-over, meanwhile, 'displays what is inaccessible to the image, what exceeds the visible: the "inner life" of the character' (Doane 1980: 41). The ways that Hendrix's voice is used in these chronotopes of performance shifts from off and over – both turning in and turning out of the character's inner world, helping us understand Hendrix's place in the film world as well as his emotional turmoil, and in this way, giving more depth to Hendrix's subjective formation.

Multiple layers of meaning are offered through these chronotopes of performance, where the fictional character of Hendrix finds his voice in and beyond the screen space. In all of these we hear the voice of the fictional Hendrix, the real-life Filipino rapper Abra, and the voice that Hendrix's character as *istambay* urban youth figure symbolically represents. This is made possible given the ways these chronotopes of performance are framed and positioned within the film narrative.

The first time we hear Hendrix's voice-over/voice-off, he is in the cemetery, captured in a medium close-up as he listens to music blaring from his headphones. As the camera pans slowly from right to left and Hendrix's rap/poetry begins, his dialogue functions both as voice-over and voice-off. This initial chronotope of performance has an expository function: Hendrix speaks in the first person about how he was orphaned at a young age and forced to grow up fast, exposed to the violence of the streets. While the voice continues the camera turns its focus to Hendrix's background – the cemetery – framing his friends, Betchai and Payaso, catching them in the innocent act of 'hanging out' in the cemetery space. This deep focus framing emplaces Hendrix in the cemetery space, just as he articulates feelings of liminality through his words: '*Why am I in this world?/Caught between troubles/ I may look like a child, my bones are young/ but heart and fist can crush stones.*'[9] This last line reverberates in the final scene, where Hendrix beats the figure of the cop to his death.

The cemetery space functions to invoke liminality as well, signifying that *Respeto*'s youth figures are always treading the line between life and death, as reports of their peers being shot dead on the streets have become commonplace. Beyond this, the cemetery space also functions to invoke the haunting of the nation's violent history of killings and human rights violations under the Martial Law regime, which *Respeto* maps directly on to the Duterte regime's extrajudicial killings. Again, the film effectively uses sound to signify this mapping of the past on to the present, as Hendrix's voice-over/voice-off in the initial chronotope of performance cuts immediately to the sound of a radio news commentary that Doc is listening to, which was about the Duterte regime's brazen proposition to bury dictator Ferdinand Marcos's corpse in the Heroes' Cemetery.[10] Male and female voices are debating the subject, with the male voice advocating for the burial, and the female voice expressing dissent. There is something uncanny about the voices coming from the radio, both in terms of the subject they are discussing (a burial) and because we cannot see the bodies from which the voices are coming.[11] There is symbolic weight in the use of the radio as the medium of sound in these spectral scenes, given the historic significance of anti-Marcos radio broadcasts during the Martial Law period. For instance, one of the most iconic voices from that period was that of Cardinal Jaime Sin, whose radio broadcast over church-owned station Radio Veritas calling for people to take to the streets, became crucial to the 1986 revolution that led to the ouster of the Marcoses.

This carrying over of Hendrix's voice into scenes that focus on the character of Doc listening to radio news broadcasts about the Marcos burial allows for a compelling transition to *Respeto*'s spectral scenes, which depict the haunting of national and personal history through Doc's disturbing visions of his late wife. We later on learn that Doc's wife took her own life after suffering torture and rape by policemen during Martial Law. Beyond the mentor-mentee relationship that develops between Hendrix and Doc as the film unfolds, this carrying over of Hendrix's voice to the scene of Doc listening to the radio broadcast (which can also be interpreted as Doc listening to Hendrix's voice) establishes what the film conveys as historical continuity, created through the dialogue between Hendrix's voice, which articulates his discontent with the current Duterte regime, and Doc's memory of his wife's torture during Martial Law.

Like Hendrix's voice in his chronotope of performance, the uncanny sounds of the radio broadcast carry over to the spectral female voice heard in the scene that follows. Immediately after the female voice says (in Tagalog): '*So many were claimed to bring down Martial Law. Will this all go to waste in the hands of Duterte?*' – a haunting layering of noise follows, dominated by the ghostly sound of a female voice uttering words we are unable to coherently string together. The scene's images are a series of jump cuts of a woman on the floor, smoking, screaming or staring. The spectral scene closes with a flutter of loose pages slowly falling to the floor. The scene uses the disconnect between the female voice and the body to create the sense of haunting. As Michael Chion (1999: 154) explains, ghostly sounds in films are created by this mismatch between the voice and the body through the technique of dubbing, where 'Sound loiters around the image like the voice around the body.'

Hendrix's second chronotope of performance follows the same pattern of scenes and setting as the first identified performance. Hendrix and his friends are in a cemetery, his voice leads into a radio broadcast commentary about the Marcos burial that Doc is listening to, which in turn provokes visions of Doc's dead wife. This second voice-over occurs after the young characters have a run-in with Doc's son, Fuentes, who harasses them while they are working at the bookshop. Fuentes violently frisks all three, and gropes Betchai's breasts, while Doc helplessly watches. The scene overlaid with Hendrix's voice-over begins with a wide shot of the three characters sitting atop tombs in the cemetery, framed in the middle of the screen, caught between the stack of tombs below and the sky above (Figure 8.1). Compared to the first one, the framing of this second chronotope of performance clearly conveys that Hendrix

Figure 8.1 *The youth figures in* Respeto *on top of cemetery tombs, suggesting liminality.*

speaks for himself and his friends. His tone of voice is aggressive as he voices anger at police brutality. Consistent with the film's creative use of sound, Hendrix's words use the sense of hearing to voice indignation: '*His righteousness reaches the skies/This man with a uniform with a whistle/He doesn't have to use/But just a mere click of the trigger . . .*'[12] While this scene was mostly framed in its initial wide shot, it also cuts to a medium shot of Betchai, signalling that these words of anger in Hendrix's voice-over was indeed hers as well, she whose dignity was aggrieved all the more by the sexual assault she experienced at the hands of Fuentes.

Like the earlier technique, Hendrix's voice-over weaves directly into the radio broadcast about the remains of the former dictator being buried in the National Heroes' cemetery. The last line from the radio broadcast that triggers the spectral appearance of Doc's late wife suggests the haunting of this burial in Philippine history: '*The President may have been buried but it will still be the Filipinos who will decide if Marcos was a hero.*' The eerie noise of sheets of paper strewn across the room is mixed with the layering of female voices. This time, the ghost's mouth is mute – she stares at the screen while standing on a chair. When she jumps off, a jump cut is used to make the body disappear. The female voices linger as the camera cuts to a close-up of Doc in a trance.

Hendrix's third chronotope of performance, set on a small bridge, takes a different strategy from the first two. Once again the three young characters are framed in a medium shot from a side angle, the figures leaning against the side of the bridge. The bridge symbolically cuts through the middle of the shot, extending beyond the corner of the screen, consequently extending the space in which Hendrix's voice-over can be located, suggesting that Hendrix's inner voice extends beyond the film's fictional world. In the teen film narrative development this chronotope of performance functions as a pivotal moment in Hendrix's coming-of-age – the point at which he overcomes the obstacle or his experience of limits towards maturity. This is expressed clearly in Hendrix's voice-over, where he reflects on the words imparted by the mentor. '*For men who show no respect for rhyme or reason/ Where the essence of words no longer move him/ No matter how deep or high the prose/ Will certainly fall …*'[13]

The scene that precedes the voice-over is a charged exchange of words between Doc and Hendrix. Doc berates Hendrix for stealing his poetry to use in his rap battle, but Hendrix replies with biting words that render Doc speechless. It's a significant scene in that this is where the film's title is dropped: '*All I've ever wanted was a bit of respect. Is that too much?*'[14] Even more so, it's a line that bridges their histories, as Hendrix's question applies not just to himself but to Doc, who carries the weight of his wife's suicide in his memories. Ironically, even as Hendrix bemoans Doc for depriving him of his moment of glory at the rap battle, this scene shows just how much he's learned from reading Doc's poetry as he delivers his tirade against Doc through his impressive delivery of rhymes and verses. The scene ends with the two caught in gentle silence, denoting a truce, a resolution that sets up the third chronotope of performance where Hendrix articulates what he's learned from the film's mentor figure.

Hendrix's chronotopes of performance and the scenes that precede and follow them are further laced with understated melodramatic modality. This is done through the restrained use of tense music in the voice-over scenes as well as the use of close-ups to highlight the character's facial expressions, which connote a combination of rage, sadness and resentment. Apart from the film's tragic closing scene, there is one other scene that functions as a chronotope of performance and amplifies the film's use of the melodramatic mode – Betchai's ballad, which I turn to in the next section.

BETCHAI'S BALLAD

Although the film's main focus is obviously Hendrix, it also provides time and space for Betchai and Payaso's articulations of subjective formation. To the film's credit, the female voice is strongly audible in the character of Betchai, especially in the scene where she breaks into a melancholic song.[15] Betchai is a refreshing female character, the opposite of the meek and quiet young female stereotype. In fact, on many occasions, Betchai serves as the voice of reason for Hendrix and Payaso. In an early scene, Betchai scolds Hendrix for making an off-hand sexual comment about a young girl found dead through *tokhang* operations in their neighbourhood. She also constantly reminds Hendrix to be cautious, given that he is an easy *tokhang* target.

Through Betchai's ballad, the film affords time and space for its young female character to articulate her discontent in a way that is both similar and different from Hendrix's. Like Hendrix, Betchai composes her verses on the spot, granting her the same level of wit and sharpness as Hendrix's capacity for spontaneous rap. Betchai's ballad converses with the poetic history of Pandacan as performance space, the old record referencing the romantic past of this Manila district known as the birth of *balagtasan*. Betchai's song is in the Bisaya language, which in itself is a groundbreaking feature in a Manila-based film. Through using the Bisayan language, Betchai brings attention to the continuing rural-urban exodus, referencing the tragic reality that many slum inhabitants make their way to cities in search of livelihood, only to end up bearing the worst of the city's poverty.

By using a ballad rather than the rhythm of rap or spoken word, Betchai's words articulate the injustice of growing up in poverty, and rework the melodramatic mode of excessive affect, while still achieving the melodramatic aim of moral legibility. Betchai's brief ballad opens with the following lines, articulating a sense of liminality: '*What rotten luck/Don't you dare drag me into this/I'm not part of this riot/Damn it/This life, I didn't choose.*'[16] The ballad carries over to a quick montage of scenes of everyday life in the slums, by now familiar scenes from previous examples of Philippine urban cinema: images of poor housing conditions, children sleeping and playing in spaces of dirt and squalor. This is the only instance in the entire film when *Respeto* employs this familiar montage of Philippine urban slums, but it does so in a way that incites empathy rather than pity by placing it immediately after Betchai's ballad. In a way, this scene is the beating heart of *Respeto* (even roughly timed in the middle of the film's duration), as it functions to expand the spatial limits of the film's fictional characters into the lived experience of the actual inhabitants, the children especially, who reside in Pandacan's slums.

SEEKING SPATIAL JUSTICE IN THE MELODRAMATIC SPECTACLE OF *RESPETO*

In this final section I turn to the final scenes in *Respeto* where sound and space are manipulated to bring to a head Hendrix's subjective formation as tragic youth figure, where the film amps up its understated use of melodramatic elements. In terms of narrative development, the shock elicited by this final scene of violent death derives from the unexpected turn in Hendrix's character. Following the melodramatic confessional scene where Doc parallels his inability to save his wife to Hendrix's inability to intervene when he sees

Candy being sexually assaulted before his eyes, Hendrix's mood changes from confrontational to reflective.

In the last quarter of the film, Hendrix's actions seem almost like a return to innocence, having realised he does not want to become just another brute in the harsh space he inhabits. When taunted by his rival rapper on the streets across from the bar where Candy works, instead of fighting as he normally would, Hendrix motions to Betchai and Payaso to just walk away. In this scene, Hendrix turns to the power of silence to make a stand for self-respect, just as he used the power of silence to articulate his remorse for failing Candy in an earlier confrontation scene. This confrontation between Candy and Hendrix, completely devoid of words, is as heartbreaking as it is potent: they stand opposite each other, not finding the words to articulate the injustice of the space and time they live in, where those who symbolically have the power of voice are the ones who emerge unscathed. And so at this point *Respeto* leads its viewers onto a false road of redemption for Hendrix, only to pull the rug from under us when Payaso is killed unceremoniously by Fuentes, the jokester character becoming collateral damage in the shooting of Hendrix's sister and her partner.

In its last few minutes, *Respeto* shifts drastically from realism to melodrama, provoking our affective response to Hendrix's act of killing Doc's son through the build-up of melodramatic elements: the slowing down of time, facial close-ups of those watching the killing, the melancholic score, and more importantly, the loudness of the sound of the stone landing blows on the body of the person being murdered. The pathos-action dialectic in these final slowed-down scenes, beginning with Hendrix walking towards Fuentes with a rock in his hand, is amplified by the sound of beating interspersed with the horror seen on the faces of Doc and Betchai. The temporal manipulation is crucial in this scene because it gives us time to appreciate the brutality of killing, rupturing the virtuous character that Hendrix had the promise of becoming.

The final image is manifestly allegorical, excessive to the point of melodramatic spectacle (Figure 8.2). It is staged in front of Doc's bookshop, *Malaya* ('Freedom'), the characters all representing figures of national history: Fuentes the fascist state, Doc the older generation that has failed to protect the younger generation from the horrors of today. The flutter of papers that appears in the background bridges this final image to the spectral appearances of Doc's wife, where the sheets of paper bearing Doc's poetic words first appeared, suggesting the haunting of history as Hendrix re-enacts Doc's murder of the cop who tortured his wife. A faint musical score accompanies this final image, in contrast to the volume of noise that dominates the film's opening scene. If, throughout the narrative, Hendrix sought spatial justice,

Figure 8.2 Respeto's *final tableau: a powerful melodramatic spectacle.*

or attempted to carve space for his time of youth through the production of sound, this final scene's aural landscape renders him silent, and places him in the same wide frame alongside other characters including the man he killed by his feet. The backdrop of the Freedom bookshop and the sheets of paper seem to suggest that words, and the articulation of words, are simply not enough to overcome historical injustice, which in the film is not simply repeated – it is perpetuated.

There are no clear heroes and villains in this final scene – even Fuentes, himself a victim of Martial Law, who as a child was forced to watch his mother's torture. This tragic ending of *Respeto* is not about the history of Martial Law repeating itself from one generation to the next; rather, it is about history perpetuating itself in the cruellest ways, where all figures, including the film's spectators, are liminal figures caught in-between equally oppressive histories of past and present. Thus, when *Respeto* rolls to credits from this disturbing final image, it cuts to a recording of Betchai's ballad, throwing her lines back at the audience: '*What rotten luck/Don't you dare drag me into this/I'm not part of this riot/Damn it/This life, I didn't choose.*'

Conclusion

Respeto is a novel example of Philippine urban cinema organised by the slum chronotope, imagined in the previously unexplored urban district of Pandacan, which offers a rich narrative precisely as it draws from its chosen locality's rich history of poetry, performance and rebellion. Doing so allowed the film to imbue its narrative and characters with what, to my mind, are new ways of imagining Manila through its interplay of space and sound. It is a film that literally and symbolically gives voices to Pandacan's urban inhabitants through its unabashed references to the Duterte regime's war against the urban poor.

Framed through the teen film genre, and combined with the film's undercurrent of melodrama, I argued that *Respeto* enables the configuration of liminal youth characters who constantly struggle for spatial justice through the production of noise. In the film's chronotopes of performance, the characters use their voices to express self-awareness and the critical apprehension of their own subjective formation, which they understand to be configured by oppressive structures that they did not choose, but nevertheless find themselves growing up in. *Respeto*, moreover, effectively used sound in uncanny scenes to illustrate how the national history of state violence in the dictatorial regime has mapped itself on to the present spate of extrajudicial killings.

Respeto's melodramatic spectacle in its closing scene, which locates the film's allegorical characters in a single wide frame, provides time and space for viewers to apprehend the violence of the unfolding drama. Instead of noise, the film makes use of silence and slowness to allegorise the perpetuation of a national history of violence and injustice. The final melodramatic image, combined with the film's chronotopes of performance, amplifies *Respeto*'s value, and volume, as one of the most recent examples of Philippine urban cinema that enables imaginaries of spatial justice.

Notes

1. For critical reviews, see David (2017a) and Marasigan (2017).
2. *Balagtasan* is a form of debate done through verses of poetry that emerged in Manila in the 1920s, named after Filipino poet Francisco Balagtas. 'Fliptop' refers to the rap battles that took off in 2010, which traces their history from the tradition of *balagtasan*. See Nadera Jr. and Mooney-Singh (2019)
3. Rodrigo Duterte's war on drugs was called *Operation Tokhang*, the word tokhang meaning a combination of sound of knocking '*toktok*' and the Tagalog word, '*hangyo*' which means to plead or beg. See Gregorio (2018).
4. *Florante at Laura* is a well-known Tagalog epic poem, essentially borrowing from the tradition of courtly love. In an article about the poem, Filipino National Artist for Literature, Bienvenido Lumbera, examines how Francisco Balagtas's writing formalised the tradition of Tagalog poetry in the 1920s, also a key period in Manila's urbanisation. See Lumbera (1967)
5. See Pickering and Rice (2017) where they establish the discursive links between noise and dirt by analysing Mary Douglas's line about dirt being 'out of place' in relation to theories of sound and noise.

6. See Rose (1994).
7. Hendrix's rap in Tagalog: '*Maingay ba? Maingay ba? Yan tuloy nagising si lolo!*'
8. This is, of course, not a direct equivalent. In British popular imagination, 'chav' is a term synonymous with the white working class – a racial dimension that is absent in the Philippine notion of the *istambay*.
9. The article uses the English subtitles from the film, but I think it is useful to include here for reference the Tagalog lines used, as to me they are even more poignant and powerful in the original. The lines read: '*Bakit ba ganito ang aking mundo? Lagi na lang bang maiipit sa gulo? Bata man ang aking mukha, mura ang buto, puso't kamao kayang dumurog ng bato.*'
10. Despite fierce opposition from the public, especially martial law survivors, Duterte endorsed the burial of dictator Ferdinand Marcos in the National Heroes' Cemetery in November 2016.
11. The uncanny voice coming from the radio can be linked to some early accounts of radio technology as a fascinating and even ghostly medium. See Sconce (2000).
12. The Tagalog lines: '*Kasinglawak ng langit ang pananagutan ng taong unipormadong hindi silbato ang pinahihiyaw/kundi ang nguso ng kinalabit na gatilyo/Mas malaki sa kanya ang sariling anino.*'
13. The Tagalog lines: '*Taong walang respeto sa salita's katwiran ng kapwa/Wala sa kanyang talab ang talim ng talinhanga/Gaano man kataas ang lipad ng diwa, tiyak na babagsak sa lupa.*'
14. The Tagalog lines: '*Hangad ko lang naman, katiting na respeto.*'
15. In his correspondence with *Respeto*'s producer and director and his published review of the film, critic Joel David notes that *Respeto* exhibited progressive gender dynamics compared to *Tribu*. See David (2017a, 2017b).
16. Here the Tagalog audience (myself included) relies on the English subtitles to understand Betchai's ballad, making the ballad a truly interruptive moment in the film, which was first screened at the Manila-based Cinemalaya festival.

Conclusion

By the time this book is published in mid-2021, the world will still be struggling with the implications of living in and through pandemic times and spaces.

In the early phase of the pandemic's unfurling, we experienced and witnessed in real-time how the COVID-19 pandemic thoroughly exposed and intensified social inequalities all over the world. As reports of lockdowns and bodies scrambling to find shelter streamed onto our screens, it became apparent how the spatiality of justice and the injustice of spatiality could be used to grasp an important facet of how the pandemic was taking place. The pandemic laid bare, in the most striking ways, how space is not just a given but is produced, contested and appropriated, in literal and symbolic terms. In fact, the initial rallying call from governments across the globe, was a statement that revealed the spatial facet of the pandemic crisis: 'Stay at home.' For the global underclass on our planet of slums, this seemingly straightforward campaign was almost like a death sentence. Footage from urban centres in the Third World, Manila included, showed bodies crammed in shanties waiting for government aid that never came, crowds walking miles to get to their homes outside city centres, the homeless left to fend for themselves. In the Philippines, pandemic deaths piled on the body count of the casualties of Duterte's extrajudicial killings, alongside reports of activists being gunned down in both urban and rural spaces.

It is undeniable that the pandemic has ushered in a new era in global history, just as it has exacerbated all the more the existing crisis of the urbanisation of poverty. While the films I've discussed in this book belong to a pre-COVID-19 age, the need to view the social from a spatial perspective resounds at a time when there is an even more urgent need to imagine the production of spaces of justice in post-pandemic times. I contend that films, and the films in this study that are now part of Philippine film and urban history, remain useful for helping us understand our stakes in producing the spaces and times we live in.

This study of the imaginaries of spatial justice in Philippine urban cinema has responded to the challenge to strengthen the cinema-city nexus, or the dialectical relations between urban and film studies. In the matter of human geography, the study has contributed to enriching the discourse of spatial justice as applied to the study of film. In film studies, the study has offered new ways of using Bakhtin's chronotopic approach in the study of film narratives from a particular non-Western context. The study has contributed to the cinema-city nexus in two major ways, which I recapitulate in what follows.

First, this study has offered a novel, interdisciplinary theoretical framework for examining the ways social justice is revealed in and through film narratives set in the particularities of Manila's slums and its larger urban landscape. While recognising the problematic discourse of poverty pornography invoked by the urban imaginary of slums in the Third World, this study has formulated the theory of the slum chronotope as a means to think through the social, political and ethical issues raised in the films. By formulating the slum chronotope as a theoretical tool towards the purpose of locating and examining spatial in/justice, the study has been able to diverge from the limiting route of poverty pornography, shifting attention to the ways the narratives are productive in examining the workings of the production of space.

The study has argued that the slum chronotope enables narrative and subjective configurations which imagine the struggle for spatial justice through tracking the characters' movements through distinctive urban spaces. In the coming-of-age chapter, the child figures are compelled to pass through the space of childhood, which in the films are sites imagined as chronotopes of passage. Focused on the movements of the children of the slums, the films reconfigure the space of childhood not just as a time of innocence, but as a period in which children learn to come to terms with violence and injustice in order to shape their future. The two films also showed a contrast between the spaces of *byuti* produced by the queer figure in *Ang Pagdadalaga*, versus the masculine spaces the child follows at the heels of the youth gangs of Tondo in *Tribu*.

In the following melodrama chapter, the mothers and grandmothers struggle for justice and survival through the spatial practice of walking that dialogues with affective chronotopes, or key moments of melodramatic excess. These affective chronotopes are assertions of life in the face of death, care in the face of oppression, and resilience in the face of injustice. In contrast to readings that might find weakness in the slow, laborious pacing of these restrained melodramatic films, I have argued that the act of walking as rendered in these films is a form of female affective labour the reveals moments of spatial justice, where women literally and symbolically walk for the sake of their family's survival.

The chapter on Manila noir ventures beyond immediate slum spaces through increased mobility. By covering more ground in the urban space, the chapter examined the male characters' struggle for spatial justice through the politics of mobility, which is also indicative of a masculine desire to master urban space. Compared to the previous chapters, the male-centred narratives in Manila noir end in the death of their lead characters (in the case of *Kinatay*, the death of innocence). However, their deaths reveal the injustice of spatiality by suggesting that those who reinforce injustice are the gatekeepers of mobility, or the ones behind the wheel. All three films implicate the state and its figures of authority as those behind the injustice of spatiality.

The following chapter exports the slum chronotope and places it in dialogue with the migrant narrative of *Transit*. The chapter likens the slum inhabitant to the migrant figure, who struggles for spatial justice through strategically inhabiting chronotopes of in/visibilty in the foreign space. I have argued that *Transit* is a significant expansion of the slum chronotope into the OFW genre which is unique to Philippine cinema. The film privileges the politics of survival in the struggle over the foreign space, which is disassociated from the state's rhetoric of national sacrifice that has been used to justify the country's labour export policy.

The book's last chapter returns to Manila's urban space in the age of Duterte's extrajudicial killings, specifically grounded on the imaginary of Pandacan whose history as a site of poetry, performance and rebellion dialogues with the configuration of the film's liminal youth figures. I have argued that the film enables its youth figures to participate in the production of space through the disruptive production of noise. The film's chronotopes of performance allow the characters' voices to amplify their stakes in space, while also enabling the haunting of history through the film's dialogue with the spectre of the Martial Law period. The film's use of silence in the final scene amplifies the film's ability to invoke the haunting of national traumatic history through the tableau of symbolic characters occupying the final frame.

As its second contribution to the city-cinema nexus, this study of Philippine urban cinema has argued for the significance of Philippine urban and cinematic development as crucial to understanding the workings of neoliberal global capitalism, gleaned from the narratives of subjective formation in the films set in the backdrop of the urbanisation of poverty. While firmly grounded in the sociopolitical conditions of Manila's urban landscape, the study's general contextualisation in the colonial and postcolonial history of slum formation immediately situates the films in the intersections of the local and global production of spatial injustice. The history of Manila's slum formation reveals how the capitalist logic of accumulation by dispossession takes place in such a context, creating culturally specific built environments and social conditions that configure and are configured by the city's inhabitants.

All the films included in this study implicitly or overtly dialogue with the transnational urban imaginary, not just through the global scope of the urbanisation of poverty, but through the mode of genre analysis enabled by the film's chronotopic readings. In each chapter, I have shown how Philippine urban films inarguably converse and appropriate Western genre conventions in ways that are more meaningful when situated in the Philippine context.

In the coming-of-age chapter, the *Bildungsroman* narrative has been reconfigured and grounded in Maxi's *looban* and Ebet's Tondo, prompting a rethinking of what justice means for children who come of age in spaces where childhood is not a time of innocence. *Ang Pagdadalaga*, in particular, is exceptional in how it locates its queer child figure in the space of *kabaklaan*, its negotiations of *labas* and *loob* that is particular to Philippine queer culture. *Tribu*, meanwhile, is laudable in its reimagining of how children and young people actively stake their claims in producing the space of Tondo that occupies a significant place in popular urban imaginary.

Meanwhile, the chapter on melodrama has reconfigured melodramatic excess, as channelled through the spatial practice of walking that tactically displaces emotions at narrative moments that reveal the subjective power of the films' female protagonists. The melodramatic narratives surface affects particular to the social conditions of the female-centred narratives: the fear and grief in *Kubrador* in which the movements of the protagonist are structured by the illegal numbers game and her son's spectral presence; the mixed affects of shame and care that underpin the business of fostering in *Foster Child*; the powerful affects the underscore the resilience of the elderly female protagonists in *Lola*.

The Manila noir chapter has examined the politics of mobility as central to the masculine myths that run through the modality/genre of noir. The crimes in Manila noir strongly locate the films in the Philippine context, implicating figures of state authority as the masterminds behind the male leads' descent into darkness. In *Kinatay*, the male lead's long journey in the van symbolises his future as a dirty cop; *Metro Manila* reconfigures the naive rural migrant who hijacks the heist for his family's escape; while *On the Job*'s whodunit narrative unfolds through chase scenes that signify collisions of masculinities in Manila's urban landscape.

Transit offers a powerful reconfiguration of the nationalist rhetoric of migrant labour in the Overseas Filipino Worker film, a genre that is unique to Philippine cinema. The film's non-modular narrative and the choice of Tel Aviv as a location distinguish the film from canonical OFW films. Following in the tracks of the previous chapters, this chapter has shown how the struggle for spatial justice exceeds the contours of Manila's slums. The very production of *Transit* alongside the other films in this chapter suggests the inevitable expansion of the slum chronotope beyond Manila's landscape, suggesting the slum inhabitant's potential grounds for solidarity with the migrant figure, as both figures belong to the growing global underclass.

Finally, the last chapter on *Respeto* reconfigures the youth film genre alongside the melodramatic mode, unique in its eloquent and explosive use of Tagalog rap, poetry and Bisayan ballad throughout its narrative. The film configures the teen film genre's intergenerational conflict through its effective parallelism of the traumas of its youth and mentor figures. The film's final melodramatic spectacle poignantly captures in a single frame the tragic experience of violence and injustice, passed on from one generation to the next. Released roughly a decade after the films discussed in this book's first chapter, *Respeto* is a compelling example of how Philippine urban cinema has developed over the years, providing a promising glimpse of what else Philippine filmmakers can offer in the future.

Bibliography

Abacan, Crispin Mahrion (2015) 'INFOGRAPHIC: Fast Facts on Overseas Filipino Workers'. *ABS-CBN News*, 19 December, <http://news.abs-cbn.com/focus/v2/12/19/15/infographic-fast-facts-on-overseas-filipino-workers> (last accessed 6 September 2017).

Abella, Manolo I. (1993) 'Labor Mobility, Trade and Structural Change: The Philippine Experience'. *Asian and Pacific Migration Journal* 2(3): 249–68.

ABS-CBN News (2010) 'Instead of Gang Riots, This Group Prefers Rap Music'. *ABS-CBN News*, 19 May, <https://www.youtube.com/watch?v=CUV5_ba8Aho> (last accessed 2 March 2017).

ABS-CBN News (2012) 'Mendoza Denies Indie Films Are "Poverty Porn"'. *ABS-CBN News*, 12 January, <http://news.abs-cbn.com/entertainment/01/12/12/mendoza-denies-indie-films-are-poverty-porn> (last accessed 10 January 2018).

Agbayani, Susan Claire (2017) 'What to Know about Cinemalaya 2017 Best Film, "Respeto"'. *Rappler*, 22 September, <https://www.rappler.com/entertainment/movies/182887-respeto-movie-fun-facts-treb-monteras> (last accessed 10 October 2019).

Aguilar, Jr, Filomeno V. (2003) 'Global Migrations, Old Forms of Labor, and New Transborder Class Relations'. *Southeast Asian Studies* 41(2): 137–51.

Ahmed, Sara (2014) *The Cultural Politics of Emotion*. Edinburgh: Edinburgh University Press.

Aitken, Stuart C. and Leo Zonn (1994) *Place, Power, Situation, and Spectacle: A Geography of Film*. Lanham, MD and London: Rowman & Littlefield.

Alcazaren, Paulo, Luis Ferrer, Benvenuto Icamina and Neal M. Oshima (2011) *Lungsod Iskwater: The Evolution of Informality as a Dominant Pattern in Philippine Cities*. Mandaluyong City: Anvil Publishing, Inc.

Alfonso, Gigi Javier (2009) 'Lola: An Ode to Women and to Life | Manunuri Ng Pelikulang Pilipino (MPP)'. *Manunuri Ng Pelikulang Pilipino*. <http://www.manunuri.com/reviews/lola_an_ode_to_women_and_to_life> (last accessed 17 September 2017).

Aljazeera News (2020) '"Shoot Them Dead": Duterte Warns against Violating Lockdown'. *Aljazeera*, 2 April, <https://www.aljazeera.com/news/2020/04/dead-duterte-warns-violating-lockdown-200401164531160.html> (last accessed 5 July 2020).

Andersson, Johan and Lawrence Webb (2016) *Global Cinematic Cities: New Landscapes of Film and Media*. New York: Columbia University Press.

Antolihao, Lou (2004) *Culture of Improvisation: Informal Settlements and Slum Upgrading in a Metro Manila Locality*. Quezon City: Institute of Philippine Culture, Ateneo de Manila University.

Appadurai, Arjun (1996) *Modernity at Large: Cultural Dimensions in Globalization*. Minneapolis: University of Minnesota Press.

Arabindoo, Pushpa (2011) 'Rhetoric of the "Slum": Rethinking Urban Poverty'. *City* 15(6): 636–46.

Arcilla, Chester Antonio C. (2015) '"Lumaban Na Tayo! Wala Na Tayong Pupuntahan!" [We

Must Fight! We Have Nowhere to Go!]: An Ethnography of a State-Sponsored Demolition and "Barikadang Bayan" [Slum Community Barricade]'. Ateneo De Manila, Quezon City.

Arguillas, Marie Joy B. and Lindy Williams (2010) 'The Impact of Parents' Overseas Employment on Educational Outcomes of Filipino Children'. *International Migration Review* 44(2): 300–19.

Arn, Jack (1995) 'Pathway To The Periphery: Urbanization, Creation Of A Relative Surplus Population, And Political Outcomes In Manila, Philippines'. *Urban Anthropology and Studies of Cultural Systems and World Economic Development* 24(3/4): 189–228.

Asis, Maruja Milagros B. (2008) 'The Social Dimensions of International Migration in the Philippines', in *Moving Out, Back and Up: International Migration and Development Prospects in the Philippines*, ed. Maruja M. B. Asis and Fabio Baggio. Quezon City: Scalabrini Migration Center, pp. 77–108.

Atanacio, Glenn (2007) '"Tribu" Is Cinemalaya 2007 Best Full-Length Feature Film'. *PEP.Ph*, 30 July, <http://www.pep.ph/guide/arts-and-culture/934/tribu-is-cinemalaya-2007-best-full-length-feature-film-> (last accessed 2 March 2017).

Attali, Jacques (1985) *Noise: The Political Economy of Music*. Manchester: Manchester University Press.

Auge, Marc (2009) *Non-Places: Introduction to an Anthropology of Supermodernity*. New edition. London and New York: Verso Books.

Austria Jr, Fernando A. (2009) 'In the Vortex of Violence'. *Plaridel Journal* 6(1): 153–60.

Badiou, Alain (2013) *Cinema*. Cambridge and Malden: Polity Press.

Bakhtin, Mikhail Mikhaï (1981) *The Dialogic Imagination: Four Essays*, ed. Michael Holquist. Austin: University of Texas Press.

Bakhtin, Mikhail Mikhaï (2010) 'The Bildungsroman and Its Significance to the History of Realism (Toward a Historical Typology of the Novel)', in *Speech Genres and Other Late Essays*, ed. Caryl Emerson and Michael Holquist. Austin: University of Texas Press, pp. 10–59.

Ballesteros, Marife M. (2010) *Linking Poverty and the Environment: Evidence from Slums in Philippine Cities. Working Paper.* 2010–33. PIDS Discussion Paper Series.

Ballesteros, Marife M. (2011) 'Why Slum Poverty Matters'. *Philippine Institute for Development Studies* 2011(02): 1–6.

Bartram, David V. (1998) 'Foreign Workers in Israel: History and Theory'. *The International Migration Review* 32(2): 303–25.

Batan, Clarence M. (2010) 'Istambay: A Sociological Analysis of Youth Inactivity in the Philippines'. Dalhousie University, Halifax, Nova Scotia.

Baumgartel, Tilman (ed.) (2012) '"An Inexpensive Film Should Start with an Inexpensive Story" Interview with Brillante Mendoza and Armando Bing Lao', in *Southeast Asian Independent Cinema*. Hong Kong: Hong Kong University Press, pp. 155–170.

Baytan, Ronald (2008) 'Evolving Identities in Philippine Cinema', in *AsiaPacifiQueer: Rethinking Genders and Sexualities*, ed. Fran Martin. Champaign: University of Illinois Press, pp. 181–96.

Bazin, André (1967) *What Is Cinema? Vol. I*. Oakland: University of California Press.

Bazin, André (1971) *What Is Cinema? Vol II*. Oakland: University of California Press.

Beller, Jonathan (2012) 'Wagers within the Image: Rise of Visuality, Transformation of Labour, Aesthetic Regimes'. *Culture Machine* 13.

Benjamin, Walter [1982] (2002) *The Arcades Project*. Cambridge, MA: Harvard University Press.

Berehulak, Daniel (2016) '"They Are Slaughtering Us Like Animals"'. *The New York Times*, 7 December.

Berghahn, Daniela (2010) 'Coming of Age in "the Hood": The Diasporic Youth Film and Questions of Genre', in *European Cinema in Motion: Migrant and Diasporic Film in Contemporary*

Europe, Palgrave European Film and Media Studies, ed. Daniela Berghahn and Claudia Sternberg. London: Palgrave Macmillan, pp. 235–55.

Berner, Erhard (1997) 'Opportunities and Insecurities: Globalisation, Localities and the Struggle for Urban Land in Manila'. *The European Journal of Development Research* 9(1): 167–82.

Berner, Erhard (2000) 'Poverty Alleviation and the Eviction of the Poorest: Towards Urban Land Reform in the Philippines'. *International Journal of Urban and Regional Research* 24(3): 554–66.

Boehringer, Gill H. (2009) 'Class and Ondoy: The Philippine Daily Inquirer's Ideological Distortions – Bulatlat'. *Bulatlat*, 23 October.

Bolay, Jean-Claude (2006) 'Slums and Urban Development: Questions on Society and Globalisation'. *The European Journal of Development Research* 18(2): 284–98.

Bolisay, Richard (2009) 'Lola (Brillante Mendoza, 2009)'. *Lilok Pelikula*, 21 October, <https://lilokpelikula.wordpress.com/2009/10/21/lola-brillante-mendoza-2009/> (last accessed 17 September 2017).

Bolisay, Richard (2019) '"Yes, You Belong to Me!": Reflections on the JaDine Love Team Fandom in the Age of Twitter and in the Context of Filipino Fan Culture'. *Plaridel Journal* 16(2): 41–61.

Boo, Bernard (2013) 'Interview: Erik Matti of On the Job Interview'. Way Too Indie, 26 September, <http://waytooindie.com/interview/interview-erik-matti-job/> (last accessed 31 May 2017).

Borde, Raymond and Etienne Chaumeton (2012) 'Towards a Definition of Film Noir', in *Film Noir Reader*, ed. Alain Silver and James Ursini. Köln, pp. 17–26. London: Taschen.

Braester, Yomi and James Tweedie (2010) *Cinema at the City's Edge: Film and Urban Networks in East Asia*. Hong Kong: Hong Kong University Press.

Broe, Dennis (2014) *Class, Crime and International Film Noir: Globalizing America's Dark Art*. London: Palgrave Macmillan.

Brooks, Peter (1976) *The Melodramatic Imagination: Balzac, Henry James, Melodrama, and the Mode of Excess*. New Haven, CT: Yale University Press.

Buckley, Jerome Hamilton (1974) *Season of Youth: The Bildungsroman from Dickens to Golding*. Cambridge, MA: Harvard University Press.

Bulatao, Jaime C. (1964) 'Hiya'. *Philippine Studies* 12(3): 424–38.

Bureau of Jail Management and Penology (2017) 'Congestion Rate'. *Bureau of Jail Management and Penology*, <https://www.bjmp.gov.ph/datstat.html> (last accessed 31 May 2017).

Cabalfin, Edson (2014) 'The Politics of Nation in the Urban Form of Informal Settlements in Quezon City, Philippines', in *Reading the Architecture of the Underprivileged Classes*, ed. Nnamdi Elleh. Farnham: Ashgate Publishing, pp. 153–70.

Campos, Patrick F. (2011) 'The Intersection of Philippine and Global Film Cultures in the New Urban Realist Film'. *Plaridel* 8(1).

Campos, Patrick F. (2013) 'Ghostly Allegories: Haunting as Constitution of Philippine (Trans) National (Cinema) History'. *Kritika Kultura* (21/22): 611–43.

Campos, Patrick F. (2016) *The End of National Cinema: Filipino Film at the Turn of the Century*. Quezon City: University of the Philippines Press.

Candaliza-Gutierrez, Filomin (2012) 'Pangkat: Inmate Gangs at the New Bilibid Prison Maximum Security Compound'. *Philippine Sociological Review* 193–237.

Caoili, Manuel A. (1988) *The Origins of Metropolitan Manila: A Political and Social Analysis*. Quezon City: New Day Publishers.

Capino, Jose B. (2006) 'Philippines: Cinema and Its Hybridity (or You're Nothing but a

Second-Rate, Trying Hard Copycat)', in *Contemporary Asian Cinema: Popular Culture in a Global Frame*, pp. 32–44. New York: Berg Publishers.

Capino, José B. (2010) *Dream Factories of a Former Colony: American Fantasies, Philippine Cinema*. Minneapolis: University of Minnesota Press.

Carballo, Bibsy (2007) 'Encounter with Greatness'. *Philstar*, 16 June.

Celis, Noel (2016) 'Dead Bodies and Hellish Prisons on the Philippines Police Graveyard Shift'. *Correspondent*, 5 August <https://correspondent.afp.com/dead-bodies-and-hellish-prisons-philippines-police-graveyard-shift> (last accessed 31 May 2017).

Chakrabarty, Dipesh (2002) *Habitations of Modernity: Essays in the Wake of Subaltern Studies*. Chicago: University of Chicago Press.

Chambers, Deborah, Tracey Skelton and Gill Valentine (2005) 'Cool Places: An Introduction to Youth and Youth Cultures', in *Cool Places: Geographies of Youth Cultures*, ed. Tracey Skelton and Gill Valentine. London: Routledge, pp. 1–34.

Chandola, Tripta (2012) 'Listening into Others: Moralising the Soundscapes in Delhi'. *International Development Planning Review* 34(4): 391–408.

Chion, Michel (1999) *The Voice in Cinema*. New York: Columbia University Press.

Clarke, David B. (1997) *The Cinematic City*. Hove: Psychology Press.

CNN (2017) 'City of the Dead: A Neighbourhood Destroyed by Duterte's War on Drugs'. *CNN*, March, <http://www.cnn.com/interactive/2017/03/world/city-of-the-dead/> (last accessed 19 July 2017).

Collin, Robbie (2013) 'Metro Manila, Review'. *The Telegraph*, 19 September, <http://www.telegraph.co.uk/culture/film/filmreviews/10320301/Metro-Manila-review.html> (last accessed 6 March 2016).

Commission on Human Rights – Philippines (2015) 'A Study of the Human Rights Situation in Police Lock-Up Cells in the National Capital Region'.

Conde, Carlos H. (2007) 'In "Tribu," Real-Life Filipino Gangs Collaborate Onscreen'. *The New York Times*, 1 November.

Cowie, Elizabeth (1993) 'Film Noir and Women', in *Shades of Noir: A Reader*, ed. Joan Copjec. London: Verso, pp. 121–65.

Cresswell, Timothy (2012) *On the Move: Mobility in the Modern Western World*. London: Routledge.

Cruz, Isagani R. (1988) 'Portraits of Youth in Philippine Films'. *Media Asia* 15(1): 17–21.

Cruz, Marinel and Bayani San Diego Jr (2007) 'RP Goes to Cannes – Again'. *Inquirer*, 22 April.

Cu-Unjieng, Phillip (2013) 'Film Review: On The Job: It's "Bitter" in the Philippines'. *Philstar. Com*, 29 August, <http://www.philstar.com/entertainment/2013/08/29/1145601/film-review-job-its-bitter-philippines> (last accessed 31 May 2017).

Dasgupta, Rana (2006) 'The Sudden Stardom of the Third World City', <http://www.ranadasgupta.com/texts.asp?text_id=36> (last accessed 22 June 2015).

David, Joel (1990) *The National Pastime: Contemporary Philippine Cinema*. Quezon City: Anvil Publishing.

David, Joel (1995) *Fields of Vision: Critical Applications in Recent Philippine Cinema*. Quezon City: Ateneo de Manila University Press.

David, Joel (2012) 'Introduction to FORUM KRITIKA: A Closer Look at "Manila by Night"'. *Kritika Kultura* (19): 6–13.

David, Joel (2013a) 'OFWs in Foreign Cinema: An Introduction'. *Kritika Kultura* (21/22): 557–9.

David, Joel (2013b) 'Phantom in Paradise: A Philippine Presence in Hollywood Cinema'. *Kritika Kultura* (21/22): 560–83.

David, Joel (2014) 'Millennial Traversals – The Golden Ages of Philippine Cinema: A Critical

Reassessment'. *Ámauteurish!*, 17 March, <https://amauteurish.com/2014/03/17/the-golden-ages-of-philippine-cinema-a-critical-reassessment/> (last accessed 26 June 2016).

David, Joel (2015a) 'A Desire Named Oscar'. *Ámauteurish!*, 22 June, <https://amauteurish.com/2015/06/22/local-film-reviews-new-millennium/> (last accessed 31 May 2017).

David, Joel (2015b) 'On The Edge'. *Ámauteurish!*, 22 June, <https://amauteurish.com/2015/06/22/local-film-reviews-new-millennium/> (last accessed 31 May 2017).

David, Joel (2017a) 'Film May Be Dead, but Film Culture Is Alive and Well'. *Ámauteurish!*, 18 September, <https://amauteurish.com/2017/09/18/film-may-be-dead-but-film-culture-is-alive-and-well/> (last accessed 16 May 2020).

David, Joel (2017b) 'Source Exchange for Review of Respeto'. *Ámauteurish!*, 20 August, <https://amauteurish.com/2017/08/20/source-exchange-for-review-of-respeto/> (last accessed 16 May 2020).

Davis, Mike (2006) *Planet of Slums*. London and New York: Verso.

De Certeau, Michel (2011) *The Practice of Everyday Life*. Berkeley: University of California Press.

De Chavez, Jeremy (2016) '"Love Is …": An Inaesthetic Inquiry on Love and Attention in Aureus Solito's The Blossoming of Maximo Oliveros'. *Kritika Kultura* (27): 45–62.

De La Cruz, Khavn (2010) *Philippine New Wave: This Is Not a Film Movement*. Kamias Road.

Deleuze, Gilles (2013) *Cinema II: The Time-Image*. London: Bloomsbury Publishing.

Deleuze, Gilles and Félix Guattari (2004) *A Thousand Plateaus: Capitalism and Schizophrenia*. London: A&C Black.

Del Mundo Jr, Clodualdo (1998) *Native Resistance: Philippine Cinema and Colonialism, 1898–1941*. Manila: De La Salle University Press.

Del Mundo Jr, Clodualdo (1999) 'Philippine Cinema: An Historical Overview'. *Asian Cinema* 10(2): 29–66.

Del Mundo Jr, Clodualdo (2013) 'Philippine Movies in 2001: The Film Industry Is Dead. Long Live Philippine Cinema!', in *The Urian Anthology, 2000–2009: The Rise of the Philippine New Wave Indie Film*, ed. Nicanor G. Tiongson. Quezon City: University of the Philippines Press, pp. 48–55.

Deocampo, Nick (2007a) *Cine: Spanish Influences on Early Cinema in the Philippines* (Kindle Edition). Quezon City: Anvil Publishing.

Deocampo, Nick (2007b) 'Cinema and Colonization: American Colonization and the Rise of Cinema in the Philippines'. *Comparative American Studies* 5(2): 147–71.

Deocampo, Nick (2009) 'City, Nation, Cinema: Manila's Representation on Screen'. *Manila* 5(1):1–1.

Deocampo, Nick (2011) *Film: American Influences on Philippine Cinema* (Kindle Edition). Quezon City: Anvil Publishing.

Desser, David (2003) 'Global Noir: Genre Film in the Age of Transnationalism', in *Film Genre Reader III*, ed. Barry Keith Grant. Austin: University of Texas Press, pp. 516–36.

Devilles, Gary (2008) 'The Pornography of Poverty in Serbis and Tribu'. Quezon City: Ateneo de Manila University.

Diaz, Robert (2018) 'Biyuti from BelowContemporary Philippine Cinema and the Transing of Kabaklaan'. *TSQ: Transgender Studies Quarterly* 5(3): 404–24.

Dikeç, Mustafa (2001) 'Justice and the Spatial Imagination'. *Environment and Planning A* 33(10): 1785–1805.

Dikeç, Mustafa (2007) *Badlands of the Republic: Space, Politics and Urban Policy*. n.p.: Wiley.

Dikeç, Mustafa (2015) *Space, Politics and Aesthetics*. Edinburgh: Edinburgh University Press.

Dimaculangan, Jocelyn (2007) '"Foster Child" Opens in Cinemas Nationwide Starting September 12 | PEP.Ph', 2 September, <http://www.pep.ph/guide/movies/1042/

foster-child-opens-in-cinemas-nationwide-starting-september-12> (last accessed 31 August 2017).
Dissanayake, Wimal (1993) *Melodrama and Asian Cinema*. Cambridge: Cambridge University Press.
Doane, Mary Ann (1980) 'The Voice in the Cinema: The Articulation of Body and Space'. *Yale French Studies* (60): 33–50.
Doeppers, Daniel F. (1984) *Manila 1900–1941*. Quezon City: Ateneo de Manila University Press.
Dogra, Nandita (2013) *Representations of Global Poverty: Aid, Development and International NGOs*. Repr. London: I. B. Tauris.
Doherty, Thomas Patrick (2002) *Teenagers and Teenpics the Juvenilization of American Movies in the 1950s*. Philadelphia: Temple University Press.
Douglas, Mary (2003) *Purity and Danger: An Analysis of Concepts of Pollution and Taboo*. London and New York: Routledge.
Driscoll, Catherine (2019) *Teen Film: A Critical Introduction*. Oxford and New York: Berg.
Dussere, Erik (2013) *America Is Elsewhere: The Noir Tradition in the Age of Consumer Culture*. New York: Oxford University Press.
Dychiu, Stephanie (2010a) 'In Many Places, Bettors Still Prefer Jueteng over Lotto'. *GMA News Online*, 10 December, <http://www.gmanetwork.com/news/story/208002/news/specialreports/in-many-places-bettors-still-prefer-jueteng-over-lotto> (last accessed 17 April 2017).
Dychiu, Stephanie (2010b) 'To Real-Life Kubrador, Life Is Worth *Jueteng* For'. *GMA News Online*, 10 December, <http://www.gmanetwork.com/news/story/208000/news/special reports/to-real-life-kubrador-life-is-worth-jueteng-for> (last accessed 17 April 2017).
Dyer, Richard (1993) *The Matter of Images: Essays on Representations*. London and New York: Routledge.
Dyos, H. J. (1967) 'The Slums of Victorian London'. *Victorian Studies* 11(1): 5–40.
Ebert, Roger (2009) 'Cannes #4: What Were They Thinking of? | Roger Ebert's Journal | Roger Ebert', 16 May, <http://www.rogerebert.com/rogers-journal/cannes-4-what-were-they-thinking-of> (last accessed 31 May 2017).
Edensor, Tim (2010) 'Walking in Rhythms: Place, Regulation, Style and the Flow of Experience'. *Visual Studies* 25(1): 69–79.
Elsaesser, Thomas (2002) 'Tales of Sound and Fury', in *Home is where the heart is: studies in melodrama and the woman's film*, ed. Christine Gledhill. London: BFI Publishing, pp. 43–69.
Fabe, Marilyn (2004) 'Italian Neorealism: De Sica's The Bicycle Thief: Chapter of Closely Watched Films: An Introduction to the Art of Narrative Film Technique', in *Closely Watched Films: An Introduction to the Art of Narrative Film Technique*, pp. 99–119. Berkeley: University of California Press.
Fay, Jennifer and Justus Nieland (2009) *Film Noir: Hard-Boiled Modernity and the Cultures of Globalization*. London: Routledge.
Feng, Pin-chia (1998) *The Female Bildungsroman by Toni Morrison and Maxine Hong Kingston: A Postmodern Reading*. Pieterlen and Bern: Peter Lang Publishing.
Fisher, Jaimey (2007) 'On the Ruins of Masculinity: The Figure of the Child in Italian Neorealism and the German Rubble-Film', in *Italian Neorealism and Global Cinema*, ed. Laura E. Ruberto and Kristi M. Wilson. Detroit: Wayne State University Press, pp. 25–53.
Flanagan, Martin (2009) *Bakhtin and the Movies: New Ways of Understanding Hollywood Film*. Basingstoke and New York: Palgrave Macmillan.

Flores, Patrick (1998) 'Philippine Cinema and Society', in *Filipiniana Reader*, ed. Priscelina Patajo-Legasto. Quezon City: University of the Philippines Open University, pp. 420–9.

Flores, Patrick (2007) 'Look After: Critique of "Foster Child" (2007)'. *Young Critics Circle Film Desk*, 22 February, <https://yccfilmdesk.wordpress.com/2017/02/22/look-after-critique-of-foster-child-2007/> (last accessed 17 September 2017).

Flores, Patrick (2012) 'The Long Take: Passage as Form in the Philippine Film'. *Kritika Kultura* 19: 070–089.

Flores, Wilson Lee (2005) 'Proud to Be a Tondo Boy'. *Philstar.Com*, 20 February.

Fluck, Winfried (2001) 'Crime, Guilt, and Subjectivity in "Film Noir"'. *Amerikastudien / American Studies* 46(3): 379–408.

Franciso, Butch (2007) 'Foster Child: Cherry Pie Simply Brilliant'. *Manunuri Ng Pelikulang Pilipino*. <http://www.manunuri.com/reviews/foster_child_cherry_pie_simply_brilliant> (last accessed 17 September 2017).

Frank, Nino (1946) 'A New Kind of Police Drama: The Criminal Adventure', in *Film Noir Reader 2*, ed. Alain Silver and James Ursini. New York: Limelight Editions, pp. 15–19.

Gairola, Rahul K. (2005) 'Deterritorialisations of Desire: "Transgressive" Sexuality as Filipino Anti-Imperialist Resistance in Jessica Hagedorn's Dogeaters'. *Philament* 7: 22–41.

Garcia, J. Neil C. (2000) 'Performativity, the Bakla and the Orientalizing Gaze'. *Inter-Asia Cultural Studies* 1(2): 265–81.

Garcia, J. Neil C. (2006) 'Paradoxical Philippines: Ang Pagdadalaga Ni Maximo Oliveros.' *L Magazine*, 1 November.

Garcia, J. Neil C. (2008) *Philippine Gay Culture: Binabae to Bakla, Silahis to MSM*. Quezon City: University of the Philippines Press.

Garcia, J. Neil C. (2013) 'Nativism or Universalism: Situating LGBT Discourse in the Philippines'. *Kritika Kultura* (20): 48–68.

Garrido, Marco (2008) 'Civil and Uncivil Society: Symbolic Boundaries and Civic Exclusion in Metro Manila'. *Philippine Studies: Historical and Ethnographic Viewpoints* 56(4): 443–65.

Gavilan, Jodesz (2015) 'What You Need to Know about Overseas Filipino Workers'. *Rappler*, 5 December, <http://www.rappler.com/newsbreak/iq/114549-overseas-filipino-workers-facts-figures> (last accessed 8 June 2017).

Gilbert, Alan (2007) 'The Return of the Slum: Does Language Matter?'. *International Journal of Urban and Regional Research* 31(4): 697–713.

Giovacchini, Saverio and Robert Sklar (2011) *Global Neorealism: The Transnational History of a Film Style*. Mississippi: University Press of Mississippi.

Gledhill, Christine (1986) 'Dialogue: Christine Gledhill on "Stella Dallas" and Feminist Film Theory'. *Cinema Journal* 25(4): 44.

Gledhill, Christine (1991) *Melodrama and Realism in Twenties British Cinema*. London: British Film Institute.

Gledhill, Christine (2000) 'Rethinking Genre', in *Reinventing Film Studies*, ed. Linda Williams and Christine Gledhill. London and New York: Arnold; New York: Oxford University Press, pp. 221–42.

Gledhill, Christine (2002) 'The Melodramatic Field: An Investigation', in *Home is Where the Heart is: Studies in Melodrama and the Woman's Film*, ed. Christine Gledhill, pp. 5–39. London: BFI Publishing.

GMA News Online (2006) 'Kubrador Wins 8th International Award in Rome'. *GMA News Online*, 29 November, <http://www.gmanetwork.com/news/story/22350/showbiz/kubrador-wins-8th-international-award-in-rome> (last accessed 17 April 2017).

Goffman, Erving (1959) *The Presentation of Self in Everyday Life*. New York: Doubleday Anchor Books.
Gonzaga, Elmo (2017) 'The Cinematographic Unconscious of Slum Voyeurism'. *Cinema Journal* 56(4): 102–25.
Gonzalez, Joaquin Lucero (1998) *Philippine Labour Migration: Critical Dimensions of Public Policy*. Singapore: Institute of Southeast Asian Studies.
Gordin, Michael D., Helen Tilley and Gyan Prakash (2010) *Utopia/Dystopia: Conditions of Historical Possibility*. Princeton: Princeton University Press.
Gregorio, Xave (2018) '"Tokhang" Named 2018 Word of the Year'. *CNN Philippines*, 26 October, <https://cnnphilippines.com/news/2018/10/26/tokhang-named-2018-word-of-the-year.html> (last accessed 16 May 2020).
Guarnieri, Mya (2010) 'Children Are Just Israel's Latest Victims | Mya Guarnieri'. *The Guardian*, 20 July.
Guerrero, Rafael Ma (1983a) 'Lino Brocka: Dramatic Sense, Documentary Aspirations', in *Readings in Philippine cinema*, ed. Rafael Ma. Guerrero. Manila: Experimental Cinema of the Philippines, pp. 226–35.
Guerrero, Rafael Ma (ed.) (1983b) *Readings in Philippine Cinema*. Manila: Experimental Cinema of the Philippines.
Guerrero, Rafael Ma (1983c) 'Tagalog Movies: A New Understanding', in *Readings in Philippine Cinema*, ed. Rafael Ma. Guerrero. Manila: Experimental Cinema of the Philippines, pp. 109–16.
Guieb III, Eulalio (2012) '"Engkwentro": Like Most Pinoy Indie Films, It Is about Poverty; Unlike Most Pinoy Indie Films, It Does Not Feast on Poverty'. *Young Critics Circle Film Desk*, 13 October <https://yccfilmdesk.wordpress.com/tag/engkwentro-review/> (last accessed 7 June 2016).
Guillermo, Alice (2000) 'The Filipina OCW in Extremis', in *Geopolitics of the Visible: Essays on Philippine Film Cultures*, ed. Rolando B. Tolentino. Quezon City: Ateneo de Manila University Press, pp. 106–24.
Hagedorn, Jessica (2013) *Manila Noir*. New York: Akashic Books.
Halberstam, Judith (2005) *In a Queer Time and Place: Transgender Bodies, Subcultural Lives*. New York: New York University Press.
Harrison, Anthony Kwame (2012) 'Post-Colonial Consciousness, Knowledge Production, and Identity Inscription within Filipino-American Hip-Hop Music'. *Perfect Beat; London* 13(1): 29–48.
Harvey, David (1973) *Social Justice and the City*. Baltimore, MD: Johns Hopkins University Press.
Harvey, David (1997) *Justice, Nature and the Geography of Difference*. Hoboken, NJ: Wiley-Blackwell.
Harvey, David (2000) *Spaces of Hope*. Berkley: University of California Press.
Harvey, David (2008) 'The Right to the City'. *New Left Review* 53: 23–40.
Harvey, David (2009) 'The "New" Imperialism: Accumulation by Dispossession'. *Socialist Register* 40(40).
Hau, Caroline Sy (2011) '"Patria é Interes"": Reflections on the Origins and Changing Meanings of Ilustrado'. *Philippine Studies* 59(1): 3–54.
Heisler, Barbara Schmitter (1991) 'A Comparative Perspective on the Underclass: Questions of Urban Poverty, Race, and Citizenship'. *Theory and Society* 20(4): 455–83.
Hernandez, Eloisa May P. (2014) *Digital Cinema in the Philippines, 1999–2009*. Quezon City: University of the Philippines Press.
Hincks, Joseph (2017) 'National Geographic Film Shows Horrors of Duterte's Drug War'.

Time, 6 March <http://time.com/4689742/national-geographic-philippines-drug-war/> (last accessed 19 July 2017).
Hochschild, Arlie Russell (2000) 'Global Care Chains and Emotional Surplus Value', in *On the Edge*, ed. Anthony Giddens. London: Random House, pp. 130–46.
Hodkinson, Paul (2007) 'Youth Cultures: A Critical Outline of Key Debates', in *Youth Cultures: Scenes, Subcultures and Tribes*, ed. Wolfgang Deicke and Paul Hodkinson. New York: Routledge, pp. 1–22.
Hollnsteiner, Mary R. (1972) 'Becoming an Urbanite: The Neighbourhood as a Learning Environment', in *The City as a Centre of Change in Asia*, ed. D. J. Dwyer. Hong Kong: Hong Kong University Press, pp. 29–40.
Holquist, Michael (2002) *Dialogism: Bakhtin and His World*. London and New York: Routledge.
Human Rights Watch (2017) '"License to Kill"'. *Human Rights Watch*, 2 March, <https://www.hrw.org/report/2017/03/02/license-kill/philippine-police-killings-dutertes-war-drugs> (last accessed 19 July 2017).
Husock, Howard (2015) 'Slums of Hope'. *City Journal*. <https://www.city-journal.org/html/slums-hope-13147.html> (last accessed 6 July 2017).
Hutchison, Jane (2007) 'The "Disallowed" Political Participation of Manila's Urban Poor'. *Democratization* 14(5): 853–72.
Huyssen, Andreas (ed.) (2008) *Other Cities, Other Worlds: Urban Imaginaries in a Globalizing Age*. Durham, NC: Duke University Press.
Inton, Mikee N. (2015) 'The Bakla and Gay Globality in Chris Martinez's Here Comes the Bride'. *Intersections: Gender and Sexuality in Asia and the Pacific* (38): 12.
Inton, Mikee N. (2017) 'The Bakla and the Silver Screen : Queer Cinema in the Philippines'. PhD thesis, Lingnan University, Hong Kong.
Inton, Mikee N. (2018) 'Exploring the Dolphy Bakla: Queerness in Philippine Cinema', in *The Palgrave Handbook of Asian Cinema*, ed. Aaron Han Joon Magnan-Park, Gina Marchetti and See Kam Tan. London: Palgrave Macmillan UK, pp. 583–605.
Jackson, Vivienne (2011) 'Belonging against the National Odds: Globalisation, Political Security and Philippine Migrant Workers in Israel'. *Global Society* 25(1): 49–71.
Jaucian, Don (2017) 'How "Respeto" Became a Movie about the War on Drugs'. *CNN*, 19 September, <https://cnnphilippines.com/life/entertainment/film/2017/09/19/respeto-movie-war-on-drugs.html> (last accessed 16 May 2020).
Jocano, F. Landa (1975) *Slum as a Way of Life: A Study of Coping Behavior in an Urban Environment*. Quezon City: University of the Philippines Press.
Jones, Owen (2011) *Chavs: The Demonization of the Working Class*. London and New York: Verso.
Kaiser, Matthew (2011) 'From London's East End to West Baltimore: How the Victorian Skum Narrative Shapes The Wire', in *Neo-Victorian Families: Gender, Sexual and Cultural Politics*, ed. Marie-Luise Kohlke and Christian Gutleben. Amsterdam: Rodopi, pp. 45–70.
Kim, Susie Jie Young (2010) 'Noir Looks and the Flash of Transgression: Trauma and the City's Edge(s) in A Bittersweet Life', in *Cinema at the City's Edge*, ed. Yomi Braester and James Tweedie. Hong Kong: Hong Kong University Press, pp. 119–36.
Koolhaas, Rem, Stefano Boeri, Sanford Kwinter, Nadia Tazi, Hans-Ulrich Obrist (2000) Arc en rêve centre d'architecture, and Harvard Project on the City. *Mutations*. Barcelona: ACTAR.
Krause, Linda and Patrice Petro (2003) *Global Cities: Cinema, Architecture, and Urbanism in a Digital Age*. New Brunswick, NJ: Rutgers University Press.
Krstić, Igor (2016) *Slums on Screen: World Cinema and the Planet of Slums*. Edinburgh: Edinburgh University Press.

Krutnik, Frank (1991) *In a Lonely Street: Film Noir, Genre, Masculinity*. London: Routledge.

Lacaba, Jose F. (1983) 'Notes on "Bakya": Being an Apologia of Sorts for Filipino Masscult', in *Readings in Philippine Cinema*, ed. Rafael Ma. Guerrero. Manila: Experimental Cinema of the Philippines, pp. 117–23.

Lagman, Marco Stefan B. (2012) 'Informal Settlements as Spatial Outcomes of Everyday Forms of Resistance: The Case of Three Depressed Communities in Quezon City'. *Philippine Social Sciences Review* 64(1).

Lee, Daryl (2014) *The Heist Film: Stealing with Style*. New York: Columbia University Press.

Lee, Maggie (2007) 'Tribe (Tribu)'. *The Hollywood Reporter*, 8 October, <http://www.hollywoodreporter.com/review/tribe-tribu-158616> (last accessed 2 March 2017).

Lefebvre, Henri [1974] (1991) *The Production of Space*. Oxford and Cambridge, MA: Blackwell.

Lefebvre, Henri [1992] (2013) *Rhythmanalysis: Space, Time, and Everyday Life*. Trans. Stuart Elden and Gerald Moore. London: Bloomsbury Academic.

Lefebvre, Henri (1996) *Writings on Cities*. Cambridge, MA: Wiley-Blackwell.

Lico, Gerard (2003) *Edifice Complex: Power, Myth, and Marcos State Architecture*. Quezon City: Ateneo de Manila University Press.

Liebelt, Claudia (2011) *Caring for the 'Holy Land': Filipina Domestic Workers in Israel*. New York: Berghahn Books.

Lim, Bliss Cua (2011) 'Gambling on Life and Death : Neoliberal Rationality and the Films of Jeffrey Jeturian', in *Neoliberalism and Global Cinema: Capital, Culture, and Marxist Critique, Routledge Advances in Film Studies*, ed. Jyotsna Kapur and Keith B. Wagner. New York: Routledge, pp. 279–308.

Lim, Yvette Yanwen (2016) 'Beyond Str8tus Quo: Urbanization and Queerness in Tropical Southeast Asia'. *ETropic: Electronic Journal of Studies in the Tropics* 15(2).

Lodge, Guy (2009) 'Tarantino Cheers "Kinatay"'. *In Contention*, 20 October, <http://www.incontention.com/2009/10/20/tarantino-cheers-kinatay/> (last accessed 31 May 2017).

Luhr, William (2012) *Film Noir (New Approaches to Film Genre)*. Oxford: Wiley-Blackwell.

Lumbera, Bienvenido (1967) '"Florante at Laura" and the Formalization of Tradition in Tagalog Poetry'. *Philippine Studies* 15(4): 545–75.

Lumbera, Bienvenido (1983) 'Problems in Philippine Film History', in *Readings in Philippine Cinema*, ed. Rafael Ma. Guerrero. Manila: Experimental Cinema of the Philippines, pp. 67–82.

Lury, Karen (2010) *The Child in Film: Tears, Fears and Fairy Tales*. London: I. B. Tauris.

Lynch, Frank (1962) 'Philippine Values II: Social Acceptance'. *Philippine Studies* 10(1): 82–99.

McCoy, Alfred W. (2000) 'RAM and the Filipino Action Film', in *Geopolitics of the Visible: Essays on Philippine Film Cultures*, ed. Rolando B. Tolentino. Quezon City: Ateneo de Manila University Press, pp. 194–216.

McKirdy, Euan (2016) 'Life inside the Philippines' Most Overcrowded Jail'. *CNN*, 21 August, <http://www.cnn.com/2016/08/21/asia/philippines-overcrowded-jail-quezon-city/index.html> (last accessed 31 May 2017).

McWilliams, Ellen (2009) *Margaret Atwood and the Female Bildungsroman*. Farnham: Ashgate Publishing.

Mahmud, Tayyab (2010) '"Surplus Humanity" and Margins of Legality: Slums, Slumdogs, and Accumulation by Dispossession'. *Chapman Law Review* 14: 1–75.

Malone, Karen (2002) 'Street Life: Youth, Culture and Competing Uses of Public Space'. *Environment and Urbanization* 14(2): 157–68.

Manalansan, Martin (2003) *Global Divas: Filipino Gay Men in the Diaspora*. Durham, NC: Duke University Press.

Mangahas, Mahar (2015) 'OFW-Households Are 10 Percent', 5 December, <http://opinion.inquirer.net/90891/ofw-households-are-10-percent> (last accessed 12 June 2017).
Marasigan, Teo (2017) 'Hindi Hinihingi Ang Respeto'. *Gaslight*, 9 October, <https://www.gaslight.online/post/hindi-hinihingi-ang-respeto> (last accessed 16 May 2020).
Marcantonio, Carla (2015) *Global Melodrama*. New York: Palgrave Macmillan.
Marcuse, Peter (2009) 'From Critical Urban Theory to the Right to the City'. *City* 13(2–3): 185–97.
Margalit, Ruth (2017) 'Israel's Invisible Filipino Work Force'. *The New York Times*, 3 May.
Martin, Adrian (2018) 'Live to Tell: Teen Movies Yesterday, Today and Tomorrow', in *Mysteries of Cinema: Reflections on Film Theory, History and Culture 1982–2016*. Amsterdam: Amsterdam University Press, pp. 291–300.
Martin-Jones, David (2011) *Deleuze and World Cinemas*. London: Bloomsbury Publishing.
Massey, Doreen, John Allen and Phil Sarre (1999) *Human Geography Today*. Cambridge: Polity.
Massey, Doreen (1994) *Space, Place, and Gender*. Minneapolis: University of Minnesota Press.
Massood, Paula (1996) 'Mapping the Hood: The Genealogy of City Space in "Boyz N the Hood" and "Menace II Society"'. *Cinema Journal* 35(2): 85.
Massood, Paula (1998) 'The Urban Chronotope: Cinematic Representations and Transformations of the African-American City'. PhD thesis, New York University.
Massood, Paula (2003) *Black City Cinema African American Urban Experiences in Film*. Philadelphia: Temple University Press.
Massood, Paula (2011) *Black City Cinema: African American Urban Experiences In Film*. Philadelphia: Temple University Press.
Matti, Erik (2013) 'On The Job. Director's Statement. Cannes Director's Fortnight', 19 August, <http://katumbal.blogspot.co.uk/2013/08/on-job-directors-statement-cannes.html> (last accessed 31 May 2017).
Mazumdar, Ranjani (2007) *Bombay Cinema: An Archive of the City*. Minneapolis: University of Minnesota Press.
Medel, Fidel Antonio (2009) 'Lola Gives a Heartbreaking Portrait of Two Grandmothers'. *PEP.Ph*, 17 October, <http://www.pep.ph/guide/movies/4921/pep-review-lola-gives-a-heartbreaking-portrait-of-two-grandmothers> (last accessed 17 September 2017).
Mennel, Barbara Caroline (2008) *Cities and Cinema*. London and New York: Routledge.
Merrifield, Andrew (2013) *Henri Lefebvre: A Critical Introduction*. New York: Routledge.
Michel, Boris (2010) 'Going Global, Veiling the Poor Global City Imaginaries in Metro Manila'. *Philippine Studies* 58(3): 383–406.
Migrante International (2015) '#SONA2015 Number of OFWs Leaving Daily Rose from 2,500 in 2009 to 6,092 in 2015'. *Migrante International*, 29 July, <https://migranteinternational.org/2015/07/29/sona2015-number-of-ofws-leaving-daily-rose-from-2500-in-2009-to-6092-in-2015/> (last accessed 13 June 2017).
Modleski, Tania (1984) 'Time and Desire in the Woman's Film'. *Cinema Journal* 23(3): 19.
Mohan, Megha (2016) 'The Philippines: No Country for Poor Men'. *BBC News*, 3 December.
Montgomery, Michael V. (1993) *Carnivals and Commonplaces: Bakhtin's Chronotope, Cultural Studies, and Film*. New York: Peter Lang Publishing.
Moretti, Franco (2000) *The Way of the World: The Bildungsroman in European Culture*. London: Verso.
Morson, Gary Saul and Caryl Emerson (1990) *Mikhail Bakhtin: Creation of a Prosaics*. Palo Alto: Stanford University Press.
Moya, George (2014) 'The Floating World of Artex', <http://www.rappler.com/move-ph/62516-floating-world-artex> (last accessed 18 April 2017).

Murphet, Julian (1998) 'Film Noir and the Racial Unconscious'. *Screen* 39(1): 22–35.

Murphet, Julian (2001) *Literature and Race in Los Angeles*. Cambridge: Cambridge University Press.

Nachtwey, James (2017) 'In Manila, Death Comes by Night: Photographs From the Front Lines of Philippines' Drug War'. *TIME.Com*. <http://time.com/philippines-drug-war/> (last accessed 19 July 2017).

Nadera Jr, Victor Emmanuel Carmelo D. and Chris Mooney-Singh (2019) 'Balagtasan Beyond Balagtas: Debate Poetry, a Filipino Tradition'. *SARE: Southeast Asian Review of English* 56(1): 26–44.

Naerssen, Ton van (2003) 'Globalization and Urban Social Action in Metro Manila'. *Philippine Studies* 51(3): 435–50.

Naficy, Hamid (2001) *An Accented Cinema: Exilic and Diasporic Filmmaking*. Princeton: Princeton University Press.

Nagib, Lúcia (2011) *World Cinema and the Ethics of Realism*. New York: Continuum.

Nandy, Ashis (1998) *The Secret Politics of Our Desires: Innocence, Culpability and Indian Popular Cinema*. London: Palgrave Macmillan.

Naremore, James (2005) 'Something More than Night: Tales of the Noir City', in *The Cinematic City*, ed. David B. Clarke. Hove: Psychology Press, pp. 87–112.

Naremore, James (2008) *More than Night: Film Noir in Its Contexts*. Berkeley: University of California Press.

Novak, David (2015) 'Noise', in *Keywords in Sound*, ed. Matt Sakakeeny and David Novak. Durham, NC: Duke University Press, pp. 125–38.

Nowell-Smith, Geoffrey (2002) 'Minnelli and Melodrama', in *Home is Where the Heart is: Studies in Melodrama and the Woman's Film*, ed. Christine Gledhill. London: BFI Publishing, pp. 70–4.

Olan, Sarah Jayne (2014) 'Looking Back: The Records of Ondoy'. *Rappler*. <http://www.rappler.com/move-ph/issues/disasters/70240-ondoy-records> (last accessed 31 August 2017).

Ortega, Arnisson Andre (2016a) 'Manila's Metropolitan Landscape of Gentrification: Global Urban Development, Accumulation by Dispossession & Neoliberal Warfare against Informality'. *Geoforum* 70: 35–50.

Ortega, Arnisson Andre (2016b) *Neoliberalizing Spaces in the Philippines: Suburbanization, Transnational Migration, and Dispossession*. Lanham: MD: Rowman & Littlefield.

Osteen, Mark (2008) 'Noir's Cars: Automobility and Amoral Space in American Film Noir'. *Journal of Popular Film and Television* 35(4): 183–92.

Osumare, Halifu (2001) 'Beat Streets in the Global Hood: Connective Marginalities of the Hip Hop Globe'. *Journal of American & Comparative Cultures* 24(1–2): 171–81.

Palmer, R. Barton (2004) '"Lounge Time" Reconsidered: Spatial Discontinuity and Temporal Contingency in Out of the Past (1947)', in *Film Noir Reader 4: The Crucial Films and Themes*, ed. Alain Silver and James Ursini. Pompton Plains, NJ: Limelight Editions, pp. 53–66.

Pante, Michael D. (2014) 'A Collision of Masculinities: Men, Modernity and Urban Transportation in American-Colonial Manila'. *Asian Studies Review* 38(2): 253–73.

Parreñas, Rhacel Salazar (2000) 'Migrant Filipina Domestic Workers and the International Division of Reproductive Labor'. *Gender and Society* 14(4): 560–80.

Parreñas, Rhacel Salazar (2001) 'Transgressing the Nation-State: The Partial Citizenship and "Imagined (Global) Community" of Migrant Filipina Domestic Workers'. *Signs: Journal of Women in Culture and Society* 26(4): 1129–54.

Parreñas, Rhacel Salazar (2005) *Children of Global Migration: Transnational Families and Gendered Woes*. Palo Alto: Stanford University Press.

Paterson, Mark (2009) 'Haptic Geographies: Ethnography, Haptic Knowledges and Sensuous Dispositions'. *Progress in Human Geography* 33(6): 766–88.
Pettey, Homer B. and R. Barton Palmer (eds) (2014) *International Noir*. Edinburgh: Edinburgh University Press.
Phelps, David (2008) 'Foster Child | Film Review'. *Slant Magazine*, 12 March, <http://www.slantmagazine.com/film/review/foster-child> (last accessed 18 April 2017).
Philippine Embassy in Israel (2019) 'Filipinos in Israel'. *Embassy of the Philippines, Tel-Aviv, Israel*, 6 March, <https://tel-avivpe.dfa.gov.ph/filipinos-in-israel> (last accessed 20 July 2020).
Philippine Overseas Employment Administration (2015) 'Philippine Overseas Employment Administration: Oversease Employment Statistics, Deployed Overseas Filipino Workers, 2014–2015'.
Philippine Statistics Authority (2013) 'Stock Estimates of Overseas Filipinos: 2009–2013'.
Phillips, Richard (2010) 'Brillante Mendoza Discusses Lola – World Socialist Web Site', 10 July, <https://www.wsws.org/en/articles/2010/07/mend-j10.html> (last accessed 18 April 2017).
Pickering, Hugh and Tom Rice (2017) 'Noise as "Sound out of Place": Investigating the Links between Mary Douglas' Work on Dirt and Sound Studies Research'. *Journal of Sonic Studies* 14.
Pile, Steve (2010) 'Emotions and Affect in Recent Human Geography'. *Transactions of the Institute of British Geographers* 35(1): 5–20.
Pinches, Michael (1994) 'Modernisation and the Quest for Modernity: Architectural Form, Squatter Settlements and the New Society in Manila', in *Cultural Identity and Urban Change in Southeast Asia: Interpretative Essays*, ed. William Stewart Logan and Marc Askew. Melbourne: Deakin University Press, pp. 13–42.
Piocos III, Carlos (2016) 'On Being Moved: Affect and Politics in Narratives of Southeast Asian Migration'. PhD dissertation, University of Hong Kong.
Planta, Ma Mercedes G. (2008) 'Prerequisites to a Civilized Life: The American Colonial Public Health System in the Philippines, 1901 to 1927'. PhD dissertation, National University of Singapore.
Prakash, Gyan (ed.) (2010) *Noir Urbanisms: Dystopic Images of the Modern City*. Princeton: Princeton University Press.
Probyn, Elspeth (2004) 'Everyday Shame'. *Cultural Studies* 18(2–3): 328–49.
Pühringer, Julia, Alexandra Ganser and Markus Rheindorf (2006) 'Bakhtin's Chronotope on the Road: Space, Time, and Place in Road Movies Since the 1970s'. *FACTA UNIVERSITATIS-Linguistics and Literature* 4(1): 1–17.
Qin, Amy (2016) 'Filipino Filmmakers Shed Light on the Forgotten. They Hope It Can Last.' *The New York Times*, 28 November.
Rafael, Vicente L. (2000) *White Love and Other Events in Filipino History*. Durham, NC: Duke University Press.
Rao, Vyjayanthi (2013) 'Slum as Theory: Mega-Cities and Urban Models', in *The SAGE Handbook of Architectural Theory*. Los Angeles: SAGE Publications, pp. 671–86.
Reed, Robert Ronald (1978) *Colonial Manila: The Context of Hispanic Urbanism and Process of Morphogenesis*. Berkeley: University of California Press.
Reyes, Emmanuel A. (1989) 'The World on Her Shoulders: Women in Melodrama', in *Notes on Philippine Cinema*. Manila: De La Salle University Press, pp. 43–50.
Robinson, Jennifer (2010) 'Living in Dystopia: Past, Present, and Future in Contemporary African Cities', in *Noir Urbanisms: Dystopic Images of the Modern City*, ed. Gyan Prakash. Princeton: Princeton University Press, pp. 218–40.

Rodriguez, Robyn Magalit (2010) *Migrants for Export: How the Philippine State Brokers Labor to the World*. Minneapolis: University of Minnesota Press.

Rose, Tricia (1994) *Black Noise: Rap Music and Black Culture in Contemporary America*. Middletown, CT: Wesleyan University Press.

Rotbard, Sharon (2015) *White City, Black City: Architecture and War in Tel Aviv and Jaffa*. London: Pluto Press.

Roy, Ananya (2011) 'Slumdog Cities: Rethinking Subaltern Urbanism: Rethinking Subaltern Urbanism'. *International Journal of Urban and Regional Research* 35(2): 223–38.

Roy, Arundhati (2009) 'Caught on Film: India "not Shining"'. *Dawn.Com*, 2 March, <https://www.dawn.com/news/921599> (last accessed 11 June 2020).

San Juan Jr, Epifanio (1990) 'Encircle the Cities by the Countryside: The City in Philippine Writing'. *Journal of South Asian Literature* 25(1): 189–213.

San Juan Jr, Epifanio (2009) 'Overseas Filipino Workers: The Making of an Asian-Pacific Diaspora'. *The Global South* 3(2): 99–129.

Santiago Jr, Fernando A. (2006) 'Isang Maikling Kasaysayan Ng Pandacan, Maynila 1589–1898'. *MALAY* 19(2): 1–1.

Santiago Jr, Fernando A. (2007) 'A Preliminary Study of the History of Pandacan, Manila, during the Second World War, 1941–1945'. *Manila: Studies in Urban Cultures and Tradition* 3(1): 108–24.

Schrader, Paul (1972) 'Notes on Film Noir', in *Film Noir Reader*, ed. Alain Silver and James Ursini. New York: Limelight Editions, pp. 53–64.

Sconce, Jeffrey (2000) *Haunted Media: Electronic Presence from Telegraphy to Television*. Durham, NC: Duke University Press.

Seabrook, Jeremy (2009) 'Myths of Victorian Squalor | Jeremy Seabrook'. *The Guardian*, 12 July.

Selzer, Kelvin Lee (2019) '[Herald Interview] Hip-Hop Film Seeks to Show Realities of Life in the Philippines', 17 January, <http://www.koreaherald.com/view.php?ud=20190117000673> (last accessed 16 May 2020).

Shapiro, Michael J. (2008) *Cinematic Geopolitics*. New York: Routledge.

Shary, Timothy (2002) *Generation Multiplex the Image of Youth in Contemporary American Cinema*. Austin: University of Texas Press.

Shary, Timothy (2003) 'Teen Films: The Cinematic Image of Youth', in *Film Genre Reader III*, ed. Barry Keith Grant. Austin: University of Texas Press, pp. 490–515.

Shary, Timothy and Alexandra Seibel (2007) *Youth Culture in Global Cinema*. Austin: University of Texas Press.

Shatkin, Gavin (2004) 'Planning to Forget: Informal Settlements as "forgotten Places" in Globalising Metro Manila'. *Urban Studies* 41(12): 2469–84.

Shiel, Mark (2012) *Italian Neorealism: Rebuilding the Cinematic City*. New York: Columbia University Press.

Shiel, Mark and Tony Fitzmaurice (eds) (2001) *Cinema and the City: Film and Urban Societies in a Global Context*. Oxford and Malden, MA: Blackwell.

Shin, Chi-Yun and Mark Gallagher (2015) *East Asian Film Noir: Transnational Encounters and Intercultural Dialogue*. New York: I. B. Tauris.

Silver, Alain and James Ursini (eds) (2006) *Film Noir Reader*. New York: Limelight Editions.

Simmel, George (2014) 'The Metropolis and Mental Life', in *The People, Place, and Space Reader*, ed. Jen Jack Gieseking, William Mangold, Cindi Katz, Setha M. Low and Susan Saegert. London: Routledge, pp. 223–6.

Sinnerbrink, Robert (2015) *Cinematic Ethics: Exploring Ethical Experience through Film*. Abingdon and New York: Routledge.
Sobchack, Vivian (1998) 'Lounge Time: Postwar Crises and the Chronotope of Film Noir', in *Refiguring American Film Genres: History and Theory*. Berkley: University of California Press, pp. 129–70.
Soja, Edward W. (2010) *Seeking Spatial Justice*. Minneapolis: University of Minnesota Press.
Sorlin, Pierre (2000) 'Children as War Victims in Postwar European Cinema', in *War and Remembrance in the Twentieth Century*, ed. Emmanuel Sivan and Jay Winter. Cambridge: Cambridge University Press, pp. 104–24.
Sotto, Agustin L. (1987) 'Notes on the Filipino Action Film'. *East-West Film Journal* 1(2): 1–14.
Special Committee Report (1968) 'Squatting and Slumdwelling in Metropolitan Manila'. *Philippine Sociological Review* 16(1/2): 92–105.
Spicer, Andre and Helen Hanson (2013) *A Companion to Film Noir*. Hoboken, NJ: John Wiley & Sons.
Stam, Robert (1989) *Subversive Pleasures: Bakhtin, Cultural Criticism, and Film*. Baltimore, MD: Johns Hopkins University Press.
Stam, Robert (2000) *Film Theory: An Introduction*. Malden, MA and Oxford: Blackwell.
Standing, Guy (1999) 'Global Feminization Through Flexible Labor: A Theme Revisited'. *World Development* 27(3): 583–602.
Stephens, Sharon (1995) *Children and the Politics of Culture*. Princeton: Princeton University Press.
Sumsky, Victor V. (1992) 'The City as Political Actor: Manila, February 1986'. *Alternatives: Global, Local, Political* 17(4): 479–92.
Syjuco, Miguel (2010) *Ilustrado*. Basingstoke: Pan Macmillan.
Tadiar, Neferti Xina M. (2004) *Fantasy Production: Sexual Economies and Other Philippine Consequences for the New World Order*. Hong Kong and London: Hong Kong University Press.
Tadiar, Neferti Xina M. (2009) *Things Fall Away : Philippine Historical Experience and the Makings of Globalization*. Durham, NC: Duke University Press.
Tadiar, Neferti Xina M. (2013) 'Life-Times of Disposability within Global Neoliberalism'. *Social Text* 31(2 (115)): 19–48.
Talabong, Rambo (2018) 'Nearly 3,000 "tambays" Arrested in Metro Manila since Duterte Order'. *Rappler*, 18 June, <https://www.rappler.com/nation/205186-number-arrested-loiterers-metro-manila> (last accessed 16 May 2020).
Teather, Elizabeth Kenworthy (1999) *Embodied Geographies: Spaces, Bodies and Rites of Passage*. London: Routledge.
Teodoro, Luis (2018) 'Standby Regime'. *Bulatlat*, 1 July, <https://www.bulatlat.com/2018/07/01/standby-regime/> (last accessed 16 May 2020).
Tharoor, Ishaan (2009) 'The Manila Floods: Why Wasn't the City Prepared?' *Time*, 29 September.
The Economist (2016) 'Slowly Does It'. *The Economist*, 25 February, <http://www.economist.com/news/asia/21693631-rising-car-ownership-and-appalling-transport-policies-block-roads-slowly-does-it> (last accessed 31 May 2017).
Thrift, Nigel (2004) 'Intensities of Feeling: Towards a Spatial Politics of Affect'. *Geografiska Annaler: Series B, Human Geography* 86(1): 57–78.
Tiongson, Antonio T. (2013) *Filipinos Represent: DJs, Racial Authenticity, and the Hip-Hop Nation*. Minneapolis: University of Minnesota Press.
Tiongson, Nicanor G. (ed.) (1983a) *The Urian Anthology, 1970–1979: Selected Essays on Tradition*

and Innovation in the Filipino Cinema of the 1970s by the Manunuri Ng Pelikulang Pilipino. Manila: M. L. Morato.
Tiongson, Nicanor G. (1983b) 'From Stage to Screen: Philippine Dramatic Traditions and the Filipino Film', in *Readings in Philippine cinema*, ed. Rafael Ma. Guerrero. Manila: Experimental Cinema of the Philippines, pp. 83–94.
Tiongson, Nicanor G. (1992) 'The Filipino Film Industry: Profile, Problems And Prospects'. *East-West Film Journal* 6(2): 23–61.
Tiongson, Nicanor G. (ed.) (2013) *The Urian Anthology, 2000–2009: The Rise of the Philippine New Wave Indie Film*. Quezon City: University of the Philippines Press.
Tioseco, Alexis (2007) 'Shifting Agendas: The Decay of the Mainstream and Rise of the Independents in the Context of Philippine Cinema'. *Inter-Asia Cultural Studies* 8(2): 298–303.
Tiquia, Ma. Lourdes (2019) 'Dugyot'. *The Manila Times*, 19 November, <https://www.manilatimes.net/2019/11/19/opinion/columnists/dugyot/657039/> (last accessed 30 April 2020).
Tobias, Scott (2013) 'On The Job'. *The Dissolve*, 26 September, <https://thedissolve.com/reviews/225-on-the-job/> (last accessed 31 May 2017).
Tolentino, Roland B. (2001) *Sa loob at labas ng mall kong sawi kaliluha'y siyang nangyayaring hari: ang pagkatuto at pagtatanghal ng kulturang popular*. Quezon City: University of the Philippines Press.
Tolentino, Rolando B. (2009a) 'Globalizing National Domesticity Female Work and Representation in Contemporary Women's Films'. *Philippine Studies* 57(3): 419–42.
Tolentino, Rolando B. (2009b) 'Macho Dancing, the Feminization of Labor, and Neoliberalism in the Philippines'. *TDR/The Drama Review* 53(2): 77–89.
Tolentino, Roland B. (2014) *Contestable nation-space: cinema, cultural politics, and transnationalism in the Marcos-Brocka Philippines*. Quezon City: University of the Philippines Press.
Toro, Gabe (2013) 'Review: Filipino Thriller "On The Job" A Familiar But Exciting Echo Of "The Departed"'. *IndieWire*, 27 September, <http://www.indiewire.com/2013/09/review-filipino-thriller-on-the-job-a-familiar-but-exciting-echo-of-the-departed-93183/> (last accessed 31 May 2017).
Torres, Cristina Evangelista (2010) *The Americanization of Manila, 1898–1921*. Quezon City: University of the Philippines Press.
Tuan, Yi-fu (2014) *Space and Place: The Perspective of Experience*. Minneapolis and London: University of Minnesota Press.
UN-Habitat (2003) *The Challenge of Slums*. London: Earthscan.
UN-Habitat (2004) *The State of the World's Cities: Globalization and Urban Culture*. London: Earthscan.
United Nations, Department of Economic and Social Affairs, and Population Division (2019) *World Urbanization Prospects: The 2018 Revision*.
US State Department (2013) 'US State Department Human Rights Country Report 2013: Philippines'.
Valerio, Elvin Amerigo (2012) 'Defining the Aesthetics of Philippine Independent Cinema: An Interview with Brillante Mendoza'. *Asian Cinema* 22(2): 47–73.
Velasco, Jovenal D. (2004) 'Filipino Film Melodrama of the Late 1950s: Two Case Studies of Accommodation of Hollywood Genre Models'. *Plaridel* 1(1): 31–46.
Vera, Noel (2005) 'Lino Brocka: The Heart of Philippine Cinema'. *Center for Asian American Media*. <http://caamedia.org/blog/2010/03/07/essay-lino-brocka-the-heart-of-philippine-cinema/> (last accessed 17 April 2017).
Vice, Sue (1997) *Introducing Bakhtin*. Manchester: Manchester University Press.

Vieira, João Luiz (2009) 'The Transnational Other: Street Kids in Contemporary Brazilian Cinema', in *World Cinemas, Transnational Perspectives*, ed. Natasa Durovicová and Kathleen E. Newman. Abingdon: Taylor & Francis, pp. 226–43.

Villegas, Dan (2010) 'Artex, Malabon: A Waterworld Compound | The Philippine Online Chronicles'. *The Philippine Online Chronicle.* <http://thepoc.net/index.php/artex-malabon-a-waterworld-compound/> (last accessed 18 April 2017).

Virola, Romulo A. (2010) 'Statistically Speaking – Now Showing: Panday Nag-Shake, Rattle and Roll'. *Philippine Statistics Authority.* <http://nap.psa.gov.ph/headlines/StatsSpeak/2012/021312_rav_mpg.asp> (last accessed 12 September 2017).

Wallace, Lee (2011) *Lesbianism, Cinema, Space: The Sexual Life of Apartments.* London: Routledge.

Wang, Oliver (2015) *Legions of Boom: Filipino American Mobile DJ Crews in the San Francisco Bay Area.* Durham, NC: Duke University Press.

Warner, Koko (2010) 'Global Environmental Change and Migration: Governance Challenges'. *Global Environmental Change* 20(3): 402–13.

Weiss, Jeff (2015) 'How Filipino-American DJs Came to Dominate West Coast Turntablism'. *L.A. Weekly*, 27 May, <http://www.laweekly.com/music/how-filipino-american-djs-came-to-dominate-west-coast-turntablism-5616157> (last accessed 2 March 2017).

Weissberg, Jay (2009) 'Review: "Kinatay"'. *Variety*, 17 May.

Wells, Matt (2017) 'Philippines: Duterte's "war on Drugs" Is a War on the Poor'. *Amnesty International*, 4 February, <https://www.amnesty.org/en/latest/news/2017/02/war-on-drugs-war-on-poor/> (last accessed 19 July 2017).

Whaley, Floyd (2012) 'New Ambitions in Philippine Film Business'. *The New York Times*, 7 May.

Willen, Sarah S. (2003) 'Perspectives on labour migration in Israel'. *Revue européenne des migrations internationales* 19(3): 243–62.

Willen, Sarah S. (2007) 'Toward a Critical Phenomenology of "Illegality": State Power, Criminalization, and Abjectivity among Undocumented Migrant Workers in Tel Aviv, Israel'. *International Migration* 45(3): 8–38.

Williams, Linda (1998) 'Melodrama Revised', in *Refiguring American Film Genres: History and Theory*, ed. Nick Browne. Berkeley: University of California Press, pp. 42–88.

Wise, Damon (2013) 'Metro Manila's Sean Ellis: "You Don't Need to Know What an Actor Is Saying"'. *The Guardian*, 16 September.

Wood, Robin (2006) *Personal Views: Explorations in Film.* Detroit: Wayne State University Press.

Wunderlich, Filipa Matos (2008) 'Walking and Rhythmicity: Sensing Urban Space'. *Journal of Urban Design* 13(1): 125–39.

Yapan, Alvin (2008) 'The Aesthetic of the Meandering Camera'. Paper read during the 5th Annual Southeast Asian Cinemas Conference, 22 November, Ateneo de Manila University.

Yeates, Nicola (2009) *Globalizing Care Economies and Migrant Workers: Explorations in Global Care Chains.* Basingstoke: Palgrave Macmillan.

Zafra, Jessica (2009) 'A Filipino Director Dares Viewers Not to Look Away'. *Newsweek*, 11 June.

Zafra, Jessica (2011) 'Mainstream Movies vs. Indie Cinema: We All Lose'. *Philstar.Com*, 27 March, <http://www.philstar.com/sunday-life/669770/mainstream-movies-vs-indie-cinema-we-all-lose> (last accessed 12 September 2017).

Zarzosa, Agustín (2013) *Refiguring Melodrama in Film and Television: Captive Affects, Elastic Sufferings, Vicarious Objects.* Lanham, MD: Lexington Books.

Zhang, Yingjin (2010) *Cinema, Space, and Polylocality in a Globalizing China.* Honolulu: University of Hawaii Press.

Žižek, Slavoj (2009) *In Defense of Lost Causes*. London: Verso.
Zulueta, Lito B. (2014) 'The Indie Fire Spreads', in *Making Waves: 10 Years of Cinemalaya*. Mandaluyong City: Anvil Publishing, pp. 22–39.

Filmography

Anak (Rory B. Quintos, 2000) Star Cinema Productions.
Anak Dalita (Lamberto V. Avellana, 1956) LVN Pictures.
Ang Babae Sa Septic Tank (Marlon Rivera, 2011) Cinemalaya Foundation, Martinez Rivera Films, Quantum Filmd, Straight Shooters Media.
Ang Pagdadalaga Ni Maximo Oliveros (*The Blossoming of Maximo Oliveros*) (Auraeus Solito, 2006) Cinemalaya Foundation, UFO Pictures.
A Portrait of the Artist as Filipino (Lamberto V. Avellana, 1965) Diadem Pictures, Cinema Artists Philippines.
Aswang (Arumpac, Alyx Ayn G. Arumpac, 2019) Cinematografica, Les Productions de l'Oeil Sauvage, Razor Film Produktion GmbH.
Bagets (Maryo J. de los Reyes, 1984) Viva Films.
Barcelona (Gil Portes, 2006) G5 Media Productions.
Barcelona: A Love Untold (Olivia M. Lamasan, 2016) ABS-CBN Film Productions, Star Cinema Productions.
Batch '81 (Mike De Leon, 1982) MVP Pictures.
Bicycle Thieves (Vittorio De Sica, 1948) Ente Nazionale Industrie Cinematografiche (ENIC).
Blade Runner (Ridley Scott, 1982) The Ladd Company, Shaw Brothers, Warner Bros.
Bona (Lino Brocka, 1980) NV Productions.
Children's Show (Roderick Cabrido, 2014) Cornelsen Films, One Big Fight Productions.
City After Dark (Ishmael Bernal, 1980) Regal Films.
City of God (Fernando Meirelles and Kátia Lund, 2004) O2 Filmes, VideoFilmes, Globo Filmes (co-production), Lumière (co-production), Wild Bunch (co-production).
Dubai (Rory B. Quintos, 2005) ABS-CBN Film Productions, Star Cinema Productions.
Foster Child (Brillante Mendoza, 2007) Seiko Films, Centerstage Productions.
Germany Year Zero (Roberto Rossellini, 1948) Tevere Film, SAFDI Union Générale Cinématographique (UGC), Deutsche Film (DEFA).
Hello, Love, Goodbye (Cathy Garcia-Molina, 2019) Star Cinema.
Infernal Affairs (Wai-Keung Lau, 2004) Media Asia Films, Basic Pictures.
Insiang (Lino Brocka, 1976) LVN Pictures.
Jaguar (Lino Brocka, 1979) Bancom Audiovision.
Katas Ng Saudi (Jose Javier Reyes, 2007) Maverick Films.
Kinatay (Brillante Mendoza, 2009) Swift Productions, Centerstage Productions.
Kubrador (Jeffrey Jeturian, 2007) MLR Films, Inc.
Le Fantôme de la Liberté (Luis Buñuel, 1974) Greenwich Film Productions.
Lola (Brillante Mendoza, 2010) Swift Productions, Centerstage Productions.
Los Olvidados (Luis Buñuel, 1950) Ultramar Films.
Lumuha Pati Mga Anghel (Lino Brocka, 1971) Lea Productions.

Magnifico (Maryo J. de los Reyes, 2003) Unico Entertainment, GMA Films.
Maynila Sa Mga Kuko Ng Liwanag (Lino Brocka, 1975) LVN Pictures.
'Merika (Gil Portes, 1984) Adrian Films.
Metro Manila (Sean Ellis, 2013) Chocolate Frog Films.
Milan (Olivia M. Lamasan, 2004) ABS-CBN Film Productions, Star Cinema Productions.
On the Job (Erik Matti, 2013) Reality Entertainment, Star Cinema Productions, ABS-CBN Film Productions.
Out of the Past (Jacques Tourneur, 1947) RKO Radio Pictures.
Pepot Artista (Clodualdo Del Mundo Jr, 2005) Buruka Films.
Reflections in a Golden Eye (John Huston, 1967) Warner Bros./Seven Arts.
Respeto (Treb Monteras II, 2017) Cinemalaya, Arkeo Films, Dogzilla.
Roberta (Olive La Torre, 1951) Sampaguita Pictures.
Rome, Open City (Roberto Rossellini, 1945) Excelsa Film.
Sampaguita, National Flower (Francis Xavier Pasion, 2010) Quantum Films, Pasion Para Pelicula Productions, Voyage Studios.
Sana Maulit Muli (Olivia M. Lamasan, 1995) Star Cinema Productions.
Slumdog Millionaire (Danny Boyle, 2008) Warner Bros, Celador Films, Film4, Pathé Pictures International.
The Flor Contemplacion Story (Joel Lamangan, 1995) Viva Films.
Transit (Hanna Espia, 2013) Cinemalaya Foundation, Ten17P.
Tribu (Jim Libiran, 2007) 8 Glasses Productions, Cinemalaya Foundation.

Index

1974 Labour Code, 134; *see also* labour export policy

accumulation by dispossession, 16, 177
action film, 45, 49–50, 11
affect, 46, 54, 74, 82–3; *see also* affective chronotopes
affective chronotopes, 7, 44, 46, 82–3, 85–9, 90–6, 100–5, 176
affective labour *see* care
Ahmed, S., 85; *see also* fear
amor propio, 91–2; *see also* shame
Anak (Quintos, 2000), 52, 52, 64, 136
Anak Dalita (Avellana, 1956), 32
Ang Babae sa Septic Tank (Rivera, 2011), 34
Ang Pagdadalaga ni Maximo Oliveros (Solito, 2006), 7, 59–68, 70, 71–2, 79–80
any-space-whatever, 66, 78, 126
Arabindoo, P., 21–2
Arcilla, C., 31; *see also* right to the city
Artex Compound, 97; *see also* Sitio Ilog
Asis, M. M. B., 134
Auge, M. *see* non-place

Badiou, A., 25; *see also* cinematic ethics
Bagets (de los Reyes, 1984), 41
bakbakan see action film
Bakhtin, M., 4, 5, 16–18, 60, 176; *see also* chronotope
bakla, 61–2
balagtasan, 156, 170; *see also* Fliptop Rap Battle League
ballad 169–70, 172
baril-barilan 71–2
Batan, C. *see istambay*
Bernal, I., 32, 33; *see also* Manila by Night (Bernal, 1980)
Berner, E., 27, 28, 30, 31, 51
Bicycle Thieves (De Sica, 1948), 24
Bildungsroman, 36
Black City, 138–9; *see also* Tel Aviv

Bolisay, R., 41
Boris, M., 59
bridge, 168–9
Brocka, L., 32–3, 35, 39, 41, 45–6, 50, 70
Buckley, J., 36, 178
Burnham Plan, 29; *see also* Manila
byuti, 61–2, 67–8, 176

Campos, P., 33, 35, 46, 52, 53, 85, 132, 136
care, 95–6, 104; *see also* feminised labour
cemetery, 88, 157, 166–8
Central Bus Station, 138; *see also* Tel Aviv
Chakrabarty, D., 93; *see also* dirt
Chandola, T., 161
chase, 107, 118, 125–7, 128, 129, 178; *see also* mobility
chavs, 164; *see also istambay*
child in film, 37
child seer, 37, 74, 149
childhood, 7, 37–9, 40, 59, 60, 62, 65, 67, 71–4, 176, 178; *see also* coming-of-age
Chion, M., 167
chronotope, 4, 16–20
chronotopes of in/visibility, 8, 54, 132, 133, 136, 139–52, 153
chronotopes of mobility, 8, 107–9, 129, 112–14, 117, 124–8
chronotopes of passage, 7, 59–60, 62–5, 72–5, 78, 79–80, 82, 156, 176
chronotopes of performance, 8, 157, 159, 163–73
Cinema Novo, 24
cinema-city nexus, 2–3, 175–6
Cinemalaya festival, 9, 33, 34, 39, 68, 156
cinematic ethics, 25; *see also* poverty pornography
City after Dark see Manila by Night
City of God (Mereilles, 2004), 22
coming-of-age, 7, 36–42, 59, 60–1, 67, 68, 71, 79–80
COVID-19, 1, 175–6

Index

Cresswell, T., 108; *see also* mobility
crime film, 47, 50; *see also* film noir
crisis of masculinity, 108

David, J., 34, 50, 52–3
Davis, M., 2, 15–16, 21, 30, 38, 48
De Certeau, 83; *see also* walking
deep focus 65, 113–14, 166
Deleuze, G., 37, 66, 74, 82
Deocampo, N., 31–2, 36, 44, 49
Desser, D., 48
diaspora *see* Overseas Filipino Worker genre
Diaz, L. *see* rural chronotope
Diaz, R. *see byuti*
digital realisms, 24, *see also* Krstić, I.
Dikec, M., 14
dirt, 93, 161, 162; *see also* noise
Doane, M., 165; *see also* voice-over
Driscoll, C., 158; *see also* teen films
driving, 108–9, 110, 113, 117, 118, 125, 129; *see also* mobility
dugyot, 162; *see also* dirt
Duterte, Rodrigo, 1, 5–6, 122, 156–7, 160, 164, 166, 167, 173, 175, 177; *see also* extrajudicial killings

Ellis, S., 116
emasculation, 50, 121, 143, 153
Epifanio de los Santos Avenue (EDSA), 31, 108, 112, 118
eskinitas, 6, 41, 68, 72, 78, 80, 86–8, 90, 126
ethics of realism, 24, 62, 71, 74; *see also* Nagib, L.
extrajudicial killings, 1, 5–6, 156–7, 160, 166, 173, 175, 177

fear, 48, 84, 86–7, 88–90, 113–14, 137, 141–2, 143, 146–7, 178
feminised labour, 95, 109, 153
femme fatale, 46, 121, 124–5
Filipino migrant spaces *see* Tel Aviv
Filipino Plan, 138; *see also* Overseas Filipino Worker (OFW)
film noir, 8, 18, 46–51, 108, 110, 128–9; *see also* Manila noir
Fliptop Rap Battle League, 75, 156, 161, 164; *see also* Pinoy rap
Flor Contempacion Story (Lamangan, 1995), 53
foster care, 91
Foster Child, 7, 43, 82, 90–6

geographical imagination, 3; *see also* Harvey, D.

Germany Year Zero (Rossellini, 1948), 79
ghosts *see* spectral scenes
Gledhill, C., 42; *see also* melodrama
global noir *see* Desser, D.
global underclass, 3, 132, 133, 135, 152, 179
global youth film, 158
Guerrero, R., 39, 45, 50

Harvey, D., 3, 13–14, 16
haunting *see* spectral scenes
heist film, 119
Hello, Love, Goodbye (Garcia-Molina, 2019), 52
heteronormative spaces, 61, 64
hiya see shame
hood films, 40, 74–5, 158
Huyssen, A., 9; *see also* urban imaginary

imaginary, 3, 4
Imperial Manila, 9
Insiang (Brocka, L., 1976), 32, 33, 41, 46, 70
International Monetary Fund (IMF), 15, 16, 30; *see also* neoliberal global capitalism
Intramuros, 28–9, 32, 159
iskwater, 27–8
Israel *see* Overseas Filipino Worker (OFW)
istambay, 163–4

Jaguar (Brocka, 1979), 50
jueteng, 83–4, 88, 104; *see also Kubrador* (Jeturian, 2007)

Kaiser, M., 39
Kinatay (Mendoza, 2009), 7, 22, 34, 107, 109–15
Krstić, I., 24, 38
Kubrador (Jeturian, 2007), 7, 43, 82–9

labour export policy, 51, 134–5, 136, 177
Le Fantôme de la liberté (Buñuel, 1974), 94
Lefebvre, H., 1, 13, 84
Libiran, J., 68, 76
Liebelt C., 138–9
Lim, B. C., 89
liminal space, 113
liminal youth, 8, 157, 159, 173, 177
liminality, 40, 153, 163, 168, 170
location shooting, 24, 35; *see also* neorealism
Lola (Mendoza, 2013), 6, 43, 82, 97–105
looban, 7, 28, 41, 43, 59, 61, 62, 64, 66, 67, 78, 80, 87, 90, 91, 123, 125, 126, 178
Los Olvidados (Buñuel, 1950), 38

Lumuha Pati Mga Anghel (Brocka, 1971), 39
Lury, K., 37

machismo, 45, 50
Magnifico (de los Reyes, 2003), 39
Mahmud, T., 16
Malabon *see Sitio Ilog*
Malone, K., 163
Manila
  in Philippine film history, 31–2
  slums, 2, 6, 20, 27–31
Manila Avenue, 138; *see also* Tel Aviv
Manila by Night (Bernal, 1980), 32
Manila City Hall, 127
Manila noir, 8, 48–51
Marcantonio, C., 45
Marcos, Ferdinand, 30, 32–3, 45, 69, 134–5, 156, 160, 166–7; *see also* Martial Law
Marcos, Imelda, 32, 46
Marcus, P., 192; *see also* right to the city
Martial Law, 30, 134, 156, 166, 167, 172, 177 *see also* Marcos, Ferdinand
Martin-Jones, D., 126
masculinity, 37, 46, 50, 107, 108, 109, 111–13, 113, 118, 121, 125, 144
masochismo, 45
Maynila sa mga Kuko ng Liwanag, 32; *see also* Brocka, L.
McCoy, A., 111; *see also* action film
melodrama, 7, 21, 33, 42–6
melodramatic excess, 136–76
melodramatic realism, 45
melodramatic spectacle, 171–3, 179
Mendoza, Brillante, 9, 22, 23, 33, 34, 98
Merrifield, A., 13; *see also* production of space
Metro Gwapo, 59, 109
Metro Manila (Ellis, 2013), 8, 107, 115–21, 128–9, 178
migrant narrative, *see* Overseas Filipino Worker (OFW)
mobility *see* Cresswell, T.
Modleski, T., 89
Montgomery, M., 20
Murphet, J., 19
music *see* ballad

Naficy, H., 18–19, 21
Nagib, L., 24–5
national sacrifice, 8, 154, 177; *see also* Overseas Filipino Worker (OFW)
neoliberal global capitalism, 12, 15–16, 133, 134, 135, 177; *see also* accumulation by dispossession
neorealism, 24, 35, 45
noise, 8, 74–7, 156–7, 161–3; 165, 173, 177; *see also* rap
non-modular narrative, 137, 141, 153, 178
non-place *see* Auge, M.
Nowell-Smith, G., 43

On the Job (Matti, 2013), 8, 107, 122–9
Ortega, A. A., 30, 99
Osumare, H., 75; *see also* rap
Overseas Filipino Worker (OFW)
  genre, 7, 8, 21, 36, 51–4, 132, 178
  figure, 52, 54, 135–6
  in Israel, 137–9

Palmer, R. B., 49
Pandacan, 8, 42, 155–7, 159–60, 162–3, 170, 173, 177
Pante, M., 108–9
Parreñas, R. S., 134, 136, 147
partial citizen, 136, 140–1, 153; *see also* Parreñas, R. S.
pathos-action dialectic, 42, 83, 171
Pepot Artista (Del Mundo Jr, 2005), 39
performativity, 158
Philippine cinema golden ages, 32
Philippine independent cinema, 9, 33–5, 38, 68
Philippine urban cinema, 2, 4, 6, 8–9, 13, 16, 18, 20–3, 27, 31–6
Pinoy rap, 69, 75; *see also* Fliptop Rap Battle League
piss, 92–2, 113
planet of slums, 2, 15, 175; *see also* Davis M.
Prakash, G., 48
prisons, 19, 122–3, 124
Probyn, E., 91; *see also* shame
production of space, 4, 5, 8, 13–14, 16, 19, 41, 46, 59, 62, 64, 80, 82, 83, 90, 108, 133, 176, 177; *see also* Lefebvre, H.
poverty pornography, 22–3

queer coming-of-age *see Ang Pagdadalaga ni Maximo Oliveros* (Solito, 2006)
queer figure *see bakla*
queer spaces, 64–5, 79

radio broadcast, 166–8
Rao, V., 21
rap, 75; *see also* Pinoy rap
realism, 19, 23–4; *see also* cinematic ethics

resilience, 7, 99, 104, 176, 178
Respeto (Monteras II, 2016), 8, 75, 156–73
right to the city, 1, 3, 14, 31, 51, 162, 164; *see also* Lefebvre, H.
rite of passage, 150, 158, 164
Roberta (La Torre, 1951), 39
Robinson, J., 48
Rodriguez, R., 134–5
Roy, A., 21; *see also* poverty pornography
rural chronotope, 9
rural migrant, 32, 116, 178

San Juan, E., 28, 132, 133, 135
Santiago Jr, F., 160; *see also* Pandacan
shame, 91–6, 104, 178; *see also hiya*
shit, 84, 162
silence, 74, 75, 11, 146, 161, 169, 171, 173, 177
Sitio Ilog, 43, 97
slum
　criticism of term, 21
　rise of, 4, 13, 15–16
　theory, 21–2
　see also urbanisation of poverty
slum child, 37–6, 39, 60
slum chronotope, 1, 4–10, 18–20, 20–4, 27, 31–5, 36, 38–9, 42–4, 46–7, 49, 50–1, 60–1, 74, 76, 79–80, 82, 84, 104, 107, 109, 110, 117, 118, 122, 124, 128–9, 132–5, 153, 156–8, 172, 176–7
slum imaginary, 1, 4, 21, 24, 32
slum voyeurism *see* poverty pornography
Slumdog Millionaire (Boyle, 2009), 22, 48, 162
slumification, 4, 6, 15, 48, 133, 134; *see also* urbanisation of poverty
Sobchack, V., 18–19, 46–7, 49
social justice, 4, 5, 13–14, 23, 25, 133, 176; *see also* spatial justice
social realism, 33, 46, 116
Soja, E., 4, 14; *see also* spatial justice
Sotto, A., 49–50
sound, 41, 76, 157, 159, 161–73; *see also* noise
space *see* production of space
spatial consciousness *see* geographical imagination
spatial justice, 1, 3–4, 5–6, 6–8, 9–10, 13–15, 16, 19–20, 23, 25, 42, 59, 66, 68, 74, 75, 77, 79–80, 82, 89, 104, 107, 116, 129, 132, 140, 147, 151–4, 156–7, 161, 163, 170–3, 175–7, 178–9
spatial practice *see* walking
spatiality of justice *see* Dikec, M.

spectral appearances, 85–6, 88, 89, 171; *see also* affective chronotopes
spectral scenes, 165–7
squatter colonies, 31, 32
staircase, 62–4, 100–3, 146
Stam, R., 17–18, 24
static images, 152
Stephens, S., 38
street children *see* slum child
street urchin *see* slum child
structuring presence of home, 115, 127, 129
structuring presence of return, 136–7
suffering *see* melodrama
surplus humanity, 16; *see also* Davis, M.

Tadiar, N., 95, 109, 133–4, 135, 161
tae bombs, 31, 162; *see also* shit
Teather, E., 60
teen film, 7, 21, 40, 157, 169, 173, 179; *see also* coming-of-age
Tel Aviv, 132, 136–9; 141–2, 147, 148, 152, 153, 154; see also *Transit* (Espia, 2016)
Third Cinema, 24, 46
threshold chronotope, 65, 66, 78, 79, 119
Tiongson, N. G., 33, 40–1, 44
tokhang see extrajudicial killings
Tolentino, R., 22, 32–3, 34, 46, 53–4, 136
Tondo, 7, 4, 32, 33, 41, 42, 68–72, 73–4, 75, 76–7, 78–9, 117, 119, 159–60, 164, 176, 178; *see also Tribu* (Libiran, 2007)
Tondo Tribes, 68, 73, 74, 76
topography of fear, 138; *see also* fear
Torres, C. E., 29
tracking shots, 61, 68, 83, 85, 98, 118, 120, 123
Transit (Espia, 2016), 8, 54, 132–54, 177, 178–9
Tribu (Libiran, 2007), 7, 41–2, 59–60, 68–80
typhoons *see* resilience

United Nations (UN), 2, 15, 15–16, 27–8; *see also* urbanisation of poverty
urban dystopia, 48
urban excess, 134–5, 161
urban imaginary, 3, 5, 7, 8, 20, 46, 117, 144, 176, 178
urban realist films, 22, 33, 35
urbanisation of poverty, 2, 4, 9–10, 14, 132, 175, 177, 178

Velasco, J., 41, 44
Vice, S., 18
Vieira, J., 38

voice-off, 164–6
voice-over, 71, 74, 78–9, 121, 143, 144, 164–9

walking, 7, 44, 63, 67, 82–3, 83–9, 90–1, 95–6, 97–100, 101, 104–5
water *see* resilience
Western Wall, 148, 150
White City, 138–9; *see also* Tel Aviv
wide establishing shots, 68, 123, 136
Willen, S., 139

Williams, L., 42, 54, 82; *see also* melodrama
women *see* walking
World Bank (WB), 15, 16, 30; *see also* neoliberal global capitalism

Yapan, A., 35
youth culture, 40, 163
youth film, 40–1, 58, 159; *see also* teen film

Žižek, S., 16

EU representative:
Easy Access System Europe
Mustamäe tee 50, 10621 Tallinn, Estonia
Gpsr.requests@easproject.com